Accumulation   Power

& Power

Accumulation & Power

An Economic History of the United States

Richard B. Du Boff

M. E. Sharpe, Inc.
ARMONK, NEW YORK
LONDON, ENGLAND

Library of Congress Cataloging-in-Publication Data

Du Boff, Richard B.
    Accumulation and power : an economic history of the United States
/ by Richard B. Du Boff.

        p.   cm.
    Bibliography: p.
    Includes index.
    ISBN 0-87332-516-8 — ISBN 0-87332-559-1 (pbk.)
    1. Saving and investment—United States—History. 2. Capital
investments—United States—History. 3. Monopolies—United States—
History. 4. Competition—United States—History. 5. Capitalism—
United States—History. I. Title.
HC110.S3D8 1989
339'.0973—dc19   *HB*   88-39542
                                                                      CIP

Printed in the United States of America

Contents

Figure and Tables

Preface

Just after the Second World War, economists of the Keynesian, Marxian, and institutionalist schools shared one vision—that nothing in the workings of a capitalist economy assured compatibility between the demand side and the supply side requirements for steady growth with full employment. For several reasons this approach to economic history soon fell by the wayside (if in fact there were ever any attempts to make use of it). This book represents an effort to revive it.

Dissatisfaction with neoclassical microtheory and mainstream social science has already produced a number of important contributions to U.S. economic history, dealing mainly with the evolution of the labor process under capitalism and the impact of accumulation on the workforce (see, in the References, Braverman [1974]; Edwards [1979]; Matthaei [1982]; D. Gordon, Edwards, and Reich [1982]). This book, by contrast, focuses on what I conceive to be the central organizing process of capitalism in the United States—private investment carried out to assure profitable growth for the corporate sector of the economy.

This line of analysis means that other sectors must be de-emphasized, particularly agriculture and small business. My assumption is that the power of these sectors to shape markets, technologies, the labor process, and other aspects of the production of goods and services is secondary, or derivative of what is occurring in corporate America. To a degree the same may be said for government monetary and fiscal policy, which is more independent of corporate power than decisionmaking by farmers and small business operators, but not completely so, as I shall argue at several points.

During the various drafts of this book, I had the good fortune to receive a stream of criticism and comments on the entire manuscript from Gregg Huff, Edward Herman, Louis Ferleger, and Allen Fenichel. Others offered their help on several chapters or particular sections: Gar Alperovitz, Fred Block, James

Cypher, Noel Farley, John Bellamy Foster, Jay Mandle, and Howard Sherman. Support was provided by Bryn Mawr College, in the form of a sabbatical leave, which permitted me to do the first draft, and released time, which facilitated the inevitable rewriting process. The final draft benefited from a thorough review by copy editor Clement Russo. The encouragement and advice of M. E. Sharpe editor Richard Bartel are gratefully acknowledged, as are the critical suggestions that came from Alfred Eichner. Al was responsible for an overhaul of the middle chapters that, I believe, greatly improved the formulation and exposition of the basic theme. It is a small measure of what many of us have lost with his untimely passing in 1988.

I thank the Brookings Institution, Harvard University Press, Prentice-Hall, Inc., *Business Week*, and *The New York Times* for permission to quote and to reprint copyrighted material. Thanks of a special kind go to Solange Du Boff, possibly the planet's most relentless proofreader for errors of all sorts.

Richard B. Du Boff
Bryn Mawr, Pennsylvania
December 1988

Accumulation & Power

1

The Flow of Economic History: Accumulation, Monopolization, Competition

We live in an age of information overload. It comes not only through electronic media but also through an exploding number of textbooks and teaching materials at all levels of the U.S. education system. Under circumstances like these, how can a fundamental issue like the long-term development of the American economy be understood or even approached? How can students find their way amid all the competing versions of our economic history?

A look at the recent past may help. Of the several schools of thought vying for attention, the dominant one in the United States over the past three decades has been the "new economic history." Its explanation for U.S. economic growth is clear and concise: the free market is what lies behind America's success.[1] Whether the issue is the long-run productivity performance of the nation, the economic viability of slavery in the Old South, or the suburbanizing of the landscape since the 1920s, the verdict of new economic historians is the same: "the market worked." There are rational cost-price explanations for the production decisions and technical innovations that helped shape the American economy. The competitive market created demands for goods and services that unleashed the energies of enterprising individuals, who responded to these opportunities by creating unparalleled economic growth.

The theme is invariably one of functional response and triumphant outcome. Financial, legal, and political institutions adapted to emerging market pressures, and per capita incomes, technological virtuosity, and international prestige all increased accordingly. In fact, the purpose of the new economic history has been to show how the American economy achieved its size and efficiency through a process of "free," unregulated decisionmaking. As the authors of a widely consulted new economic history collection state, even "irrationalities" such as "ignorance, market power, [or] government interference for social (or nonsocial) purposes . . . may turn out to be rational when subjected to the scrutiny of an ingenious logic and a sympathetic insight into the actual conditions under which they occurred. Engaging in this exercise of finding rational patterns in history is, we confess, a source of endless delight to us."[2]

The focus of this intellectual exercise is an economy consisting of interconnected markets in which activities are coordinated by the price system. Changes in technology or the size of markets or the supply of labor bring about changes in relative prices, which then provide "signals" for allocating the economy's resources. Consumers and business firms react quickly—and rationally—to these market-generated prices, thereby determining what goods and services are needed and supplied, as well as what inputs are required to produce them. Thus, they are led by something like Adam Smith's "invisible hand" to invest, produce, and consume in ways that increase overall output and distribute the income that flows from it.

Available technologies, consumer tastes, and the role the government plays in the economy are treated as exogenous or "given." The economic advantages that accrue to some market participants are treated as endogenous—incidental results of decisions made in response to relative prices. The idea that *all* these phenomena are influenced by the structure of economic and political power falls outside the realm of the new economic history. The economy may sometimes react to political shocks, but it is treated as a self-contained, independent system. Nor does there appear to be any connection between economic and social organization, since relations among individuals or classes of individuals are not seen as particularly important.

Certainly no one can deny the achievements of the new economic history, several of which are reflected in this book. But assumptions based on pure competition and uncoerced maximizing decisions can hardly be expected to serve as guides for understanding the evolving institutional characteristics of economies. The new economic history, for example, leaves us uninformed about the growth and impact of the pace-setting institution in present-day capitalism—the multinational corporation with its command over production and employment.[3] It exhibits a remarkable lack of interest in cyclical instability. Most of its cost-benefit studies have been used to determine whether a given investment or public policy represented the optimum use of resources compared to possible alternatives, while the social costs of free market growth itself, including the casualties inflicted on workers by industrialization, attract scant attention. Government is reduced to an "institutional arrangement" for defining "property rights." And by using government to reduce risk or redistribute income, groups of people are seen as acting just as anonymously competing individuals do: they spontaneously, almost robotically, follow market signals toward "reorganizational profits."[4]

A leading new economic historian has acknowledged that the "common element'' of his craft ''is the use of an explicit model with explicit assumptions. Most of the models used are neo-classical, and most of the questions asked concern either microeconomic problems, long-term growth, or price changes under conditions of essentially full employment. Keynesian models are available for use, of course, but they have been largely ignored.''[5] Another eminent new economic historian points out how the values implicit in this theoretical model ''color the questions to be asked and the range of answers admitted.'' The new economic history, he concludes, ''is viscerally conservative: the invisible hand has created the *only* world compatible with individual preferences, for if not, there would be a different one.''[6]

Some of the same comments can be applied to the ''new business history.'' It does not seem accidental that at the same time the new economic history was being introduced, Professor Alfred Chandler was recasting the foundations of business history in the United States.[7] Like the new economic historians, Chandler saw his discipline as lacking in rigor and laboring under the foibles of traditional historians. He sought a middle ground between ''progressive attacks'' on the pioneers of big business as ''robber barons'' and conservative praise of them as ''industrial statesmen.'' To ''carry out the historian's basic responsibility for setting the record straight,'' Chandler drew on economics and organizational theory to uncover systematic patterns in industrial development, making it possible to assign business enterprises to specific categories according to the nature of their products and the production techniques available to them. For him, the size and administrative structure of business firms became functions of their strategic responses to external forces over which they presumably have little control— markets and technologies.

The core of Chandler's hypothesis is that the form of a business organization adapts itself to the nature of the tasks it performs in supplying its markets efficiently. This ''strategy and structure'' theorem is the new business history equivalent of the ''market rationality'' assumption of the new economic history. Concentration of market power in the hands of relatively few giant corporations is seen as an outgrowth of the competitive process. Chandler does acknowledge a reality foreign to neoclassical theory—the displacement of atomistically competitive markets by the constrained rivalry of oligopolies. But economic power still seems to be an incidental consequence of the development of large firms; it is thrust upon managers by technological advance, widening markets, and the quest for productive efficiency. Furthermore, the interplay between business and politics is almost wholly ignored. The result is that while Chandler trains a powerful light on ''the managerial revolution in American business,'' he leaves us with a selective and partial view of the forces making for big business and its investment practices.

The analysis of America's economic development in the present work departs radically from both the new economic and new business history models. It focuses not on consumption and production choices in an allocative efficiency setting but on capitalist decisionmaking and its social consequences. That decisionmaking process is not seen as a series of adaptations to external market forces but rather as the major determinant of the pattern of economic growth and as the main element forcing change in the economy at large. In this view, the twin goals of capitalist enterprise are *accumulation* and *monopolization*.

Accumulation may be defined as "the process of mobilizing, transforming, and exploiting the inputs used in capitalist production and then selling the output."[8] The *goal* is to increase the volume of capital under the control of private interests. This will guarantee the expansion of profits, which can then be used for the further expansion of capital, in a continuous process that makes capital a self-expanding value.

Capital, in this context, refers to income-generating property. It can take the form of land, buildings, machinery and equipment, or inventories of finished and unfinished goods, as well as unique personal skills and talents. But the driving force in the accumulation process is what economists call "capital formation" or "investment"—decisions by business firms to purchase new office buildings, factories, and machines that will contribute to the expansion of output and income over a number of years into the future. During the past century, investment in "intangible capital"—like research and development, employee training, and professional services—has grown, and this also has a long-term impact on a firm's production possibilities. In any case profits are the balance wheel: capitalists will not invest unless they are reasonably confident of their rate of return. And they will spare no effort to control the external world to keep it open for making more profits.

Since the industrial revolution began over two hundred years ago, accumulation has become embedded in "the regime of capital."[9] In this sense "capital" must be regarded as something far more than just another "input" along with labor hours, raw materials, or acres of land: it implies property rights over the means of production, so that capitalists ("entrepreneurs" or "management" in the language of conventional economics) can organize the production and sale of goods and services on the basis of wage labor and reap the profits that result. This constitutes a *social relation*, the power of one class of people over another. American history is studded with examples of "heroic" entrepreneurs, but their exploits must be kept in perspective. The individual capitalist as such is an important figure only in so far as he is an owner of capital: deprived of his capital, he himself would be nothing special. Nor is it a question of "innate human propensities or instincts; the desire of the capitalist to expand the value under his control (to accumulate capital) springs from his special position in a particular form of organization of social production."[10]

Societies and economies can also be understood as systems of involuntary interdependencies, where relations among people are mutual but imbalanced.

This structured inequality creates sources of power—economic, political, psychological, often cultural. Capital as a social relation is no different. There is a minority of people who invest and produce, and they interact with a far greater number of people who own little except their own ability to work. This employer-worker relationship is distinguished by vastly unequal endowments of property, education, status, even self-confidence. Yet at the same time everybody in a private enterprise economy is dependent upon accumulation: wage and salary people need it for jobs and income, the government needs it for tax revenues. And for capitalists, accumulation is not a "choice" but a way of life. The expansion of business assets through investment makes possible the growth of output and sales, larger profits, the introduction of improved techniques, and the long-term survival of the firm, with each of these objectives essential for attaining the others.

Monopolization goes on at the same time as accumulation. It implies a drive for control over the economic environment, since the future can never be securely predicted and investment commitments are determined by profit expectations. As John Maynard Keynes explained, "the whole object of the accumulation of Wealth is to produce results, or potential results, at a comparatively distant, and sometimes at an *indefinitely* distant, date. . . . About these matters there is no scientific basis on which to form any calculable probability whatever. We simply do not know."[11] It is pointless, and dangerous, to assume that business firms react quickly and accurately to any deviations of expected demand from planned supply. Producers have always operated in a far larger universe of uncertainty and risk. During the time between investment decisions and eventual profits, virtually anything can happen to change a firm's competitive situation, in its costs of transacting business, in the value of its equipment when left idle, among so many other unanticipated developments.

But uncertainties also present themselves as opportunities for monopolization, and anything that can be done to reduce risk simultaneously diminishes a rival's prospects. In this arena, the fight for markets and profits is a zero-sum game, although there are instances where cooperative arrangements can be reached to protect all capitalists against common risk (cartels and collusive price setting, tariffs and quotas, trade associations, government regulations). This is why, as economists used to say years ago, "monopoly is not a matter of desire but of opportunity": everyone desires control over economic uncertainties but only the most astute, or the luckiest, will succeed in gaining it. Efforts to gain such control must be monopolizing by their very nature. They range from the recognizably economic to such "nonmarket" tactics as bribery and corruption, concealment and misuse of information, spying on competitors,[12] and outright coercion. All are types of behavior well known to students of business history. The father of neoclassical economics, Alfred Marshall, noted that "the feverish pursuit of wealth may induce men, capable of great work, to drift into distinctly criminal courses."[13] But unorthodox methods fair or foul must be regarded as integral parts of the quest for monopoly advantages; the ends sought are the same as those pursued in the formal marketplace. Nonmarket means of monopolization do exist, a fact that does much to break down the artificial boundary between economic and noneconomic power.

Accumulation and monopolization are both driven by the dynamics of competition. Long-term growth of the capitalist system generates an investible economic surplus, and with it come sweeping changes in technology, equipment, organization, human skills, and usable natural resources. As levels of output increase, so do the degree of specialization among individuals and the number and variety of transactions occurring in the economy. Step by step, new opportunities and constraints appear in every area of economic life. The long-run development of capitalism thus takes place under conditions that destabilize and reconstitute the networks of human interdependencies. The upshot of the process is continuous change in the nature and quantity of power resources, along with the emergence of greater numbers of pretenders to the throne (or "new independent capitals").[14] Individuals, social classes, and nation states are drawn into competition for power resources: with economic expansion, the available "chances" tend to be scarce relative to the mounting demands for them.

In this context "scarcity" is the central constraint that gives rise to the competitive process. It is not, however, the one-dimensional scarcity of conventional economics—"the science which studies human behavior as a relationship between ends and scarce means which have alternative uses."[15] Technology alone has greatly alleviated that kind of scarcity. The real problem is one of *social* scarcity: advancement in the capitalist economy becomes possible only by seizing one of the newer positions of power created by the continual revolutionizing of society's means of production. Over time the process multiplies the potential number of economic decisionmakers and intensifies the competitive contest for wealth-creating initiatives and personal status. "So the distributional struggle returns, heightened rather than relieved by the dynamic process of growth. It is an exact reversal of what economists and present-day politicians have come to expect growth to deliver."[16]

Competitive pressures force participants to adopt expansionist strategies for both offensive and defensive purposes. To stand still is to allow some rival to gain an edge in production efficiency or marketing that could soon become cumulative. Even simultaneous expansion by all businesses would breed conflict over market shares, perhaps a "battle of competition . . . fought by cheapening of commodities."[17] This is not just a feature of advanced capitalism; well before the industrial revolution in Western Europe "that competition must ultimately lead to monopoly was a truth well understood at the time."[18] The two preeminent students of capitalism—Karl Marx (1818–83) and Joseph Schumpeter (1883–1950)—thoroughly disagreed on the social costs and benefits of private enterprise, but both insisted that the very same forces within it produce competition *and* monopoly. Monopolies may well be temporary and insecure; frequently they are subject to "the perennial gale of creative destruction" coming from "competition from the new commodity, the new technology, the new source of supply, the new type of organization."[19] Nonetheless, they are the natural end product of successful competition, arising out of accumulation and the drive for control over an economy never in "equilibrium." As French economist François Perroux summarized the point:

> Competition produces results that are always thrown into question. In other words, competition is the working out of a domination effect always challenged and always changeable in the framework of the rules of the game. . . . Far from being alien to competition, the domination effect . . . is the essential element of it.[20]

Monopoly as the recurring result of the competitive process clashes with the thinking of conventional economists, who define it merely as the absence of competition in one industry or another. This view is narrow and restrictive, and as a power concept it is hopelessly inadequate. Monopoly is best seen as a relation of production inherent in capital, not as an attribute of certain product markets. It flows out of gross inequalities in powers over investment, technological innovation, pricing, labor utilization, industrial relocation, and the introduction of new goods. These are the real levers of control and command in any economy. But they are never the permanent property of any single capitalist. Competition itself is a blind, unplanned process that carries everyone along with it. "Competition makes the immanent laws of capitalist production to be felt by each individual capitalist, as external coercive laws. . . . It is, from the very outset, a process that takes place behind his back and is controlled by the force of circumstances independent of himself."[21] To survive, the "individual capitalist" must accumulate; to accumulate, he must join in a competitive free-for-all in which control over power resources is always at issue and in which the quantity of them brought under control must be defended and enlarged. The fact that only a few are successful depends more on the structure of the game than on the skills of the players or their strategies.

This is why we have been witnessing the concentration of economic power in small numbers of very large business firms, even as industries and product markets change over time, sometimes dramatically, as we shall see. It also explains why, in the face of all the changes in Western capitalism since 1800, holdings of income and wealth remain jarringly unequal, and any tendency for them to become more evenly distributed has proceeded slowly, and at times not at all.

If there is any factor which is exogenous to the interactive process of accumulation, monopolization, and competition, it is the *historical rate of accumulation* over time. "To attempt to account for what makes the propensity to accumulate high or low we must look into historical, political, and psychological characteristics of an economy.''[22] As accumulation itself has come to depend critically on private capital formation, it behooves observers of the capitalist economy to identify the determinants of investment over something more than just the standard "business cycle" of four or five years duration. Profits, of course, are essential. "To sustain a higher rate of accumulation requires a higher level of profits, both because it offers more favorable odds in the gamble and because it makes finance more readily available.''[23] But why do profitability schedules and investment horizons appear so rosy during certain periods and so bleak during others? Favorable "historical, political, and psychological" circumstances are, as we shall also see, in the eye of the beholder—the capitalist investor, increasingly in the form of the large business corporation.

At irregular intervals, new technologies, markets, and government policies have paved the way for long surges of accumulation that have raised average living standards far beyond anything imagined even a half-century ago. But such progress comes at a high, and rising, price. The "negative externalities" of capitalist growth run from environmental destruction to militarism, which is often employed to arouse the public against "threats to our national security." Invariably these turn out to be efforts by reformist or revolutionary forces to break free of domination by the international market system and the local elites who benefit from it, with China, Cuba, Vietnam, and Nicaragua the prime post-World War II examples. But even when the issue is framed in purely economic terms, bouts of stagnation have marked the U.S. historical record, leaving millions of people with no gainful work and many more living on the edge of insecurity. The root problem is that under capitalism production and employment decisions are based on the pursuit of private material gain. "The aim of capital is not to minister to certain wants, but to produce profit," wrote Marx over a century ago:

> The market must, therefore, be continually extended . . . through expansion of the outlying field of production. But the more productivity develops, the more it finds itself at variance with the narrow basis on which the conditions of consumption rest. [Thus] a rift must continually ensue between the limited dimensions of consumption under capitalism and a production which forever tends to exceed this immanent barrier.[24]

Keynes later reached essentially the same conclusion: while at any given moment economic instability can come from a variety of causes, such as serious price inflation (or deflation), a drop in profit rates, or upheavals in international trade and investment flows, the basic dilemma of a *laissez faire* economy is that "the mere existence of an insufficiency of effective demand may, and often will, bring the increase of employment to a standstill *before* a level of full employment has been reached . . . [weakening] opportunities for further investment. . . . Moreover, the evidence indicates that full, or even approximately full, employment is of rare and short-lived occurrence.''[25]

Accumulation and the Changing Structure of Business, 1790–1860

The capitalism with which we are familiar is part of a historical process, with the next stage of development latent in the forms and methods of accumulation that dominate in any one period. Many features of our own economic institutions first became visible in the mid-nineteenth century, in the years between 1840 and 1860, although the interplay between accumulation and monopolization began much earlier. The newly independent United States of 1776 was a European transplant, already in a fairly advanced state of development; "the commercial expertise, artisan skills, and capital resources for domestic industrial development had been generated in the northern cities and in the surrounding rural areas."[1] The former colonies never cut their ties to the expanding mercantile system which was beginning to subordinate so many aspects of human existence to markets and prices. In fact, the economic development of the new nation is probably the purest example of capitalism in history, free as it was from the feudal encumbrances common to all its European mentors.

The Years before 1840

Elements of capitalist accumulation were present in the United States well before 1840. By the end of the eighteenth century, labor power and instruments of production, including land, were being transformed into commodities bought and sold in the marketplace like any others. Private property, individual mobility and acquisitiveness, and commercial exchange were all prevalent. They were powerful solvents of institutions and values incompatible with capitalist expansion (subsistence farming, religion as the guide to personal behavior, social ties based on communal or nonprice norms). From colonial times, there were no independent or antagonistic modes of production that capitalism had to challenge—except those of the native Americans and the southern slaveholders. Both would be destroyed by military force well before the end of the nineteenth century.

The accumulation of wealth in the form of productive capital was firmly established in the colonial economy, and it resumed with great energy after the interruptions of the 1770s and 1780s. But it was chiefly mercantile: the major source of profits, and increasing private wealth, was trade rather than the production of goods and services for impersonal markets. The dominant business unit, or firm, was embodied in an individual known as the general merchant. ("Dominant business firm" does not mean a statistically average firm but one that exerts a disproportionate influence on economic activity. In such a firm we can see both the most advanced methods of doing business *and* the forces tending to supersede it by pointing the way toward higher forms of accumulation.) Between the 1770s and the 1820s, the general merchant, located chiefly in port and river cities, acted as "the grand distributor," to use Chandler's term. This general merchant was the key figure in the entrepôt or market-center economies of the day. He

> bought and sold all types of products and carried out all the basic commercial functions. He was an exporter, wholesaler, importer, retailer, shipowner, banker, and insurer. . . . He provided short-term loans to finance staple crops and manufactured goods when they were in transit, and he made long-term loans to planters, farmers, and artisans to enable them to clear land or to improve their facilities. . . . With other merchants, he also insured ships and cargoes. Again with others, he built wharves for the ships. In the same port town, he helped to finance the construction . . . of rum distilleries, candle works, ropewalks, and shipyards—that is, those manufacturing industries not carried on by crafstmen in small family shops.[2]

Mercantile capital coexisted, and interacted, with the most common business units of the day—small hand-trade establishments, retail proprietorships, and farms that depended almost entirely on family labor. In Philadelphia in 1776, "the core element of the town economy was the one-man shop. . . . Most Philadelphians labored alone, some with a helper or two." In the 1780s there were diverse kinds of manufacturing in that city, from carriage making to distilling, woodworking, and clock making, but the scale of operations was tiny, limited as it was largely to serving individual customers on an order-by-order basis.[3]

Still, these small units were producing for sale to an external market, as well as for their own needs. Petty commodity production is production beyond self-sufficiency, and it generates economic surpluses, quite modest in the years before 1840, that make each unit dependent on market outlets for profits to plow back into the business. It thus sets in motion forces leading toward growing volumes of output and larger scales of operation. This is not to overlook the existence, at certain times and places, of commodity production governed by basic subsistence needs, but its necessarily static character stands out in contrast to the dynamics of production for an external market, even a small one.

In these early years, the accumulation impulse led general merchants and smaller units alike to reorganize their techniques (however primitive) and output mixes in order to survive. Under such circumstances each unit attempted to accumulate—buy and sell, profit, and reinvest—to protect the value of its property and avoid falling behind any potential competitor. Its members put in longer hours of work, cut back their own consumption, and reinvested all the returns they could. Merchants, craftsmen, and family farmers were all intent on building up equities in their enterprises. In their efforts to create an independent and remunerative economic base for themselves, some of them even lived on incomes below going wages in the area. This economic behavior was particularly evident in the westward movement of agriculture to Ohio before 1830 and then Indiana, Illinois, Michigan, Iowa, and Missouri, where pioneer farmers concentrated on wheat and corn with financial returns that took time to accrue. Such farms and similar nonfarm units were "small, but germinal, units of capital."[4]

The accumulation patterns of the 1790–1840 period should be understood as part of this historical background. Several related developments were now beginning to produce significant economic growth, which brought pressure on the capacity of existing business structures. Accumulation was gaining strength, but within definite limits.

The earliest impetus to economic growth came from foreign trade, which boomed from 1793 to 1807. Revolutionary turmoil and the Napoleonic wars in Europe allowed American shippers to capture a major part of the international carrying trade and led to unprecedented volumes of exports and profits. U.S. shipping earnings rose from $6 million in 1790 to $42 million in the peak year 1807; the value of all exports increased from about $20 million in the early 1790s to $109 million in 1807 (in current dollars). For a fledgling economy, these numbers are impressive. Exports probably constituted 15 percent of the national product such as it was.[5] Cotton exports alone shot up from 189,000 pounds in 1791 to 66 million pounds worth $14 million in 1807. Some merchants amassed fortunes of over $1 million, unheard of from trade during the colonial period.

The impact on trading channels and seaport cities was pervasive. It encouraged commercial cotton growing in the South and cotton commission dealing in New York City and set off an income-multiplier chain affecting other trading centers as well. But this export-led growth process was cut short. When British-French hostilities erupted anew in 1803, both sides imposed blockades on each other and searched or seized all ships, including neutrals. Fearful of entanglement in war, President Jefferson and the Congress passed the Embargo Act of 1807, banning all vessels in the United States from traveling to foreign ports and requiring special bonds for those in the coastal trade. U.S. exports duly plunged, from $109 million in 1807 to $22 million within a year. Harbor-based cities and their economies ground to a halt, and losses sustained by shipping interests were catastrophic, especially in New England.

But the embargo did not kill the entire income-generation process. Instead, it enhanced investment and profit possibilities in goods production at home. Ready-made markets for articles no longer available from abroad gave rise to import substitution. The growing demand for cloth prompted the mechanization of weaving and the integration of spinning and weaving inside a single "mill." Before 1808 only 15 cotton mills had been constructed; by the end of 1809 the total reached 87 and continued to grow through 1812. The number of spindles involved in cotton textile production increased from 20,000 in 1809 to 135,000 in 1815.[6] The end of the European wars in 1814, however, reopened the United States to a flood of British imports that drove many American competitors out of business. Large portions of the newly expanded manufacturing base were wiped out, bringing a decade of near-stagnation, with urbanization remaining constant at 7.2 percent of the population between 1810 and 1820—the only decade to show no such change.

Nevertheless, the war-related spurts in goods production provided a learning experience and some solid economic foundations for manufacturing expansion. This occurred not only in textiles, where several large New England firms survived the post–1814 British onslaught, but in other sectors as well. Machine processes were taking hold in Philadelphia, where the nation's first independent producer of textile machinery began operating in 1810, and by 1815 the city had steam-driven furniture and carpet factories. Greater numbers of woodworking machines were being introduced, with fastest growth in the sawmills of Pennsylvania. A million houses were built in the United States between 1800 and 1820.[7] Residential construction meant a continuous demand for all types of fittings, nails, bricks, shingles, and the machines to make them—a prime example of infant industrialization without a factory system, with these first shifts from handicraft toward machine production. In all, between 1810 and 1840 the manufacturing share of the labor force tripled, from 3 to 9 percent.[8]

The expansion of trade and then manufacturing was accompanied by two more growth-promoting developments. One was the advance of the agricultural frontier westward, from New England and the Middle Atlantic region into today's Midwest and from the "Old South" into Alabama and Mississippi, where land yields and output per laborer were well above those in the East. This shift into areas of higher farming productivity contributed substantially to the increase in real product per capita in the economy from 1810 to 1840. It also released labor for use in other sectors, as agriculture's share of the labor force fell from 81 to 63 percent.[9]

The second development was the "commercial revolution" in the Northeast. The first banks, law firms, insurance companies, and trade associations were forming an array of institutions involved in an east coast flow of information, business services, and credit. The number of commercial banks, the most important financial intermediary, increased from 87 in 1816 to more than 700 by 1836, as the practice of making loans by crediting the borrower's account with demand deposits was becoming common in eastern cities. Issues of government, bank, or transportation company bonds and stocks led some erstwhile merchants to specialize in security brokerage, while business news and advertising were being supplied by 1,400 newspapers in 1840, against fewer than 100 in 1790.[10]

Governments actively furthered this process, with public works in transportation and communication. Maryland, Pennsylvania, New York, and Massachusetts assisted their own seaports with harbor and other projects. Improved highways and post roads and, above all, the construction of canals cut transport times and freight costs dramatically between 1790 and the 1830s. New York City-Buffalo shipping time was sliced from 21 days to six when the Erie Canal (a state government project) opened in 1825, with freight charges reduced by a factor of ten per ton-mile. The postal service provided faster information flows, as the number of post offices increased from 90 in 1791 to 4,500 in 1820 and 13,500 in 1840; the cost of a two-sheet letter fell from 50 cents in 1816 (for up to 400 miles) to a flat rate of 3 cents in 1850. Transmitting an order between Philadelphia and Boston required two weeks in 1790, only 36 hours in 1836.[11]

A highly significant aspect of this "commercial revolution" was the decline of the general merchant. By the 1840s, "merchants had begun to specialize in one or two lines of goods: cotton, provisions, wheat, dry goods, hardware, or drugs. They concentrated more and more on a single function: retailing, wholesaling, importing, or exporting."[12] As volumes of produce being handled increased in the West as well as the East, specialized marketing intermediaries like forwarding and commission houses sprang up along the Ohio and Mississippi Rivers and stored and dispatched grain for both farmers and merchants. Steamboats plied the western rivers, with tonnage rising from 3,300 (and 17 vessels) in 1817 to 90,000 (600 vessels) by the early 1840s.[13] A new generation of "middlemen" was being born, supplemented by banks, fire and marine insurance companies, and common carriers. Together they were taking advantage of growing demands for business services to split off functions of the old general merchant.

Here too, it might be noted, state governments provided critical help, with devices like the chartered corporation. Some of the new banks and transportation companies had relatively large financing requirements. They were drawn to the corporate form not only to procure monopoly-type privileges through public charter, but also to raise capital by gathering in the savings of many small-business people: limited liability made it seem safe to buy a few shares in a bank or turnpike company operating outside one's own locality. Corporations as devices for mobilizing capital soon became much more important in the United

States than in the European nations. American capitalists tended to have their personal wealth tied up in mercantile or manufacturing ventures or else were land poor; they lacked the accumulated reserves of funds like those of English brewers or French financiers. Thus, in 1800, when neither Britain nor France had more than a score of chartered corporations, the United States, with a far smaller population, had 300—and over 1,000 by 1815. New York State alone had 959 incorporations from 1800 through 1829, and 573 more in the 1830s.[14]

By the 1840s the net effect of these changes was to make more efficient services available to businesses. A network of banking, transportation facilities, and specialized middlemen was appearing that could link together trade, finance, and goods production over space and time. From 1810 to 1840, the share of the labor force engaged in these nonfarm, nonmanufacturing activities grew from 16 to 28 percent.[15]

Spurts in foreign trade, the spread of manufacturing, rising agricultural productivity in the West, and the "commercial revolution" combined to bring about the first sustained economic growth in American history. Between 1805 and 1840, real per capita incomes increased approximately 30 percent, substantially faster than at any time in the colonial era. By 1840 the national product was five times larger than it had been in the first decade of the century.[16] With this expansion of the economy, the urbanized portion of the population rose from 6 percent in 1800 to 11 percent forty years later (Table 2.1). Although increases were concentrated in the great seaports of New York, Philadelphia, Boston, and Baltimore, new manufacturing towns in the interior, such as Rochester and Lowell (each had 20,000 inhabitants by 1840), were also contributing to urbanization. The number of places with 8,000 inhabitants or more rose from six in 1800 to 44 by 1840.[17]

The social byproducts of this economic growth were beginning to trace out sharper capitalist profiles. The increased concentration of income and wealth hinted at deeper changes in the urban social order and the rhythm of work. "Many lower-class groups increased their material standard of living under the new system of production, but only as a result of longer and harder hours of work." By the 1830s the sense of social distance between rich and poor was growing, as the changes in business and commerce meant "proportionately fewer independent entrepreneurs with productive property of their own."[18] The shifts in the character and pace of economic activity were creating the first signs of a new class of wage-earners, who would lose virtually all their independence for slowly and painfully acquired increases in material benefits.

In summary, by the 1840s the logic of capitalist enterprise—a search for greater total profits—was prodding firms to specialize and to reach out for potentially larger markets. But this "constant" of capitalist behavior was constrained by the steep costs of increasing the output of goods under existing industrial techniques, and by serious obstacles to the movement of trade and capital among the different regions of the country. Commerce among the regions was relatively unimportant, and northeastern cities were still competitors rather

Table 2.1

Urbanization in the United States, 1775–1910

	Urbanized percent of population	Population of cities (thousands)					
		New York	Philadelphia	Boston	Baltimore	Chicago	St. Louis
1775	N.A.*	25	40	16	6		
1800	6.1%	61	62	25	27		
1820	7.2	131	109	54	63		
1840	10.8	349	220	119	102	4	16
1860	19.8	1,175	566	179	212	112	161
1890	35.1	2,507	1,047	449	434	1,100	452
1910	45.7	4,767	1,549	671	559	2,185	687

Sources: Pred (1966), 23; Taylor (1967), 311, 314-15; U.S. Bureau of the Census (1913a), 63-65.

Note: Urbanized percent of population is the percentage living in incorporated places of 2,500 people or more. For New York, figures for 1860 through 1910 are for all boroughs as constituted under the Act of Consolidation of 1898.

*N.A. = not available.

than complementary centers specializing in specific groups of industries. Even in the larger cities, industrial capital was not yet a prime mover of metropolitan growth. Less than 10 percent of all workers were engaged in manufacturing, which was limited mainly to local market production and commerce-serving activities (printing, maritime provisions, sailmaking and ship repair, coopery). In the absence of generalized wage labor, no industrial class structure existed. Though small factories began to draw in groups of workers disciplined to be dependent on wages, journeymen like teamsters, haulers, and clerks still constituted the bottom layer of the social structure. In the South, the social situation was starkly different, as white settlers were establishing an export-oriented agricultural system sustained by an army of black slaves.

In terms of size, the "dominant business firm" of 1840 looked little different from its 1790 or 1800 predecessor—considerably more specialized, but still small, and almost universally a partnership or a family affair with only a handful of employees. The nation had a more sophisticated commercial and financial structure with better "impersonal market coordination" of economic activity, but textile mills, iron "plantations," and shipyards were the only large-scale manufacturing operations.[19] The 1832 report on manufactures by Secretary of the Treasury Louis McLane identified only 36 enterprises with 250 or more employees, most of them in textiles. For most firms, fixed capital was of so little importance relative to working capital (liquid assets used to pay for labor and inventory) that modern accounting procedures were in their infancy. The distinction between fixed charges and variable costs hardly seems to have existed.[20] Basic changes in the size and nature of the dominant business firm had not occurred, indicating that despite the vigorous accumulation of the 1800–1840 years, the structure of the economy remained preindustrial.

1840–1860:
The Germs of Industrial Transformation

The modern accumulation process is driven by the interaction between profit-seeking investment and the dominant business firm. Giant enterprises made their appearance with the long-term expansion of fixed capital and the increasing resort to the corporate form of organization. But the extent and speed of this process was limited by two factors—the costs of obtaining information, negotiating exchanges, and moving materials and goods, and the efficiency with which firms could produce much larger volumes of output. Not until such technological advances as the railroad and the telegraph were in place could demands for improved business services, growing throughout the 1830s and 1840s, begin to transform the business firm itself. And not until distant markets could be reached was interregional trade a real possibility, with business units in one region of the country tending to specialize in certain kinds of output so that their scale of operations could increase to levels inconceivable in the early 1840s.

Table 2.2

Railroad Trackage, 1830–1920
Thousands of Miles

	Net additions of track	Total miles of track, end of period
1830–39	2.3	2.3
1840–49	5.1	7.4
1850–59	21.4	28.8
1860–69	18.1	46.9
1870–79	39.7	86.6
1880–89	74.7	161.3
1890–99	28.0	189.3
1900–09	47.5	236.8
1910–19	16.3	253.1

Railroad Freight Volume, 1849–1920

	Freight volume (billions of ton-miles)	Freight volume per capita (ton-miles)
1849	0.4	17
1859	2.4	78
1882	39.3	744
1890	79.2	1,256
1900	141.6	1,861
1910	255.0	2,760
1920	413.7	3,886

Sources: Fishlow (1965), 326, 337; U.S. Bureau of the Census (1975), 727–33.

The modern accumulation process began in the 1840–1860 period, with the coming of the railroads. The first rails were laid in 1830 (see Table 2.2), and most of the early construction was confined to the eastern seaboard states. During the 1840s over 60 percent of railroad additions took place in New York and New England, while in the 1850s new construction was concentrated in the Midwest. By 1860 Ohio, Indiana, Illinois, Michigan, Wisconsin, and Iowa together accounted for over a third of all railroad mileage, and Chicago was becoming the railroad hub of the nation. By contrast, the eleven southern states that seceded from the Union a year later had less than 30 percent of total trackage, most of it connecting the coast with the interior to facilitate the export of cotton and other staples. In 1860 several railroad companies had property valued at more than $20 million. Never before had economic ventures required funds on a scale like this;

even the most expensive canal project, the Erie, cost only $7 million.[21]

Meanwhile the railroads were on their way to dominating the nation's capital formation as no single industry before or since (unless construction, far more heterogeneous, is considered to be one "industry"). By 1849–58 the "iron horse" already was generating around 15 percent of gross investment in the economy and 25 percent in the peak year of 1854. It was, by itself, largely responsible for the business cycle of 1854–57—the first modern-type cycle in U.S. history.[22] Although the "golden age" of railroading followed the Civil War, in terms of trackage expansion and freight volume (Table 2.2), the railroads were already defining the characteristics of accumulation for the industrial age by the 1850s. They brought nonagricultural investment to a position of leverage on the economy, they encouraged technical change and economies of scale in industry and agriculture, and they fostered regional specialization and interregional commodity trade. For manufacturing in the Northeast, railroads stimulated a range of already developing interests through "backward linkages," or railroad demands for the output of other industries. During the prosperous late 1850s, railroads absorbed about 20 percent of domestic pig iron and 25 percent of transportation equipment output, 8 percent of machinery production, and 5 to 10 percent of lumber.[23]

The railroads' "forward linkages"—sales of their services as inputs to other industries—were even more important. A landmark study of the railroads to 1860 shows that their strongest stimulus was to the extension of agriculture and settlement through the promise, and provision, of more flexible, faster, and cheaper transportation services. The railroad extensions of the 1850s, contrary to some romantic versions of entrepreneurial history, were not "built ahead of demand." They were responses to demands by farmers for access to eastern markets, and they whipped up the tide of landseekers to the West ahead of the rails. Thus, "an exceptionally large amount of new land was improved for agricultural use during the 1850s . . . with population gains in Minnesota, Iowa, Missouri, and Kansas particularly impressive. . . . Settlers did not wait upon the railroads but entered the region in anticipation of their coming—and also in anticipation of rising land and commodity prices."[24]

The railroads not only exerted forward and backward linkage effects, they also cut transport costs, released resources for use in other economic activities, and widened markets for goods of all sorts. Their contribution to overall economic growth, sizable by the 1850s, would become greater in the last three decades of the century, the period of heaviest railroad investment, as well as administrative and technological improvements and peak productivity gains in the industry.[25] The railroad was, perhaps most fatefully, one of the two technological breakthroughs of 1840–1860 that held out visions of vastly larger markets to be penetrated and new positions of economic power to be captured.

The other was the magnetic telegraph. Within ten years of Samuel Morse's "What Hath God Wrought!" cabled from Washington to Baltimore on May 24,

1844, more than 20,000 miles of telegraph lines reached every commercial center of any significance east of the Mississippi, from Boston to New Orleans to Chicago to St. Louis.[26] The transcontinental wire to San Francisco was completed in 1861, eight years before the railroad spanned the continent. By then there were 36,000 miles of pole line and 60,000 miles of wire with some six million messages per year being dispatched over them; and it took only two decades more for these totals to multiply from three- to five-fold.

With this rapid rate of diffusion, the telegraph began to change the face of business operations. Very soon the "lightning wires" began to sweep away institutional rigidities that still hobbled the American economy through the early 1840s—the inability of markets to break through barriers of space and time. Beginning in 1846–1850, Morse's invention was undergoing intensive commercial exploitation and bringing about widespread and often spectacular reduction in intermarket price differentials, information costs, and transactions costs. Merchants, farmers, bankers, shippers, and others soon learned the "great advantages of . . . this mode of instantaneous communication of intelligence [which] is with them not so much a matter of choice as of necessity, for, without availing themselves of it, they must necessarily be behind others in that which is essential to the success of their business" (the observations of a telegraph entrepreneur in 1850). Already, a St. Louis journalist stated in 1847, businesses could "thus regulate their trade and commerce *every day* by the actual and existing conditions of the markets at remote and distant points, and not by speculations as to prices and the demand for the staple products of the country."

The railroad was originally conceived as a local and regional facility, an image that began to change as trackage was laid westward in the 1850s. But the telegraph was interregional in its impact from its very beginnings. The result was enthusiastic adoption by a business system that was becoming national in outlook, and soon in scope. In the westward movement of commerce through Illinois to 1850, "the telegraph was the true forerunner of the railroads." Telegraphic communication between Chicago and the East was established by 1848, nearly four years before the first rail connections. "The telegraph system in America," a leading figure in the industry wrote in 1853, "is eminently characteristic of the national mind. At its very birth, it became the handmaiden of commerce." In no other nation was the telegraph so thoroughly dominated by business interests and business use.

Historian Glenn Porter has remarked that "it was the telegraph which first brought the speed of electronic communication within reach of the potential empire builder."[27] Imperial features of the telegraph for profit-seeking enterprises were prominent—and clearly recognized as such—from the outset: speed, secrecy, control, and intelligence.[28] Immediate transmission of orders and instructions was assured. Agents could be controlled and geographically scattered units brought under centralized supervision. Commercial intelligence took on new dimensions as elaborate codes guaranteed secrecy for users of the wires.

The spatial reach made possible by the telegraph system, in tandem with the railroads, expanded as information and transactions costs of serving a given market began to plunge. As early as 1851 a ten-word message could be sent from New York to Boston for 20 cents, New York to Chicago for $1.00, New York to New Orleans for $2.40, and between Washington, D.C. and Cincinnati for 70 cents. The average cost of a message fell to $1.05 in 1868 and 39 cents in 1877. Real cost decreases were larger still, since the overall price level rose between 1850 and 1875.

As transportation and communication improved in the decade before the Civil War and markets began to widen, the first genuine movement toward regional specialization and interregional trade occurred. The country's manufacturing center was evolving in the Northeast, the area benefiting from fast-growing per capita incomes, urbanization tied to commerce and trade, and markets for both consumer and producer goods. Through the 1830s, by contrast, it had been intraregional trade that initiated greater specialization in the domestic economy. Demand for manufactured wares and raw materials within a city's own hinterland and coastal trading areas caused the first widening of markets within the Northeast. In those days, "Philadelphians rarely sold goods in more distant markets. . . . Effective national integration postdated 1840."[29] For New York too, hinterland incomes earned from shipments of farm products and timber, and from New York City's consumption of these goods, created an expanding market for the city's manufacturers; over 80 percent of the Erie Canal's total revenues were derived from New Yorkers trading with New Yorkers.[30] In the West a similar story unfolded, though on a smaller scale. Active trade first developed within city-hinterland areas—Pittsburgh, Cincinnati, Louisville, St. Louis, Detroit.

In the 1840s, however, interregional trade began growing at a rapid rate, from a gross flow of $178 million in 1839 to $657 million in 1860 (current dollars; wholesale prices were stable over the period).[31] But this trade was heavily bilateral, involving the Northeast (or North) and the West, rather than trilateral among North, West, and South. In the North, per capita incomes, and consumer demand, were rising faster than the national average, and in 1860 the region was earning 15 percent of its total income from exports to other regions. The West was earning 23 percent of its total income from exports, and household spending power was growing there too.[32] In 1860, the North sold $164 million to the West and imported $147 million worth of goods from that region. The North sold $214 million to the South and bought but $69 million from it. For the West, commerce with the South was "a minor matter"; trade flows each way averaged only $30 million.

The tenuous West-South link shows that the South was primarily self-sufficient in foodstuffs. Cotton production on plantations required intensive use of slaves at picking time, but for the rest of the year planters had a labor surplus for grain and meat production.[33] At the same time the South failed to develop an active internal trade between city and countryside as the North and West were doing, and it was becoming more dependent on foreign markets. The North, meanwhile, was turning into a food-deficit region. Some of the North's consumption was supplied from the grain belt of the upper South, but the ties between North and West strengthened during the 1850s, as western prosperity increasingly depended on the growth in demand for grains, grain products, and livestock in the Northeast. Furthermore, the South was becoming a marginal market for northern manufactures.[34] Its shallow home market, a result of its specialization in cotton, left the South trailing in the industrialization process. It now lagged behind the North in all categories of industry, and manufacture was usually limited to auxiliary or local needs (sugar refining, rope, hand-made garments). The New England and Middle Atlantic states accounted for 72 percent of American manufacturing production by 1860; in that year the ratio of manufacturing and mining output to agricultural output for nonsouthern states was 8.7 times that of the South.[35]

Specialization and growth in the size of industries and firms were becoming the hallmarks of economic change in the Northeast. New York City was the emerging center for printing, apparel, and financial and shipping services. Philadelphia emphasized iron and coal, metals, food processing, and haberdashery, while Boston became known for textiles, shoes and leather products, hardware, and machinery. The latter complemented the machine tool industry of western New England and its "American System" that could make interchangeable parts for the mass production of Colt firearms, Yale locks, Waltham watches, Jerome clocks, McCormick reapers, and, after 1850, locomotives, sewing machines, typewriters, and other goods.

At the same time, the westward movement of agriculture was steering people away from self-sufficient pioneer farming toward market-oriented production and sensitivity to economic opportunity near and far. World-renowned technological innovations in farm machinery increased labor productivity in the West. John Deere's steel plow spread rapidly in the 1850s, along with various reapers, threshers, seed drills, mowers, and other labor-saving devices. By 1860 Deere turned out more than 10,000 steel plows annually, and 80,000 reapers had been bought by farmers.[36] Farms became larger and more specialized in cash crops, particularly in wheat in the north-central states.

The economic currents running between the North and the West were transforming a mercantile economy into an industrial capitalist one. Manufacturing was coming to depend on processed agricultural products and the output of goods that farmers purchased as means of consumption and production. Extending the agricultural frontier augmented the productive capacity of farms and further stimulated economic growth in the North.

"King Cotton" ruled the southern economy—and the contrasts could not have been sharper. Cotton exports may have been booming (they increased 2.4 times in constant dollars between 1840 and 1860[37]). Slavery, too, may have "paid" in terms of the rate of return on a dollar invested in a plantation compared to a dollar invested in a northern factory.[38] But noncapitalist relations of production had

Table 2.3

Measures of Economic Growth, 1839–1859

	GNP, 1860 prices (billion dollars)	Real GNP per capita (dollars)	Sector shares of value added in commodity output*		
			Agriculture	Manufacturing	Construction
1839	$1.62	$ 95	72%	17%	10%
1849	2.43	104	60	30	9
1859	4.10	130	56	32	11

Sources: Robert Gallman, "Commodity Output, 1839–1899," in National Bureau of Economic Research (1960), 26; Gallman, "Gross National Product in the United States, 1834–1909," in National Bureau of Economic Research (1966), 26.

*In each year, mining accounted for the remaining 1 percent of output.

already isolated the South from the impulses that were forging a national market elsewhere. The South's plantation economy was becoming an obvious obstacle to the dominance, and open-ended expansion possibilities, of industrial capital and free markets for labor. And the spread of an aggressive, restless, and innovative capitalist order was an equally obvious threat to the way of life of the Old South.

A number of other developments also mark the 1840–1860 period as one of strong capitalist accumulation in the North and West. First, the long economic expansion of 1843–1857 was bringing a surge in per capita incomes, along with other typical signs of a capitalist boom. By 1859, gross national product (GNP) per head was some 37 percent higher than in 1839 (see Table 2.3), indicating a two-decade rise greater than the increase over the entire 1790–1840 period. The growth spurt was led by manufacturing, whose share of total commodity output nearly doubled. Agriculture's share of the labor force declined from 64 percent in 1840 to 53 percent in 1860; in the North the decrease was even greater, from 63 to 34 percent.[39] A rise in capital formation and a decline in the relative prices of producers goods and raw materials are additional indicators of the vigor of this upswing. Most notably, the proportion of net national product devoted to investment rose from an average 9.5 percent during 1834–43 to over 12 percent in 1849–58.[40]

Second, the distribution of income and wealth was becoming more skewed between 1820 and 1860. Owners of capital, as well as some skilled craftsmen, began to enjoy disproportionately large shares of the economic rewards flowing from the changes in production and markets. Real wages did rise for working people during these years. But for common labor they lagged behind overall economic growth, as pay differentials widened substantially during the antebellum era. By 1860 income disparities had risen to a "high plateau of inequality" that persisted for the better part of a century.[41] The acceleration of economic activity increased demands for both skilled and unskilled labor, but the supply of unskilled hands became more elastic with the waves of immigration that began in the 1840s. During that decade, some 1.7 million foreigners arrived, keeping down the wages of unskilled labor even as labor productivity was rising.[42] For businesses, this situation was an invitation to wage cutting and speedups. It should be stressed that this picture excludes black slaves, whose consumption levels are variously estimated to have been about one-third the level of free workers in the 1850s.

Wealth, or property (which has always been more unequally distributed than income), was highly concentrated in the colonial period even in the nonslave North. It too became even more unequally distributed in the antebellum decades. By 1860 the wealthiest 2 percent of the nation's families owned one-third of all physical assets, the richest 10 percent held three-quarters, and the richest 50 percent possessed virtually everything—half of all households had zero wealth.[43] These trends were probably aggravated by urbanization and immigration to the United States from 1845 to 1860; inequality tends to be greater in urban than rural areas, and immigrants are usually younger people in the low-saving phase of their life cycle. Still, these findings of marked and growing inequalities in wealth not only pose a challenge to the "egalitarian tradition" in American history; they also offer testimony to the inherent tendencies of market capitalism. Here, if anywhere, was a test-tube case of a brand-new and expanding capitalist economy, with no landed aristocracy and no preexisting feudal structures to break down. Yet in its periods of most buoyant growth it generated increasing inequality, which, even a century later, was only partially moderated by the government-supported growth of the post–1940 era.

The third sign of strong capitalist accumulation in the 1840s and 1850s was "the revulsion against internal improvements."[44] The phrase refers to the wide-spread reaction against public works. At least through the 1820s, Americans had taken a pragmatic attitude toward the role of government. Public funds, as noted earlier, had been liberally used to improve transportation and the flow of commercial information. There was general understanding that huge projects like the Erie Canal (1817–25) simply could not be carried out by private enterprise. The 1808 *Report on Roads and Canals* by Albert Gallatin, Secretary of the Treasury in the administration of Thomas Jefferson, asserted that though such improvements may sometimes be left to "individual exertion, without any direct aid from Government," there were obstacles that made a private enterprise solution unfeasible in America—scarcity of capital and "the extent of the territory compared to the population. . . . The General Government can alone remove these obstacles."

The defeat of national planning for internal improvements was no doubt related to the growing sectional conflicts, especially between the North and the South, and agitation for "states' rights." But the private business sector was also starting to oppose "government interference" in the economy. The ideological

reaction apparently began with the great expansion of 1843–1857, when a generation of capitalists began to sense the burgeoning opportunities that lay in free-
wheeling exploitation of new technologies and new markets. The telegraph provides evidence. The industry embarked upon its first growth phase in the late
1840s, after Morse's experimental line between Baltimore and Washington had
been financed by $34,000 in federal subsidies.[45] With the swift commercial
success of telegraphy, a campaign for public ownership was undertaken by a
number of congressmen and private citizens. Opposition was strong and effective
from the outset. "Who should own the Magnetic Telegraph?" asked the New
York *Mercantile Advertiser* in 1846. Surely not the Post Office was the reply,
because of "its utter inefficiency, and its absolute inability to meet the wants of
the public . . . in comparison with *individual* enterprise it is perfectly contempt-
ible . . . a bungling concern."

Similar "government incompetence" language was heard from several of the
early telegraph entrepreneurs. By 1868 Western Union had established the nation's first industrial monopoly, and only in the United States and Canada did
telegraph systems remain in private hands. A decade later, Western Union was
taken over by speculator Jay Gould and saddled with heavily watered stock. Its
efficiency remained spotty, its message-pricing structures were discriminatory,
and technological improvements in the industry were mostly the work of inventors unconnected with Western Union. Nonetheless, Wall Street's *Commercial
and Financial Chronicle* was charging editorially (December 2, 1882) that a
government-run telegraph would be "communistic."

Henceforth, if government wished to subsidize private business operations,
there would be no objection. But if public power were to be used to control
business actions or if the public sector were to undertake economic initiatives on
its own, it would run up against the determined opposition of private capital.

The Economy of 1860: The Limits of Change

By 1860 the main barriers to market enlargement were falling—transport costs,
transactions costs, information costs. Such resource savings encourage growth in
the size of business firms, as owners perceive that they can now reach out for
larger markets. Eventually, the size of enterprise would grow precisely because of
the effects of "market perfection" on a national scale. Companies could then
move toward high-volume, high-speed operations. Realization of these possibilities followed the Civil War, but the threshold of increasing returns was falling by
1860. Real value added per establishment in manufacturing increased by nearly
half between 1850 and 1860, to a level of $8,243 (in 1929 dollars), not surpassed
until the late 1870s.[46]

Americans were affluent by international standards. On the eve of the Civil
War real income per head was 25 percent above income per capita in France, one
of the more developed countries in Europe at the time. Only the British enjoyed

higher average incomes, but Americans were to surpass them within thirty years.[47] American producers were creating distinctive forms of industrial technology. They had taken the undisputed lead in inventing labor-saving machinery for agriculture and interchangeable parts techniques for mass production of several types of household articles. Specialized human skills were being replaced by specialized machinery for making goods that could be assembled with no hand-tooling of parts. In the process, a new industry was being born—machine tools.

These 1840–1860 changes must be kept in perspective. They were critical but still small compared with what would occur after 1870. The lion's share of manufacturing assets in 1860 was held by proprietorships and partnerships, not corporations. There was no concentration as we know it, with a few hundred corporations controlling a third or more of the nation's industrial output and assets. No industrial working class yet existed; nor was there any white-collar stratum composed of administrative and technical personnel often possessing a substantial degree of formal education.

What was happening, however, was unmistakable. Once again capitalist enterprise was transforming its own material base, rendering the commercial improvements of the 1800–1840 period obsolete. The process of accumulation, competition, and innovation, and the localized markets it was simultaneously widening and leapfrogging, provided the foundation of industrial capitalism in the United States. That appeared after the Civil War; its characteristics were massive increases in investment, large bureaucratized business firms, and a class of propertyless wage earners forced to sell their labor power to private capital to obtain the wherewithal to survive. The sum total of the economic order remained as complex as ever, with farms run by individual proprietors and scores of small businesses clustered in cities and towns across the land. But the texture of the economy was soon to be altered beyond recognition. Henceforth, giant business organizations would dominate the pace and pattern of economic life, and social attitudes and practices would increasingly reflect the corporate way of doing things.

3

The Grand Traverse of
the American Economy,
1865–1900

The history-making developments of the last three decades of the nineteenth century had their origins in the 1850s. Structural trends in the economy were probably unaffected by the bloody 1861–1865 conflict—"the red business," Walt Whitman called it—although the triumph of industrial capitalism would not have been so complete without the institutional shifts the war effected. The demise of slavery marked a turning point in national politics, and it removed the last obstacle to northern industrial hegemony and the expansion of the capitalist mode of production to continental dimensions.

But the changes came at a high price. If the momentum of growth builds up over time rather than erupting in a short "take-off" period,[1] it would appear that the Civil War caused a hiatus in that growth process. Unlike the First and Second World Wars, the Civil War intruded upon a fully-employed economy, diverting resources and entrepreneurial energies and halting the process of development. Contrary to long-held beliefs, northern industrialization received no stimulus from war demands. Quantitative benchmarks also show that in the 1860s the rates of growth of real per capita income, commodity output, manufacturing employment, and investment all sank well below trend.[2] Why this should have happened is no mystery. Displacement of civilian production, interruption of normal trade channels, a falloff in immigration, the wrecking of southern agriculture for well over a decade, the shattering loss of young lives—619,000 of them—were hardly conducive to economic growth or industrial innovation.

This provides all the more reason to stress the economic changes underway by the late 1850s as marking the beginning of the Grand Traverse—"the long disequilibrium passage to higher wealth-income proportions . . . [and to] per capita output levels higher than the one left behind."[3] The Traverse represented a great surge of accumulation that was technologically-induced, with profit prospects created by the new technologies the crucial factor for a generation of extraordinarily aggressive capitalists. Rapid growth of demand for mass-produced goods provided a complement so powerful that markets and technologies stimulated each other—a "virtuous circle" of income growth and investment opportunity.

The Grand Traverse: In Quest of an Explanation

The Grand Traverse spanned the entire second half of the nineteenth century, although, due in part to the disruptive effects of the Civil War, its revolutionary phase followed 1865.

In the 1850s, the share of gross investment in the gross national product (GNP) stood at 14 to 15 percent, the share of net investment in the net national product (NNP) at 12 percent. Already these capital formation proportions were significantly higher than they had been twenty years earlier (see p. 24). By the end of the Civil War they had dropped below the rates of the late 1850s, but in the next decade, 1869–78, both gross and net investment rates jumped sharply above any levels hitherto seen and continued to rise almost through the turn of the century. These figures, in 1860 prices, show the trend of investment during the Grand Traverse:[4]

	Percentage shares of investment in	
	GNP	NNP
1839–48	11%	10%
1849–58	14–15	12
1869–78	22–23	18
1879–88	22–23	17
1889–98	28	20

For neoclassical followers of the new economic history, the cause of this investment surge was a change in relative factor prices and subsequent adjustments to it: the key is that the prices of capital goods fell compared to wage rates. Of the two cost components of capital goods—interest rates and actual production outlays—declining interest rates were "of greater importance in reducing the cost of capital," as both nominal and real interest rates declined between 1850 and 1890. The long-term decline in interest rates, in this view, must have been caused by autonomous increases in saving. Since the demand for capital was obviously increasing too, "the suggestion is that the supply of savings was increasing even faster."[5] Thus, the great leap forward in capital formation was but one more historical response to a relative price change: increases in the desired savings-to-income ratio drove down interest rates, led to a fall in the price of capital goods and a rise in investment, and industrialized America.

How is the all-important autonomous shift in saving to be accounted for? It turns out that of the various sources of savings—personal saving out of current income, government budget surpluses, business profits, and foreign loans to American investors—none can explain a major portion of the rise in the savings-income ratio. Corporate retained earnings were insignificant; public sector savings were modest relative to investment demands; foreign-supplied savings were always a small share of total savings, no more than 5 or 6 percent in the early years of the nation and less after 1840.[6] So, by process of elimination, personal savings should have been the principal factor. But why did they rise? The answer is said to be found in the development of financial markets. Improvements in financial intermediation reduced risk and uncertainty, lowered the costs of transactions (search, negotiation, administration), and increased the liquidity of holdings, with an increase in net returns to savers and a decrease in costs for capital-users.

This formulation poses some serious problems, however. First, if "financial innovation" was the prime reason for the long-term climb in the investment-income ratio, what happens to the "autonomous" character of the accompanying savings shift? Second, why should risk-averse entrepreneurs establish banks, insurance companies, and other financial institutions if profit prospects are not more or less promising to begin with? If substantial pools of savings were not already being generated, who would want to add to the not-insignificant supply of financial services existing by the 1850s?[7] Third, while speculative creation of financial institutions may increase the total volume of savings by making it easier and cheaper for savers to make initial commitments of their funds, the timing and extent of the growth of the financial sector strongly associate it with the investment process, as Schumpeter recognized.[8] Fourth, it is possible that the interest rate decline itself had less to do with increases in saving, and more to do with a fall in the risk discount on investment projects as new gambles proved their worth.

There is another major problem with the neoclassical account of the Grand Traverse. The well-documented plunge, by nearly a third, in the relative price of producers equipment through the 1890s seems more likely to have been due to technological progress—that famous "given" of neoclassical economics.[9] With advances in metallurgy and machine tools, the costs of producing plant and equipment were declining steadily through innovation, as we shall see. The result was a large increase in output in the capital goods sector and a lower relative price for fixed capital, to which a reduction in the nominal cost of funds surely did contribute. Technological forces also explain why the net rate of return to capital fell much less than neoclassical theory would predict. According to neoclassical theory, a rise in the capital-labor ratio, "all other things remaining equal," should lower the rate of profit and increase wage rates: massive capital accumulation and capital-deepening (a rising capital-labor ratio) are supposed to lower the yield on new investments just as massively. In fact the net rate of return on capital fell from 10 or 11 percent in 1800-1855 to around 7 percent in 1890-1905, and even that fall may be overstated because of the depression of the 1890s.[10] Investment-cum-technology was biased toward capital-using, labor-saving methods of production that apparently doubled the growth rate of labor productivity, "exerting upward pressure on the real rate of return . . . to all conventional property."[11]

A different story of how a specific historical process unfolds can make sense out of several things that "don't fit" the neoclassical parable. Economic change would not be seen as random but as brought about by autonomous investment by profit-seeking capitalists for reasons sometimes dictated by relative price changes but far more often by expectations of new marketplace advantages or by a drive to reduce labor requirements. Two effects of investment become vital for understanding the subsequent course of economic history—*income effects* and *embodiment effects*. Among income effects of capital accumulation would be saving itself. In the course of investment-propelled growth, the pool of savings is expanded through the familiar Keynesian multiplier process. "The traditional theory that . . . the process of capital formation necessarily involves the curtailment of consumption . . . finds no support whatever in the facts of our industrial history," one economist wrote in 1935, in a passage that must have disturbed his neoclassical colleagues still mystified over the events of the preceding six years.[12] But even in a "static" economy at full employment, when investment requires diversion of current income, saving can be "forced" through bank credit or inflation, either of which can be manipulated more readily by capitalists than consumers.[13] Income effects would also involve a distribution of income in ways congenial to capital: those who command the income-generation process from the start are not likely at a later stage to relinquish control and obey "marginal productivity" principles of factor compensation, unless compelled to do so by a superior force.

Embodiment effects, as Marx and Schumpeter recognized, are inherent in the accumulation process. Capitalists never invest simply to duplicate old or worn-out equipment: investment physically embodies the latest and best technologies designed to improve the firm's competitive position and enlarge total profits. Far from being separable, capital formation and technological change are complementary and interacting. There is no independence between what neoclassical economists refer to as "input quantities" and "technical progress."

Recast in this crucible, the Grand Traverse can be described as follows. Investment demand was the engine of growth. The historical advance to capital-intensive production "is not properly regarded as the consequence of the greater exercise of Thrift . . . [or] as an equilibrating adjustment to an autonomous, exclusively supply-driven rise of the savings rate."[14] Rising savings rates were a response to the shifts in investment demand: "the portion attributable to exogenous saving mobilization is trivial and negative."[15] Autonomous changes in investment not only destroyed any "steady state" paths the economy might have followed; they increased the investment-income proportion through "conventional capital-deepening bias in the progress of Invention during the nineteenth century."[16]

While the structure of savings is at best hard to pin down, the sources of investment demand could hardly be clearer. One industry, the railroads, accounted for 15 percent of gross private investment in the economy in the 1850s. That proportion averaged around 18 percent in the 1870s and 1880s, the years of peak construction.[17] It should be added that this increase took place during a period when the ratio of all investment to the GNP was itself rising to record heights in U.S. history—23 to 28 percent in the 1880s and 1890s. The railroad share of the aggregate stock of fixed reproducible capital rose from 14 percent in 1850 to 32 percent in 1880, then slipped to 26 percent by 1900. Only residential construction claimed a larger share, about half throughout the period.[18] Manufacturing expenditures for plant and equipment buttressed the later stages of this investment drive. Although manufacturing capital stock remained smaller than that of the railroads until after 1900, its "highest annual rate of growth . . . occurred during 1880–1890," its second-highest during 1890–1900.[19] Between 1880 and 1900, net investment in manufacturing actually exceeded net investment in railroads (a total of $5.8 billion compared to $5.5 billion in 1929 prices), as railroad investment virtually dried up between 1895 and 1898.[20]

The other main source of Grand Traverse investment demand was the nation's urban infrastructure—its factories and warehouses, office buildings, stores, ports, public utility systems, and residential housing. By the late 1880s investment in railroads had peaked, but it had just begun in street railways, electric utilities, and telephones and was accelerating in housing. Like all infrastructure overhead, these facilities are capital-intensive and require heavy outlays for construction, as opposed to producers durables (machinery and equipment), the other category of fixed capital. Table 3.1 shows that total new construction spending averaged more than three-fourths of gross capital formation (excluding changes in business inventories) through 1900. In those years, "population-sensitive capital formation" was the leader.[21] Between 1870 and 1900 alone the U.S. population grew from 40 to 76 million, and its urbanized contingent went from 26 to 40 percent (see Table 2.1), indicating a tripling of the urban population. Residential building was the biggest consumer of capital between 1869–73 and 1887–91, when its average annual absorptions increased four-and-a-half times (Table 3.1). Between 1870 and 1890 the number of urban dwelling units started more than tripled.[22]

Table 3.1

Gross Fixed Capital Formation by Categories,
Annual Averages, 1869–1931
Billions of Dollars, 1929 Prices

	Gross investment	Gross producers durables	Gross construction			
			Total construction	Nonfarm residential	Business	Public nonmilitary
1869–73	1.96	0.46	1.50	0.47	0.92	0.11
1887–91	5.69	1.32	4.37	2.09	2.01	0.27
1897–1901	7.21	1.75	5.46	1.72	3.30	0.43
1907–11	10.97	2.98	7.99	2.30	4.73	0.95
1917–21	10.31	5.09	5.22	1.31	2.99	0.92
1927–31	16.62	6.05	10.57	3.34	4.57	2.66

Source: Kuznets (1961), 576–78, 596–97.

Note: Because of rounding, detailed figures may not add up to total.

Through the early 1890s construction spending was still rising faster than investment in producers durables, a trend that was reversed thereafter, as shown by the rates of increase in Table 3.1. It marked the effective end of the Grand Traverse—the first great investment surge of the industrial era. Its features closely resemble those produced by what Paul Baran and Paul Sweezy called "epoch-making innovations," which transform the pattern of the economy "and hence create vast investment outlets in addition to the capital which they directly absorb. . . . Each produced a radical alteration of economic geography with attendant internal migrations and the building of whole new communities . . . [and] each directly or indirectly enlarged the market for a whole range of industrial products."[23]

Between 1865 and 1900 railroads and urbanization were the powerful investment forces behind industrialization, interacting with a host of other developments. The Grand Traverse gave rise to, and was perpetuated by, rapidly expanding personal incomes. Much larger volumes of savings were now being generated, inducing the founding or enlargement of financial institutions like savings banks, life insurance companies, and commercial deposit banks—savings mobilizers attuned to profit opportunities in supplying intermediation services. Financial markets broadened in size and in range of services offered; this tended to lower interest rates by reducing the costs of financial transactions, decreasing risk and uncertainty, and improving the liquidity of any given asset. The accelerating growth of national income was also laying the foundations for mass production and mass marketing, tipping the scales toward much larger business firms, a new stage in the ongoing monopolization process.

In the most rapidly expanding sectors of the economy, higher capital-labor ratios not only increased worker productivity but also made possible new forms of wealth-holding without seriously threatening the rate of return on increasingly large volumes of invested capital. During the Grand Traverse things did not "remain equal" as they do in a neoclassical world. Technical progress, designed by capitalists and embodied in new forms of capital equipment, maintained the flow of profits. While the rate of return to capital may have fallen modestly, capital's share of national income (profits plus interest) was rising, from about 30 percent in the 1850s to 36 or 37 percent in the 1890s, despite the intervening rise in the ratio of total capital to labor and national product. Labor's share, roughly 60 percent in 1850, levelled off in the 1880s at around 54 percent.[24]

The Grand Traverse was evidently giving rise to tighter management control over the labor process. The ability to purchase human labor, to subdivide it into precise tasks, and to equip it with specific types of tools, machinery, and factories places enormous power in the hands of any decisionmaker. During the last decades of the nineteenth century it was helping the new class of industrialists maintain profitability and hold wages below the value of labor's productivity.[25] The power to invest was, in addition, the power to orchestrate ethnic differences among workers and to play off craft unions against "radicals," further sapping unskilled workers' bargaining position. The fragmenting effect of immigration on potential working-class unity did the rest. Open immigration, supported by business interests against rising popular hostility and trade union opposition after 1880, kept supplies of labor plentiful and its wages lagging behind economic growth. These were among the reasons why the ratio of unskilled to skilled wages fell from 1850 through 1900.[26]

Working-class frustration over wages boiled over in the leading sector of corporate industrialism. A series of national railway strikes broke out in 1877, 1885–86, and 1894 (the Pullman strike), touching off violent labor agitation in other industries and cities across the country. All were put down, typically by heavy doses of armed force. The first phase of class struggle in the United States ended, in defeat for the trade-union movement.

The Fabric of Accumulation:
Demand and Supply 1865–1900

The "demand side" of the Grand Traverse is clear: population, urbanization, and purchasing power were all growing more rapidly between 1865 and 1900 than ever before.

The nation's population increased from 35.7 million in 1865 to 76.1 million in 1900, with the proportion living in cities rising from 22 to 40 percent. The largest absolute decennial increase in urbanization took place in the 1880s—nearly 7 percentage points.[27] Another measure of urbanization, people living in places of at least 8,000, climbed from 21 percent of the total population in 1870 to 33 percent in 1900.[28] By 1900 New York City had 3.4 million people, Chicago 1.7 million, Philadelphia 1.3 million, St. Louis and Boston nearly 600,000 each, and Baltimore over 500,000.

Unlike the commerce-induced urbanization of the antebellum period, these increases were due to manufacturing. Between 1865 and 1900 the ranks of nonagricultural workers tripled, and the manufacturing labor force increased much faster than the overall population in every one of the ten largest cities (the above six, plus Pittsburgh, San Francisco, Cleveland, and Detroit).[29] Jobs in manufacturing supported jobs in transportation, communications, law and advertising, and other business-support activities. Soon manufacturing and service specializations were providing markets for each other. Chicago was becoming "Hog Butcher for the world . . . Stacker of Wheat, Player with Railroads and the Nation's Freight Handler," New York the shipping, financial, and garment center, and Philadelphia the nation's coal and iron and haberdashery supplier.

Though extension of markets was made possible by historic breakthroughs in transportation and communication, the expansion of markets as outlets for larger volumes of production was driven by rising per capita incomes. Real income per person increased at an annual average rate of about 1.1 percent from 1800 through the 1850s; after the Civil War the rate jumped to 1.6 to 1.7 percent per year through 1900.[30] (The difference should be appreciated. Incomes increasing 1.1 percent per year will double in 64 years, while those growing at 1.65 percent per year will double in 42 years.) A distinct upswing in the scale of demand for goods was occurring. As per capita income rises the proportion spent on food tends to fall; and while the United States was still far from the "affluent society" of the post–1945 era, the combination of rising real income and urban growth intensified demand for industrially-produced consumer goods (textiles and apparel, boots and shoes, soap and cleaning agents, furniture and housewares, home appliances, processed food products).

Over the long run, however, growing demand must emanate from improvements in productivity, otherwise higher demand levels are not sustainable. Only increases in the productivity of labor and capital can give the economy the added capacity to generate or accommodate more "demand."[31] During the Grand Traverse, modern production techniques were beginning to pour out vastly greater quantities of goods under conditions of decreasing costs and real prices, expanding markets by expanding the purchasing power of consumers. As that happened, industries and firms were no longer so dependent on existing demand levels but, in effect, were creating their own markets.

On this causative—or supply side—level, the last third of the nineteenth century brought wholly new technologies based on the conscious application of science to economic production, rather than on mechanical ingenuity or "tinkering." A century of progress in electromagnetism, thermodynamics, chemistry, and geology now began to coincide with the development of mechanical engineering. The technologies of this "second industrial revolution" exerted a general, across-the-board influence on every economic sector, whether it be manufacturing, agriculture, communication, or transportation. The impacts can be broken down into four areas of innovation—metallurgy, inanimate power, capital equipment, and applied chemistry.

1. *Steel.* Steel had been known long before the late 1860s. But it was difficult to produce and remained a luxury good until an effective process was devised for regulating its carbon content, which must be an intermediate amount between pig and wrought iron. Steel possesses qualities superior to both; it can be shaped more easily than iron with the same strength and is far stronger than iron equally malleable. The breakthroughs came with the Bessemer process discovered in 1855–57 by an American and an Englishman working independently, the open-hearth method developed in Germany and France in the 1860s, and then the "basic process" for eliminating phosphorus invented by S. G. Thomas and Percy Gilchrist in Britain. Steel shortly began to replace wood, stone, iron, and clay. From the late 1870s on, mass-produced steel was incorporated into railroad cars and rails, ships, factory and office machinery, stoves, cans, wire and nails, bicycles, and later streetcars and automobiles. U.S. steel production soared from an annual average of 1.4 million metric tons in 1879–81 to 12.6 million in 1899–1901, when the United States was producing one-third of the world's steel.[32]

2. *Inanimate Power.*[33] In the early stages of American manufacturing, water was the major power source, especially in New England textile mills. The transition to steam power was slow. Not until the late 1860s did steam exceed water, with 52 percent of the total prime mover capacity of 2.35 million horsepower in manufacturing in 1869. Steam engines freed industry from having to locate along rivers and streams, where adequate power sites were becoming scarce. By 1899 steam power in manufacturing increased nearly seven times, to 8 million horsepower, and reached its relative peak, supplying 82 percent of manufacturing's power capacity.

The reign of steam was short in American manufacturing. Starting in the 1890s electric power began to make inroads. After 1900 it grew so fast that it rendered all other power forms obsolete within twenty years, accounting for 52 percent of primary power available to manufacturing enterprises by 1919. Powering each operation with its own electric motor ("unit drive") did away with the capital requirements of large steam engines to cover all power demands in a plant, even very small ones. Electricity also allowed a more flexible arrangement of production sequences than did the steam engine, with its clumsy methods of transmitting power from one centralized source. Fractionalized electric power meant that machines and materials could now be placed anywhere efficiency dictated, not where belts and shafts could most easily reach them. Electricity also affected intermediate inputs available to industry. It made possible the efficient refinement of copper, and it created the modern aluminum industry through the electrolytic reduction processes of the 1890s.

In all, between 1870 and 1900, total horsepower capacity in U.S. manufacturing grew fourfold. More significantly, the amount of inanimate power capacity per labor-hour nearly doubled.

3. *Capital Goods*. Machines, tools, and buildings have long existed for production purposes, but until the mid-nineteenth century they were simple kinds of equipment that expedited the division of labor—"machines which facilitate and abridge labor, and enable one man to do the work of many," as Adam Smith described them in *The Wealth of Nations* in 1776. A century later, as Marx observed, workers were being transformed into appendages of machinery itself, which was assuming almost-human attributes as it "takes the place of a mere implement."[34] In the United States the early shift from artisan workshops to small factories involved mainly a finer division of labor. It was after the Civil War that the modern factory grew up on the basis of large investments in fixed plant, mechanization of operations, and systematic use of inanimate power.

One special type of capital good, machine tools, was the key to "the American system" of interchangeable-part products that simplified manufacture and repair. Machine tools are metal-working tools that are at the same time machines. Their function is to cut and smooth metal into precise shapes with exceedingly strict tolerances, if they are to fit as parts of an intricate mechanism or product. Gradually it was realized that such machinery could be produced more efficiently by independent firms than in the users' own machine shops. These firms began to specialize in mechanizing the small number of operations common to virtually all metal-using industries. By the 1870s a distinct machine-tool industry existed to supply machinery for cutting, drilling, turning, grinding, planing, and polishing metals.

In the 1880s the output of "machinists' tools" became quantitatively significant, with production of metal-working machinery tripling and quadrupling in centers like Cincinnati and Rhode Island.[35] As the industry became more experienced in dealing with different production problems, it could apply similar techniques across industry lines and use the same end products—cutting machines, milling machines, turret lathes, precision grinders—for an ever larger number of industries. This "technological convergence" became cumulative, with the machine tool industry becoming a nerve center for transmitting new skills and techniques to all machine-using sectors of the economy. Its nucleus moved from firearms and sewing machines during 1850–1870 to bicycles in the 1890s and automobiles after 1900.[36]

4. *Applied Chemistry*. Chemical processes for metallurgy, tanning, and fermentation had also been known for centuries, but industrial chemistry as an independent entity did not originate until the last third of the nineteenth century. Scientific advances led the way here, too. Synthesizing organic chemicals, for example, could not have been done without an understanding of chemical transformations and the arrangement of atoms in a molecule. After 1880 this led to the production of coal tar and its derivatives for pharmaceuticals, dyestuffs, explosives, solvents, fuels, and fertilizers, and later petrochemicals. The soda and

heavy chemicals sector (inorganic) was revolutionized in 1863 by a Belgian, Ernest Solvay, who developed the ammonia-soda process for use in the manufacture of textiles, glass, paper, soap, starch, dyes, and sodium bicarbonate. Other advances took place in the production of sulfuric acid and chlorine for bleaching, and in chemical reactions carried out by means of electric current (electrolysis, electrometallurgy, electrothermal processing). Although the rapid growth phase of the chemical industry came after 1910, that industry was an integral part of the "second industrial revolution" and the increasing structural interdependencies characteristic of it. By the early 1900s the new chemicals were already becoming an essential input for metallurgy, petroleum, textiles, and paper.

The upshot of these new demand and supply forces can be succinctly described—enlarged markets absorbing far greater volumes of goods produced under techniques facilitating economies of scale. Statistics for the period remain sparse. Nevertheless, it is apparent that technological changes helped increase the size of business enterprise, as per-unit costs of production declined with rising levels of output.[37] Large, expensive plants and equipment—heavy fixed costs—did not begin to pay for themselves until a firm's output level was high enough to keep them running almost continuously. Thus, the expansion of markets was organically linked to the new scale of production. In some industries it was linked even more directly to new products. The technologies of the late nineteenth century compelled some of the "engineer-entrepreneurs" in brand-new industries (like electrical equipment and photographic supplies) actually to create the markets for their goods from scratch, all the way from informing potential customers about these new products to after-sale instruction, service, and repair.[38]

The kinds of changes that occurred are reflected in Table 3.2. Among the ten leading manufactures in value added in 1900 were six that did not appear in the 1860 list. Among the repeaters, machinery rose from seventh place to first. The increasing complexity of manufacturing and its greater capital requirements were stimulating industries that sold their products only to other industries. In 1900 three of the top four industries (and the ninth-place one) made producers (capital) goods or intermediate inputs used in producing goods for sale to the final users, whereas in 1860 three of the top four industries made consumer goods. And the lone industry that might be classified partly as a consumer goods industry among the top four in 1900 is the exception that proves the rule. Printing and publishing was a creature of the second industrial revolution. Paper made from wood pulp replaced the rag-made variety, the result of a science-derived process for using sulphur to mass-produce the new kind of paper. Labor productivity also increased with particular speed in this industry, which was the leader in electrification of its power equipment from the first years of the electrical age.[39] On the demand side, printing and publishing gained from the growth of cities, education, and business needs for printed materials. The combination of higher demand and cheaper supplies caused rapid expansion of the industry.

Table 3.2

Output and Employment in Leading Manufacturing Industries, 1860 and 1900

1860	Value added (million dollars)	Employment (thousands)	1900	Value added (million dollars)	Employment (thousands)
Cotton goods	54.7	115.0	Machinery	413.1	389.0
Lumber	53.6	75.6	Lumber and timber	396.1	508.8
Boots and shoes	49.2	123.0	Printing and publishing	291.5	195.2
Flour and meal	40.1	27.7	Iron and steel	206.3	183.3
Men's clothing	36.7	114.8	Malt liquors	185.3	39.5
Iron fabrication	35.7	49.0	Tobacco manufactures	170.8	132.5
Machinery	32.6	41.2	Cotton goods	162.7	302.9
Woolen goods	25.0	40.6	Men's clothing	155.7	157.6
Carriages, wagons, carts	23.7	37.1	Railroad cars	108.6	173.6
Leather	22.8	22.7	Slaughtering and meat packing	103.0	69.3
Manufacturing, total	854.3	1,474.0	Manufacturing, total	4,832.5	4,711.6

Sources: U.S. Bureau of the Census (1865), 733–42; (1902), clxiii; (1913b), 40.

All leading industries (including numbers 11 through 15 in 1900—boots and shoes, woolens, distilled liquors, bakery products, women's clothing) were becoming more capital-intensive, with a sharp acceleration of the flow of materials through the stages of production. Productivity increased spectacularly in industries like printing and publishing and malt liquors (beer), but all manufacturing benefited from the new demand and supply conditions. The data in Table 3.2 indicate that annual value added per worker in manufacturing rose from $580 in 1860 to $1,026 in 1900, and even more in real terms as prices fell some 20 percent over the forty-year period. In the new age of mass production, raw materials were converted into finished goods through consecutive and integrated processes, most of them mechanized with water or steam, then electric, power. Continuous processing of sorts had been introduced in a flour mill in 1784 by Oliver Evans of Delaware and in the 1850s in the hog slaughterhouses of Cincinnati, but the engineering techniques of the 1880s and 1890s made the assembly line a practical objective of manufacturing strategy (its most famous example would be Henry Ford's 1913 Highland Park plant). Mass-produced and mass-marketed for the first time were articles like bicycles, pneumatic tires and rubber footware, typewriters and sewing machines, linoleum, photographic supplies, soap, ready-made clothing and undergarments, shoes, beef and pork, canned food, beverages, cigarettes, stoves, ice boxes, plumbing fixtures.

The foregoing makes clear that while the railroads were the spearhead of the modern accumulation process, it was manufacturing that brought both industrial revolution and big business to the United States in the last third of the nineteenth century. Manufacturing production expanded 5.8 times between 1869 and 1899. In the 1880s, the decade of fastest growth, the volume of manufactures more than doubled.[40] As Table 3.3 reveals, manufacturing had made substantial gains since the early 1800s (see also Table 2.3) but still was responsible for only one-third of all commodity output in 1869, compared to agriculture's 53 percent. Just thirty years later the shares of the two sectors were reversed. Though 1865–1900 "wage earners" data are not comparable with present-day categories, it appears that by 1900 the proportion of all workers engaged in manufacturing passed the one-fifth mark, not far below the 23 to 28 percent range typical of the 1920–1970 years.[41]

During 1865–1900 the factory became the standard production unit in manufacturing, and it brought a significant increase in the average size of manufacturing establishments. Available data, again not exactly comparable with today's series, do indicate a rise from 8 employees per establishment around 1870 to about 16 in 1900. Between 1880 and 1900 alone, physical capital per establishment increased by at least 75 percent.[42] Finally, the average manufacturing plant in 1900 served an area more than three times larger than that of a typical plant as late as 1882.[43]

America's rise to manufacturing supremacy was extraordinary by any measure. By the late 1890s the United States became the ranking industrial power

Table 3.3

Sector Shares of Value Added in Commodity Output, 1859–1899

	Agriculture	Manufacturing	Mining	Construction
1859	56%	32%	1%	11%
1869	53	33	2	12
1879	49	37	3	11
1889	37	48	4	11
1899	33	53	5	9

Sources: See Table 2.3.

Table 3.4

Percentage Distribution of World Manufacturing Production, 1870–1938

	1870	1896–1900	1913	1926–29	1936–38
United Kingdom	31.8%	19.5%	14.0%	9.4%	9.2%
United States	23.3	30.1	35.8	42.2	32.2
Germany	13.2	16.6	15.7	11.6	10.7
France	10.3	7.1	6.4	6.6	4.5
Italy	2.4	2.7	2.7	3.3	2.7
Russia-USSR	3.7	5.0	5.5	4.3	18.5
Japan	N.A.*	N.A.*	1.2	2.5	3.5
Others	15.3	19.0	18.7	20.1	18.7

Source: League of Nations (1945), 13.
*N.A. = not available.

(Table 3.4). In 1913 it was turning out 35.8 percent of the world's manufactured goods, only slightly less than its three closest rivals—Britain, Germany, France—combined.

Winds of Change:
The Consequences of the New Accumulation

The paradox of the last third of the nineteenth century is that it was a Golden Age—the heyday of private enterprise if ever there was one—and yet a period of profound instability and anxiety. Commodity price levels drifted downward almost without interruption from 1865–70 through 1895–98, putting pressure on profit margins that never seemed sufficient no matter how large.[44] More significantly, the dynamic new engine of capitalism seemed unable to generate steady, crisis-free economic growth. Between 1867 and 1900, the economy went through eight complete business cycles (measured from peak to peak or trough to trough). Over these 396 months, the economy expanded during 199 months and contracted during 197—a disappointing if not ominous performance in view of the glowing images the new capitalists were fashioning of themselves and their economic system.[45]

The interplay between accumulation and monopolization was now bringing forth a regime of production dominated by giant business firms—and their investment activities. Attributes of this modern, corporatized economy first began to appear in the last third of the nineteenth century. As they did, capitalism was evolving toward a strong dependence on private autonomous investment as the prime mover of the economy, and investment was becoming the engine of growth and instability. A maturing corporate investment mode began to develop mechanisms tending to increase productive capacity and the potential output of both consumer and producers goods faster than the demand for them. To a considerable extent the new supply forces were indeed creating their own demand. But the rate at which they were doing so depended on how smoothly and steadily aggregate demand, composed of consumption and investment expenditures, was growing. It was the beginning of capitalism's endemic problem of maintaining levels of aggregate spending high enough to prevent productive capacity from outstripping demand.

The accumulation process once again was rendering past advances obsolete. It had moved the economy out of a long era of increases in living standards that were tiny and reckoned in centuries (when they were discernible at all) to a new age of productivity-generated advances in mass purchasing power. No sooner was the brave new age begun, however, than it was being undermined by science-based gains in efficiency that permitted huge expansions in productive capacity that tended to overshoot actual levels of private demand. The main problem lay in a system that encouraged efficiency gains but discouraged a distribution of income that could assure commensurate gains in worker purchasing power.

Through most of the Grand Traverse the economy's capacity for absorbing additional capital was very large compared to its ability to create and mobilize savings. But during the last decades of the century it was no longer so easy for capital accumulation to forge ahead at a faster rate than private consumption. As the modern corporate investment mode emerged out of the changes of 1865 to 1900, excess capacity no longer was simply a result of rapid expansion of fixed capital as new industries spread nationwide, with the railroad-telegraph network. Now the emerging goal of corporate enterprise was the systematic expansion of profits through labor-saving and capital-saving innovation, with the latest technologies built into the process. This kind of cost cutting tends to generate excess capacity, as a given amount of investment becomes more productive and capital-output ratios undergo a long-term decline. It explains why, in the late nineteenth century, the economic order was beginning to move "from conditions of capital scarcity to those of capital abundance."[46]

The New Age of Monopolization, 1875–1902

The structure of American industry began to change in the mid 1870s at a speed that stunned contemporaries. It threatened, and outraged, enough of them to cause a wave of "antimonopoly" agitation culminating in the Sherman Antitrust Act of 1890—whose vague language outlawing restraint of trade "in the form of trust or otherwise" simply led industrialists and financiers to look for ways of combining companies through new legal devices. By the late 1890s the corporate revolution had transformed the American business system. Small businesses persisted in the hundreds of thousands, but the dominant form of enterprise in terms of economic power and social impact was now the large corporation serving a national market. All the big business characteristics we know today were becoming evident—increasing scale of operations, formal separation of ownership from actual control, complex management structures and multiplant organization, and growing concentration of the output of many industries in a handful of firms.

What was emerging, particularly in mass production, was an industrial structure familiar to us nowadays as oligopoly, with the bulk of each market shared by a few large rivals. By 1904 one or two giant companies, usually put together by merger, controlled half the output or more in 78 different industries, from oil and steel and locomotives to biscuits and crackers. About one-fourth of the total assets of all industrial corporations was owned by the 100 largest ones, with the top 10 holding nearly half the assets of those 100. Furthermore, corporations employed 70 percent of all production workers outside agriculture in 1900, creating an industrial working class in a society that still liked to regard itself as individualistic.[1]

The Railroads: Big Business Pioneer?

The railroads were, as Chandler claims, "the nation's first big business." In the mid 1850s five railroad companies were providing service over 450 miles of track or more, posing altogether new problems of administrative coordination. The east-west trunk lines (the Erie, Pennsylvania, New York Central, Baltimore and Ohio) were capitalized at $17 to $35 million, at a time when only a few of the largest textile mills had total assets of $2.5 million.[2] In 1873 the Pennsylvania, the largest system, had 5,814 miles of track, operating revenues of $70 million, assets exceeding $140 million, and 8,000 stockholders.[3]

Soon single railroad systems managed more employees and handled more funds than all but the biggest public organizations. The Post Office, the largest government enterprise, employed 95,000 in 1891, but the majority held nonspecialized jobs in one of the 64,000 post offices. In 1890 the Pennsylvania Railroad had 64,300 employees, perhaps as many as 100,000 if affiliated lines west of Pittsburgh were included. Its "general administrative" staff numbered 2,600.[4] "The great railway systems," Chandler concludes, "were by the 1890s the largest business enterprises not only in the United States but also in the world. . . . The railroad was, therefore, in every way the pioneer in modern business administration."[5]

That may be so, but the critical impact of the railroads was not as the pioneer example of modern management techniques—as "the most relevant administrative models"—to be studied or copied by later capitalists.[6] Business leaders generally seem to have regarded their own industries as unique; "most ignored intellectual issues and concentrated on meeting immediate problems in the most expeditious manner possible."[7] The builders of the giant new industrial firms of 1880–1900, according to Thomas Cochran, "do not appear to have consulted with leaders of railroads or public utilities, the older forms of big business" on the details of management structure.[8] They were, however, keenly aware of the economic forces set in motion by the railroads after 1865, as that industry went through its own round of unregulated expansion, duplication of physical facilities, and competitive price cutting that threatened the survival of nearly every line at one time or another.

This was also the infancy of "robber baron" capitalism. One of its earliest and best-known manifestations was the 1868–1872 fight between Cornelius Vanderbilt of the New York Central and the notorious triumvirate of the Erie—Daniel Drew, Jay Gould, Jim Fisk—over control of the Erie.[9] Business leaders described the overall situation as one of "ruinous" or "destructive" competition as they faced the prospect of their capital being expropriated by a veritable "cheapening of commodities" process. The need for some kind of planning or regulation was crystal clear. Cooperative equilibrium of some sort had to replace free competition (let alone the barroom-brawl capitalism practiced by a Jay Gould), and it did, to a degree. The means employed were both private and public.

Starting in the 1880s the urgent theme in railroad finance and management was "consolidation": larger railroad systems began to absorb smaller lines through purchase, lease, or trust arrangements. Investment bankers, who combined the roles of promoter, financier, and bond and stock salesman, were perfectly placed to piece together such consolidations. Not only had they begun to handle the marketing of railroad, and some industrial, securities; they had themselves invested in several major railroads before the 1873 panic, which exacerbated the competitive squeeze for many overextended lines. Among the high priests of finance, John Pierpont Morgan (1837–1913) soon stood out for his restructuring of the New York Central in 1879. W. H. Vanderbilt wanted to sell a large block of his shares in the New York Central without driving their price down and still retain control through a minority interest device. Morgan showed Vanderbilt how it could be done. He discreetly sold $25 million of Central stock in London without disturbing the market—a "grand financial operation," the *Commercial and Financial Chronicle* called it (November 29, 1879). Morgan's goal was "communities of interest"—agreed-upon spheres of corporate influence to replace competitive rivalries. From the 1880s on he played an omnipresent role in railroads by setting up regional rail associations, settling territorial wars (he personally resolved a Pennsylvania-New York Central dispute on his yacht in 1885), and restoring credit ratings to safeguard bondholder and stockholder interests, with Morgan-designated trustees duly placed on the boards of all reorganized lines.

By the turn of the century railroad consolidation was virtually complete. Of some 200,000 miles of track in the United States, about two-thirds had been brought under the control of seven interest groups—Vanderbilt (New York-Chicago), Morgan (the Southeast), the Gould roads and the Rock Island system (Mississippi Valley), Harriman (central and southern), Hill (northwest), and the Pennsylvania (Philadelphia and Baltimore westward). The seven groups, by generally accepted estimates, took in 85 percent of all railroad profits around 1900.

Government too played a role in the rail consolidation movement—or was drawn into its vortex. By the mid 1880s popular pressures for federal action to control railroad abuses were becoming too strong to hold off much longer. Among the targets were discriminatory freight rates and rebates for special shippers, as well as the pooling of traffic and corrupt financial dealings with suppliers. Meanwhile, the railroads themselves were anxiously seeking ways to contain their competitive struggles. Thus in early 1886 a Senate committee found that railroad executives were manifesting "an increasing readiness to accept the aid of Congress in working out the solution of the railroad problem which has obstinately baffled all their efforts."[10] Rebates, savage competition, and erratic profits were just as much a problem for railroads as overcharges on freight shipments were for Iowa or Indiana farmers. The common solution was the landmark legislation of 1887, the Interstate Commerce Act, the federal government's first venture into the "regulation" of an industry. Even though the act was amended and tightened on several occasions through 1900, its significance never changed. Protecting the consuming public from the most blatant abuses of private enterprise was a providential opportunity not only to save capitalism from some of its self-destructive instincts, but also to use government power to stabilize industries themselves. For the railroads, the cost of regulation was bearable relative to the benefits it conferred—a halt to rate-cutting wars and a leap forward toward the planning of output levels, pricing, and profits.

It was a decisive precedent; a peek at one future development shows why. After 1907 the Bell system, observing the stabilizing effects of Interstate Commerce Commission (ICC) regulation on railroad markets and price structures, also opted for government regulation to improve the fortunes of the telephone industry. The ICC began to regulate telephone and telegraph companies in 1910, and the new climate spread to state government as well. The replacement of competition by regulation allowed Bell's market share to reach 89.5 percent of the nation's 11.5 million telephones in 1917. By the late 1920s American Telephone and Telegraph (AT&T) became "the largest aggregation of capital that [had] ever been controlled by a single private company at any time in the history of business . . . larger than the Pennsylvania Railroad Company and United States Steel Corporation put together," with assets approaching $5 billion.[11]

As was true since the 1840s, the business community remained basically hostile toward potential government interference in its affairs. Beginning with the Interstate Commerce Act of 1887, however, it increasingly turned to political solutions whenever the free market produced outcomes deemed undesirable in its own industries.

The Rise of Big Business, 1875–1895

The modern oligopolistic firm first appeared in the consumer goods industries in the 1880s and spread to capital goods in the next decade. Before 1880, Western Union and Montgomery Ward were among the very few nonrailroad companies operating on a national scale. By 1890, however, many industrial corporations were serving the entire nation, as specific brands of cigarettes, matches, soap, breakfast cereals, canned soups, and photographic film were becoming household words.[12]

Consumer markets were expanding to nationwide dimensions, and demands unleashed by these markets were instrumental in the development of large firms. The new technological opportunities were also pulling firms toward increased size. Not all industries went through the formative phase of "big business" at the same time. But the basic shift began in the years following the panic of September

1873, which brought on an economic crisis of unparalleled severity.

The contraction was the longest in American history, lasting sixty-five months, from October 1873 through March 1879. The blow could not easily be forgotten. Consumer demand stagnated, profits plunged, money wages were cut by 20 to 40 percent, and unemployment mounted to levels that left industrial leaders and government officials shocked.[13] In a relatively short time, business conditions seemed to become chronically depressed. The forces of supply were now proving to be more powerful than those of demand, a situation that business people had never before confronted. Just as firms were starting to compete in an increasingly national market, and just as they began to invest more heavily in fixed capital, they found that they were expanding their productive capacity faster than the demand for their products. "During the last twelve or fifteen years," a prominent Boston attorney wrote in 1887, "business men have, almost without exception, complained that . . . there has been an actual overproduction; and, unless a majority of these men have been mistaken as to the proportion of demand to production in their own specialities, general overproduction must have been, in spite of the theories of the economists, an actual existing fact."[14]

From the viewpoint of businesses caught in this trap, adjustments were made more imperative, and more difficult to achieve, by price levels that fell nearly 30 percent between 1873 and 1896 and by three long business depressions from 1873 to 1878, 1882 to 1885, and 1893 to 1897. Revenues often were driven down faster than costs, spurring both competitive price cutting and a search for greater efficiency through "integration"—combining formerly independent companies or functions at the various stages of production from raw materials all the way up to the final consumer (vertical integration), or combining similar businesses at the same stage of production or distribution (horizontal). The latter was probably the more immediate threat to "pure competition," as it frequently involved head-to-head competitors operating in the same market. The former was more closely linked to the revolutionary technological changes of the period and, as we shall see, involved various blends of efficiency and market control motives. Even the falling prices of 1873–1896 were caused, to some degree, by declining unit costs of production in the wake of both greater economies of scale and new technologies: industrial output soared while the supply of money grew much more slowly in this age of the gold standard.

A look at the first stage of this process, to the early 1880s, is revealing. "Pools," "gentlemen's agreements," and other informal market-sharing arrangements were the first reactions to the protracted depression of 1873–78 and outbreaks of cutthroat price competition. But they were legally unenforceable and unstable as well ("ropes of sand," John D. Rockefeller called them). As the experience of the railroads was also demonstrating, something more durable was needed. The cutting edge of the movement to control prices and markets was a new form of an old device—the trust agreement, worked out between 1879 and

1882 by Samuel C. T. Dodd, Standard Oil's attorney. Owners of each member firm deposited their common stock in the trust in return for certificates entitling them to share in the combined profits. Voting rights were delegated to the trustees who could then fix prices and divide up the market for the member firms, each of which still remained a legal entity. Coordinated management would replace loosely structured cartels, with their periodic instability. Between 1882 and 1887, eight such nationwide trusts were created:

Trust	Market share
Standard Oil (1882)	95 percent in 1880, 64 percent in 1911
American Cotton Oil (1884)	60 percent in 1890
National Linseed (1885)	60 or 70 percent in 1890
National Lead (1887)	70 to 95 percent in the 1890s
Distillers Corporation (1887)	50 to 60 percent in 1903
American Sugar Refining (1887)	98 percent in 1892, 49 percent in 1907
American Cattle Trust (1887)	Not known
National Cordage Association (1887)	Not known

The last two failed. The others were quite successful, the first four beginning as horizontally integrated organizations but quickly moving toward vertical integration to assure vital supplies as well as marketing outlets. The fifth and sixth—the "whisky trust" and the "sugar trust"—began as horizontal integrations and remained so until a decade later, when they got their second wind through vertical acquisitions.

Declared illegal under the Sherman Antitrust Act of 1890, six of the original trusts nonetheless survived well into the 1900s either as monopolistic firms or as oligopolistic competitors in their respective industries. The fourth and sixth survive today as NL Industries and Amstar. Distillers became Distillers-Securities in 1903 and remained the largest distiller in the nation until the Volstead Act of 1919 crippled its business. Standard Oil, built by John D. Rockefeller around the refining and marketing of oil, became the image of relentless expansion by any means it took to discipline an unruly industry and achieve satisfactory control over prices and output. Until 1900 the industry's principal product was kerosene for oil lamps, with by-products such as naphtha, lubricants, vaseline, paints, and paraffin wax. The spread of electrical lighting, reducing the demand for kerosene, and the appearance of aggressive, integrated rivals like Texaco and Gulf, which began to produce gasoline and oil for automobiles, chipped away at Standard's hold on the industry. The slow-footed giant was targeted for a federal antitrust suit in 1906 and dissolved into 34 independent companies by the Supreme Court in 1911 because of its "unreasonable restraint of trade," not its size, even though it still held 70 percent of all refinery capacity in 1906.[15]

Though the Sherman Act outlawed "every contract, combination in the form of trust or otherwise, or conspiracy, in restraint of trade or commerce," changes in the corporate law soon made the corporation a more flexible and less obtrusive method of achieving market power (although the term "trust" continued in popular usage well after 1890 to describe giant firms possessing substantial economic power). The Sherman Act was, in effect, undercut by legal innovations which were then taking place. In 1889 New Jersey, soon followed by Delaware, amended its general corporation law by permitting a corporation to acquire and hold the stock of any other company engaged in any kind of business. "Holding companies" could henceforth be organized simply to control other companies, well serving the needs of investment bankers and promoters. A new holding company could also preserve trust-type power more efficiently. It could replace the certificates of a trust with its own shares; its assets would consist of the securities of the old trust's member companies, which it now brought under a single active management. In this way the holding company could control all the operations of its firms. It could exercvise genuine centralized management, unlike the old trusts which only set prices and market quotas for their members.

The holding company and other incorporation tools were quickly resorted to so as not to clash with the "trust or otherwise" language of the Sherman Act however it might be applied. The result was a renewed spurt of "trustification," or the substance of trusts under a different legal cover. From 1890 through 1893, at least 57 "tight industrial combinations" were created. As it happened, the pace could not be continued. The nation sank into a major depression from 1894 through 1897, when only 27 tight combinations were put together.[16] But by the mid 1890s the foundations of the corporate order were solidly in place. Effectively, it was the series of legal responses to the "antimonopoly" movement that had produced a continuum of corporate births and adolescences from the 1870s right through the mid 1890s, as Table 4.1 shows.

This table by no means exhausts the list of corporations born *before* the merger explosion of 1898–1902. But it indicates the power, the breadth, and the duration of the big-business trend beginning in the late 1870s. The major corporate newcomers in Table 4.1 brought monopoly or oligopoly to many industries, from sugar, bananas, flour and canned goods to farm machinery, steel, and oil. By the mid 1890s an array of very large corporations stretched across the economic

Table 4.1

Large Monopolistic or Oligopolistic Firms, 1875–1895

	Date of founding (or corporate reorganization)	Type of integration (H = horizontal, V = vertical)
American Cereal	1888 (1901, as Quaker Oats)	H
American Telephone & Telegraph	1885	H; monopoly
American Tobacco	1884 (1890)	H→V
Babcock & Wilcox	1881	V
Campbell Soup	1881	H→V
Carnegie Steel	1873 (1884)	V
Celluloid Company	1890	H
Coca Cola	1886 (1892)	H→V
Crown Cork & Seal	1892	V
Diamond Match	1881 (1889)	H→V
A.B. Dick	1884	V
Eastman Kodak	1880 (1901)	H
General Electric	1892	V→H
H.J. Heinz	1880	H→V
McCormick (foods)	1889	H
National Cash Register	1882	H→V
Otis Elevator	1854 (1895)	H; monopoly
Pillsbury	1891	V
Pittsburgh Plate Glass	1895	V
Procter & Gamble	1834 (1879)	H→V
Remington Typewriter	1886	H; duopoly
Swift	1878	V
U.S. Rubber	1892	H→V
Westinghouse	1884	V→H

Sources: Moody's Industrial Manual, various editions; also Chandler (1977) and Thorelli (1955).

landscape. Competitive pressures in the new electrical equipment industry, for example, led to formation of the General Electric Company (GE), an 1892 Morgan combination of Thomson-Houston Electric and Edison Electric, leaving only Westinghouse between GE and monopoly of the industry. "The consolidation of companies," Thomas Edison told reporters at the time, "will do away with a competition which has become so sharp that the product of the factories has been worth little more than ordinary hardware."[17] Four years later GE and Westinghouse, following policies begun by Thomson-Houston in 1887, secretly agreed to share patents to prevent the entry of competitive producers of lighting and electrical equipment, the start of a habit that proved hard to break.[18]

The common pattern was the drive to curb competition and to erect production and distribution systems designed to cover large market areas, which blanketed the country in several cases. Inherent in this was the effort to build vertically integrated organizations to exploit the new technologies, to control raw materials, and to discourage would-be rivals. The very names of these corporations, many of them familiar today, make one realize why "the most imposing barrier to entry in these industries was the organization the pioneers had built to market and distribute their newly mass-produced products. A competitor who acquired the technology had to create a national and often global organization of managers, buyers, and salesmen if he was to get the business away from the one or two enterprises that already stood astride the major marketing channels."[19]

What had happened to cause such a transformation in the American industrial structure in barely two decades?

The Causes of Monopoly: Bigger is Better?

Did the new demand and supply universe, as described in Chapter 3, create big business? The answer of the business history school informally centered around Alfred Chandler is a virtually unqualified yes: managerial and administrative structure follows strategy, which in turn is dictated by the expansion of markets and changing technological opportunities.[20] The "managerial revolution" took place because in railroads, the telegraph and telephone, steel, oil, chemicals, mass merchandising and other industries "a managerial hierarchy had to be created to supervise several operating units and to coordinate and monitor their activities"; here "the visible hand of management" quickly demonstrated its value. Following the Civil War, "velocity of throughput" accelerated as the railroad and telegraph provided the fast, regular, and reliable transportation and communication "essential to high-volume production and distribution—the hallmark of large modern manufacturing or marketing enterprises . . . the requirements of high-volume, high-speed operations brought the large-scale managerial enterprise. . . . Concentration and oligopoly appeared as a consequence of the need for and the profitability of administrative coordination."[21]

The proposition that big business was the result of the economies of large-scale organization is, at once, partially true and seriously misleading. The fundamental reason for the emergence of the giant corporation is the cost savings derived from large-volume production runs with specialized plant and equipment and specialized workers. But what was true in later decades also turns out to be true for the nineteenth century: "in virtually every industry examined tight oligopolies are not dictated by production economies of scale."[22] In industries that did not show increases in concentration (lumber, bricks and tiles, clothing, for example) there was, as Chandler notes, no significant growth in the size of the optimal firm. But only in distilling, flour and meal, typewriters, pig iron, and iron rolling was growth in efficient firm size large enough to approach a natural monopoly or tight oligopoly outcome, and even here smaller firms would not have been at substantial cost disadvantages. In many other industries experiencing increases in concentration by the 1890s (steel, copper refining, gypsum products, chemicals, machinery, meat packing, sugar refining, cigarettes, soap and candles, leather, woolens) the size of the dominant firms "extended far beyond what was required to achieve technical efficiency . . . concentrated markets do not appear to have been compelled by changes in technology."[23]

Economic forces were very important in the growth of big business, but as enabling factors. Nobody can argue that giant corporations could have developed in the decades before the Civil War. But forces like increasing returns to scale and new technologies tell us little about the response of those who can capture them for their own purposes. The fact is that even before the spectacular merger wave of 1898–1902, big business was fast becoming the dominant, pace-setting mode of operation in industry. Powers inherent in the accumulation process were being used to shape the conditions under which technologies and markets interacted.

This phase of U.S. economic history was ushered in by the depression of 1873–78. When business activity receded, it exposed the first, primitive foundations of the excess capacity problem of modern capitalism. As market frontiers spread beyond local areas along with the railroad-telegraph network, many firms were increasing their levels of investment, not only to secure their shares of these growing markets but also to strengthen their competitive positions by adopting the technologies now becoming available. The result was duplication of capacity, with the railroads themselves a leading example. At this stage of development it was still possible to reduce overcapacity through failure of weaker firms and elimination of their fixed capital, the mechanism being the old competitive tendency to cut prices to recoup falling sales whenever the economy slowed down. But if all sellers have the same idea, bad tidings for everybody are close at hand. Such a prospect supplies a strong incentive to devise new price and output arrangements. Otherwise, gains from increasing productivity might be lost to consumers through price reductions, exactly as the theory of pure competition promises.

The long period of falling prices, bracketed by the major depressions of 1873–78 and 1893–97, made clear the connections among fixed costs (including service charges on debt, or interest and amortization), pricing policy, and market control. In new industries, the unworkability of the free market solution became painfully evident, as entrepreneurs grappled with heavy capital outlays, technological complexities, and interlocking stages of production involving raw materials, manufacture, and distribution—even after-sale service and repair when products were so new that only the manufacturer could furnish customers the advice they needed. Electrical machinery, photographic equipment, sewing machines, typewriters, and mechanical reapers were examples from the 1880s and early 1890s. These industries, along with steel, meat packing, perishable fruits, and canned soups, were leaders in moving toward vertical integration. The aim was to embrace a range of different activities so as to internalize, and reduce, transactions costs that certainly would have remained higher under a system of decentralized competitive markets. In other industries, like oil refining, sugar refining, and tobacco, the lure was rapid growth of markets, prompting industrialists to build large multiunit organizations via horizontal integration—acquiring direct competitors or merging with them to manage prices and output schedules.

From 1875 to 1895, the basic transformation of American industry came through vertical integration; the real or hoped for advantages of monopolistic control for coordinating prices and regulating production flows provided the impetus. Given the historically new, and enormous, increases in productive capacity, one lesson was quickly learned: free market solutions were dangerous in the extreme and control of prices was essential. But horizontal integration, critically important in oil, sugar, and tobacco, was not so different. Its architects could also point to anticipated efficiencies in the form of economies of scale in the production or marketing effort, and they too were haunted by the risks inherent in uncontrolled markets and the need for planning mechanisms. In short, with the uncertainties created by emerging nationwide markets and brand-new technologies, control of prices and stabilization of economic environments became obvious solutions to be pursued by any means available.

As pools, collusive agreements, and other cartel devices proved short-lived, there were large profits to be made by anyone who could invent new forms of coercive power to establish "order" over industry prices and output. The means toward this end could be economic, when economies of scale and technical innovation reduced costs and enhanced profitability and market power. They could also be financial, stemming from inequality in bargaining power, which allowed large firms to obtain lower prices from suppliers or preferred treatment from banks. They could be organizational as well. Unsuccessful cartelization led the new generation of industrialists toward more dependable forms of cooperation—trusts, then various types of incorporation that had the weight of the law behind them. Finally, the means for establishing market power could be political—or even illegal. To gain any of these advantages, it might first be necessary to achieve some other one, depending on the nature of the industry, the state of the economy, or random events.

For Chandler, the rise of big business was the result of a struggle to attain efficiency in a new era of expanding markets and expensive technologies: "administrative coordination *in turn* created formidable barriers to entry. . . . The first to integrate continued to dominate."[24] No doubt the eventual scale of operations of a Standard Oil, an American Tobacco, or a Swift gave it fresh cost-saving opportunities (pipelines for Rockefeller, snuff, cigar, and tinfoil takeovers for James Duke, refrigerated rail cars for Gustavus Swift) and allowed it to forge farther ahead of rivals. But if size itself was as great an advantage as initial cost efficiencies, or if size was a prerequisite for effecting certain cost reductions, Chandler's linear analysis (that "speed brought size'') oversimplifies a complex growth process.

In some industries, the possibilities for increasing velocity of throughput did stimulate a movement to larger size—mass retailing and the department stores of the 1860s and 1870s—[25] but so did several forces not related to technology or productive efficiency. In steel in the 1880s, the growth of the leading firm was not a direct function of efficiency advantages, even though costly new capital-intensive technologies were required. Andrew Carnegie's personal assistant stated that ''it was other considerations than increased efficiency and economy that prompted the first imperfect combination of the Carnegie [Steel Company] properties,'' citing internal discord, tariff protection, and desire to control prices.[26] Once size did increase in cases like this, other competitive possibilities opened up, some of which were cost-economizing and many of which were predatory—rebates and kickbacks, exclusive contracts, and price discrimination.

Chandler grants that by 1881 the Standard Oil trust controlled 90 percent of the nation's refining capacity and ''had demonstrated its willingness to use its economic power ruthlessly.''[27] But the Standard Oil story clashes with Chandler's ''strategy and structure'' hypothesis in yet another respect. Though scale and complexity pointed to the need for organizational adjustments, there were also cases where they guaranteed marketplace security and revenue flows that *lessened* pressures for improvements in internal efficiency. With Standard Oil's rapid expansion in the 1880s, attention was directed toward administrative reform. But it was not until the mid 1920s, according to Chandler himself, that faulty capital-budgeting, overlapping staffs, frictions between managers and top executives, and other internal inefficiencies were corrected—fifteen years after the colossus was broken up into smaller companies by the Supreme Court.[28] Cochran's judgment is that ''the market position of the trust was so strong that it could stand its somewhat slow and cumbersome management.''[29]

Rockefeller occupies a top-rung position in any ranking of ''robber barons,'' with Carnegie in steel and railroad moguls such as Gould, Cornelius Vanderbilt, and Collis Huntington. But in the search for any means—market or nonmarket—to gain economic advantage in a context of changing economic opportunity, they were no more malign, and perhaps less so, than other figures operating on a more modest scale. The National Cash Register Company, founded in 1882 and at once dubbed the ''cash register trust,'' could soon boast of considerable technical achievements that alone might have won it marketplace superiority, but it did gain monopolistic power using these tactics:

> [The company] set out deliberately to destroy its competitors. It hired their employees away from them. It bribed their employees and the employees of common carriers and telephone and telegraph companies to spy on them and disclose their business secrets. It spread false rumors concerning their solvency. It instructed its agents to misrepresent the quality of their goods, interfere with their sales, and damage the mechanism of their machines in establishments

where they were in use. It publicly displayed their cash registers under labels which read, "Junk." It made, and sold at less than cost, inferior machines called "knockers," which it represented to be just as good as theirs. . . . It intimidated prospective investors in competing plants by publishing lists of defunct competitors and by exhibiting in a "graveyard" at its factory samples of the machines which they had formerly made. Such practices, carried on over a period of 20 years, gave the company control of 95 percent of the Nation's production of cash registers.[30]

Other, less warlike means employed to curb overcapacity and to attain market control were legal or broadly political. The corporation, an old legal entity, had already become a more important accumulation device in the United States than in Europe by the early years of the century (see pp. 15–16). Beginning in the late 1830s, a wave of general incorporation acts and the addition of limited liability by state governments made the corporate form increasingly attractive to mercantile and manufacturing concerns. Limited liability made shares of stock easier to issue and sell and more readily transferable. Permanent rather than finite life now characterized the corporation, allowing it to raise far more money than proprietorships or partnerships of similar size. Thus, the corporation was becoming an extremely powerful, and unanswerable, device for mobilizing funds and deploying them over different time horizons, short-run and long, and to a variety of product development projects. Delegation of authority in the corporation meant that its executive officers could in most cases act as a self-perpetuating class largely unaccountable to smaller stockholders, let alone the general public. And these sources of economic power were sanctioned in a public charter.

Two other political tools must be mentioned. One, as already described, is government regulation, which was actively sought by several business leaders to stabilize markets in ways they could not. The other is tariffs, around which American political life swirled for a century. The era of protectionism began in 1816, with northern agitation for higher tariffs for cottons, woolens, glassware, and iron products. Support came from farmers, who counted on successful manufacturing in the Northeast to generate increased demands for western agricultural produce. Tariff rates peaked between 1860 and 1910 (and again in 1930 with the Smoot-Hawley Act).

The orthodox free-trade wisdom, first put forth by economist Frank Taussig in 1892, is that tariffs were not a major causal factor in American industrialization because for most of the 1820–1860 period the manufacture of iron and especially cotton textiles did not really require "infant industry" protection. "Probably as early as 1824, and almost certainly by 1832, the [cotton goods] industry had reached a firm position, in which it was able to meet foreign competition on equal terms."[31]

The proposition is questionable. New economic historians themselves have emphasized how U.S. industrialization was stimulated by economies of scale through specialization and by the steady advance of productivity in new industries through "learning by doing." "Experience-linked improvements in efficiency" were a powerful force in the cotton textile industry in the three decades before the Civil War.[32] What if these cumulative effects had been cut off at the start by a flood of British-made goods, as in 1815? According to one study, if the tariff had been removed in the 1830s "about half the industrial sector of New England would have been bankrupted."[33] Even if such doubts about the free trade case could be dismissed, the concrete fact would remain that the tariff became a near-permanent political institution representing government assistance to manufacturing. It kept price levels from being driven down by foreign competition and thereby shifted the distribution of income in favor of owners of industrial property to the disadvantage of workers and consumers.[34] The same story was played out in the steel industry: even as it became a formidable competitor in world markets it continued to receive protection, into the 1890s.

Finally, in appraising the full range of forces making for monopolistic power, it must be understood that there was nothing inevitable about the specific technologies that accompanied and promoted the rise of big business. No technology ever appears at birth as a single set of techniques that must be adopted all or nothing, and no technology ever implies a unique form of business organization. To state the issue another way, science and technology certainly affect society, but social structures just as surely affect the ways that advances in human knowledge will—or will not—be selectively drawn upon to produce commodities and services. The fact is that people in positions of decisionmaking power decide what to produce and how to produce it, and they hire skilled and professional personnel to help them achieve their objectives. The modern industrial era has been molded by the twin forces of science-based technology and corporate capital, unified through modern engineering.[35]

Corporate demands for applied science shaped and defined both chemical and electrical engineering, which were indispensable for intercepting the scientific advances of the nineteenth century and diverting them toward private profits. As chemical and electrical technologies flourished after 1880, entrepreneurs formed corporate entities to capture them and exploit their commercial possibilities. The giant industrial enterprise became the vanguard of "second industrial revolution" technology in the United States—and the habitat of the professional engineer. By 1895 GE and Westinghouse had emerged on the basis of inventions in electric power, lighting, and traction. AT&T, founded in 1885, grew rapidly as both the provider of telephone service and the producer of telephones. Through continuous science-based innovation, the chemical industry also channeled technologies along paths favoring the growth of corporate capital. Soon three companies were moving toward domination of the industry—Du Pont, Union Carbide and Carbon, and Allied Chemical and Dye.

The patent system too was seized upon to strengthen the bonds between science and oligopolistic enterprise. Toward the end of the century, patent lawyers and research departments of companies like AT&T, Corn Products, GE, Westing-house, and Du Pont (and later Radio Corporation of America) worked to trans-form patents into fencing-out devices for private capital—methods for preempting the frontiers of scientific technology by sowing minefields of potential lawsuits in the paths of individual inventors. Through interference and infringement suits, corporations could harass patent applicants and cause many of them to abandon their plans or sell them for a fraction of their value. The Thomas Edison Compa-ny, for example, spent more money in obtaining patents, litigating them, and preventing infringements than it received from them.[36]

Chandler suggests that these strategies were inconsequential because "the research organizations of modern industrial enterprises remained a more power-ful force than patent laws in assuring the continued dominance of pioneering mass production firms in concentrated industries."[37] In fact the two went hand in hand. For Eastman Kodak and Singer Sewing Machine, patents led the way toward strategies of continuous product innovation to reinforce market control. Each was utilized, depending on circumstances, to anticipate scientific discovery and to control the supply of technology relevant to marketable goods.[38]

In the 1880s and 1890s private capital undertook to transform technological progress into a product fashioned in its own image. "The scientific transforma-tion of America and the corporate transformation of America had become one and the same."[39]

The Great Merger Movement of 1898–1902

Around the turn of the century all those forces making for big business coalesced in a tidal wave of mergers and consolidations. Nothing like it had been seen before, nor anything like it since, although, as Figure 4.1 illustrates, at least three later merger movements have taken place in manufacturing and mining. A total of 2,653 large firms disappeared through merger from 1898 through 1902. The average of 531 firms per year absorbed in mergers may be compared with the average for all other years from 1895 through 1920—104 firms per year.[40] The 1898–1902 numbers may seem small by today's standards, but for the economy of 1900 they were staggering; in terms of real GNP that economy was fifteen times smaller than the economy of the late 1980s. By the "tight industrial combinations" measure, there were 14 new combinations created each year on average during the previous peak period, 1890–1893; during 1898–1902 the annual average was three times higher.[41] Moreover, multifirm consolidations, very rare ever since, were commonplace. Of all the independent firm disappear-ances during this merger movement, 75 percent occurred in mergers uniting at least 5 firms and 26 percent in mergers of 10 or more firms.[42]

The effects on U.S. industry were dramatic and permanent. They erected a figurative skyscraper on top of the already impressive "trust" edifice of 1882–1893. By 1903–04, some 300 industrial combinations covering most major lines

Figure 4.1
Acquisitions of Manufacturing and Mining Companies by Constant-Dollar Volume, 1895–1985

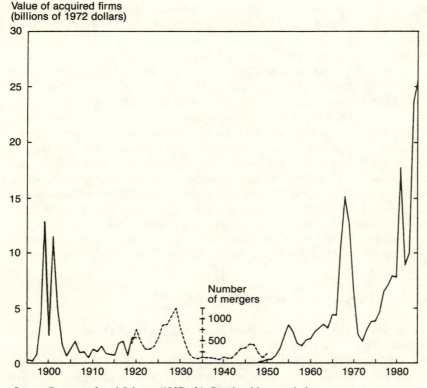

Value of acquired firms
(billions of 1972 dollars)

Source: Ravenscraft and Scherer (1987), 21. Reprinted by permission.

Note: Data on value of acquisitions are not available for 1921 to 1947. The broken line shows the number of acquisitions in those years.

of production had been formed. These combinations, by several estimates, controlled at least 40 percent of the nation's manufacturing assets, with an aggregate capitalization exceeding $7 billion. A substantially greater degree of market control was the outcome: almost half of all firm disappearances between 1895 and 1904, and seven-tenths of all merger-related assets, "were accounted for by mergers that gained a leading position in the market."[43]

Most celebrated of all was the Morgan-sponsored $1.4 billion U.S. Steel consolidation of 1901, which combined the three earlier steel combinations (Carnegie, National, Federal) and some 170 subsidiary concerns to control 65 percent of America's iron and steel output. "The new monster, the largest corporation in the world, was over-capitalized, lacked proper coordination, and functioned poorly.''[44] It was a giant holding company that resulted from Morgan's worries about price competition. Another landmark deal was the American Can Company merger of 1901. It included 120 firms with a total capital stock of $90 million and brought a 75 to 80 percent market share. The turn-of-the century merger movement also produced these giants with capitalizations of at least $50 million:

Allis-Chalmers

Amalgamated Copper (later Anaconda, taken over by Arco in 1977)

American Car and Foundry (now ACF Industries)

American Smelting and Refining (now Asarco)

American Woolen (acquired by Textron in 1955)

Corn Products Refining (now CPC International)

Distilling Company of America (now National Distillers)

Du Pont

International Harvester (now Navistar International)

National Biscuit (later Nabisco; merged with Standard Brands in 1981; acquired by R.J. Reynolds in 1985)

Pittsburgh Coal (acquired in 1966 by Continental Oil, itself acquired by Du Pont in 1981)

Pullman (taken over by Wheelabrator Frye in 1980; regained independent status in 1982)

Smaller combinations, averaging $25 million each, were International Paper, International Nickel, U.S. Gypsum, and United Shoe Machinery (acquired by Emhart in 1975). The aims of all these combinations are apparent from the list, studded with "Americans" and "Nationals" and "Internationals." Control of markets was the goal, high market shares the frequent result.

Such combinations fell under two categories—"mergers" proper, through which an existing corporation acquires the assets or voting stock of one or more corporations, not entailing the creation of a new company, and "consolidations," when two or more firms unite to form a new corporation with the former constituent firms dissolved. Both types were resorted to between 1895 and 1902, but the more common, certainly the more significant, was the consolidation of leading producers in the same industry in horizontal integration. Examples were U.S. Rubber, Du Pont, and several industrial sector "Morganizings"—U.S. Steel, American Radiator, Pullman, International Mercantile Marine, National Tube, International Harvester, and (1892) GE. The predominance of horizontal rather than vertical combinations reinforces the conclusion that market control was the overriding objective.

The first and greatest merger movement tapered off in 1902–03 and stopped by 1904 when, in the view of some business historians, industrial concentration reached a level not substantially exceeded ever since.

This extraordinary episode has been the subject of many historical writings, but one must resist the temptation to view it as an inexplicable break with the past. Its basic antecedents are clear. Combinations were already becoming an entrenched practice, an effort to assure profitable growth in a world of new technologies, new products, and rapidly expanding markets to be fought over. In this sense the 1898–1902 merger wave grew out of a long and cumulative movement, starting in the late 1870s and peaking twenty years later. The proximate causes of the outburst seem no less clear; they are found in the chain of developments linking 1890–1893 and 1893–1897.

During 1890–1893, as already noted, there was a surge in the formation of holding companies and other close-knit combinations. Trusts were being converted into corporations, and corporations were carrying out mergers and acquisitions to secure the kinds of market control the old trusts had achieved. These capitalization activities seem to have drawn toward Wall Street a substantial part of the rising volumes of savings the economy was generating. Thus, they directly stimulated growth of the market for industrial securities, mainly preferred stock at first.[45] It was during these years that capital markets were maturing: security holdings could now be acquired, manipulated, and liquidated with utter flexibility.

The long slump of 1893–1897 slowed both developments—new combinations and growth of securities markets. But it nurtured the "trustification" atmosphere in two other ways. First, the panic of 1893 caught a number of new corporations in a phase of headlong expansion. In capital-intensive industries like steel, meat packing, petroleum, and paper the result was considerable excess capacity.[46] Here, falling demand transformed profits into losses all the more swiftly, with the same deadly temptation to cut prices to rebuild sales and run at full capacity. It was by now conventional wisdom, however, that if collective control over output and prices could be worked out, monopoly profits could be extracted from society on an ongoing basis. Second, in the antitrust case against American Sugar Refining in 1895 (*United States v. E. C. Knight Company et al.*, 156 U.S. 1), the legality of the holding company form was upheld. Although the "sugar trust" controlled 95 percent of the nation's output, the Supreme Court decided that manufacture was not interstate commerce, and that American Sugar's virtual monopoly was not a restraint of trade under the Sherman Act. The Justice Department lawyers made only a perfunctory argument for applying that act, and Attorney General Richard Olney then proceeded to use it solely against labor unions. The succeeding McKinley administration brought only three suits under Sherman from 1897 through 1900. Soon "lawyers were advising their corporate clients to abandon all agreements or alliances carried out through cartels or trade associations and to consolidate into single, legally defined enterprises."[47]

Together, the fixed-cost dilemma and the executive and judicial interpretations of the Sherman Act intensified pressures to merge and consolidate. Only a return of good times was needed to release them.

The economy began to recover in mid 1897. So did the demand for corporate securities, sparking a powerful "bull market." The demand was fed by abundant reserves of liquidity held by the public. From April 1897 through September 1899 the value of industrial stocks on average doubled; railroad share prices increased 80 percent. The momentum spilled over into ready-and-waiting securities markets, which were now providing new issues for the tastes of any investor. Stocks and bonds ranging in character from virtually worthless to high quality were absorbed, and securities markets reached a speculative frenzy in early 1901.

As independent promoters exploited the changes in investor confidence, a merger boom was unleashed. Men like Judge William H. Moore, John R. Dos Passos, Charles Flint, and John W. ("bet-a-million") Gates were "quick to act. They had much to gain and little to lose . . . [and] did not let themselves be deterred by a concern for their reputation for soundness and stability. Their aim was to make quick profits from ripening opportunities."[48] Among their combinations were American Thread Company, American Can, National Biscuit, and Standard Distilling, as well as National Steel and American Steel and Wire, both absorbed in the U.S. Steel consolidation of 1901. Before the U.S. Industrial Commission in 1899, Gates was asked about "the chief causes of the formation" of his American Steel and Wire Company. "It was because we wanted to be the wire manufacturers of the world," he replied.[49]

As new combinations proliferated, larger volumes of stock were sold to the public for cash than ever before, a financing mode that increased relatively more than exchanges of company stock for the securities or assets of other companies.[50] Of the very large combinations effected during these years, only one-third were not the work of the independent promoters, and of that third, most were done by investment bankers like Morgan and Jacob Schiff of Kuhn, Loeb.[51]

For analogous reasons the most spectacular merger movement in American history ceased by 1903-04. In 1902, President Theodore Roosevelt had opened a campaign against the "trusts" to roll back some of the more abusive concentrations of power. In April 1903 a circuit court ruled that holding company activities might well be in violation of the Sherman Act, a decision upheld by the Supreme Court eleven months later. The Northern Securities Company was a jumbo consolidation by Morgan, linking the interests of the Northern Pacific and Great Northern railroads. The Court held that this particular combination was unlawful because it restrained trade by monopolizing rail transportation in the Northwest: while mergers themselves were legal, mergers destructive of competition were not. The decision stunned corporate lawyers, who had come to believe that the holding company was immune to antitrust prosecution. The final blow to the great merger movement was the "rich man's panic" of 1903. Between February and November stock prices plunged 38 to 40 percent on average. A contributing factor was failure of profits to match expectations for several of the more gaudily promoted industrial and railroad combinations of the prior decade.

The Reign of Finance Capital

The railroads were the first industry to require large amounts of funds, so large that savings had to be marshaled for bond and stock issues running into tens of millions of dollars. The result of a demand for investible funds on this scale was that during the 1850s and 1860s U.S. financial markets became "centralized where they have remained since—on Wall Street. The stocks and bonds of railroads all over the country began to be listed and actively traded on the New York Stock Exchange as the capital of investors in this country and in Europe was mobilized in support of railways."[52]

As this was occurring, about a dozen investment banking houses took over underwriting the financial needs of the railroads and other growing businesses. These investment bankers advised client companies on types and amounts of securities best suited to the market and then floated them, often buying some for their own portfolios. They also furnished advice on mergers and acquisitions, and on liquidations and reorganizations for financially troubled firms, so that it was normal for them to exercise influence in the affairs of their client firms. That influence grew, as investment bankers provided the funds and the guidance for bringing industrial order out of potential chaos.

After the Civil War, railroads and other industries were expanding so rapidly that their own financial resources were proving inadequate for their needs. It was necessary for investment bankers to mobilize funds on a regional, and soon nationwide, basis and also to contribute some of their own capital. The numerous business failures during 1873–78, 1883–85, and 1893–97 kept raising the specter of cutthroat price competition in the face of heavy fixed costs. Funds, and collective action, were needed to forestall disaster. In the 1880s and 1890s many manufacturing firms were "going public" to raise capital through the public sale of securities, and they too needed the reputation and marketing assistance of investment bankers.

During these years the power of "finance capital" grew, as consolidated railroads and industrial firms took shape and were dominated by one or more investment banks.[53] There seems to have been a greater incidence of outside financial control in railroads, but the influence of investment banking houses like Drexel Morgan, Kidder Peabody, and Kuhn Loeb was strong in life insurance, steel, copper, electric traction, and electrical equipment. A continental European-type capitalism was developing, with direct linkages between industry and investment banking. Banks often combined investment banking functions, commercial banking (taking deposits and making short-term loans), and stock ownership in client companies.

J. P. Morgan's power derived from the centralization of financial markets and banking resources in New York. The Morgan firm not only serviced the demands of railroads and industry but also the federal government, whose securities it floated in larger amounts when they had to be placed with banking syndicates and other reliable buyers. Morgan's financial capacity extended to international markets as well, further strengthening his power and reputation at home and abroad. In addition to his investment banking connections, Morgan was allied with the First National Bank and the National City Bank; the latter had a gold reserve rivaling the U.S. Treasury's and held deposits for 200 large out-of-town banks. Two more New York banks, Bankers Trust and Guaranty Trust, were Morgan-controlled.

Life insurance companies joined the ranks of Morgan customers in the 1890s. As their surpluses from premium and investment income swelled, they became large net buyers of corporate securities. The value of bonds and stocks held by the five largest insurers (Equitable, Metropolitan, Prudential, Mutual, New York Life) climbed from $164 million in 1890 to $935 million in 1905.[54] Investment bankers purchased significant blocks of stock in these insurance companies to make sure that they did not deal directly with corporations needing funds—that was the bankers' own turf. In most industries in which Morgan had interests, railroads or insurance or commercial banking, his representatives would sit on the boards of two or more competing firms, in which case "order" would be imposed and competition minimized. Such interlocking directorates were common in the age of finance capital.

The Morgan-led "money trust" was so widely denounced that in 1911 Congress launched an investigation into "the concentration of control of money and credit."[55] The 1913 Pujo Report (after Arsène Pujo, chairman of the House Banking and Currency Committee) found that a "combination or understanding or community of interest" existed at the apex of the nation's financial sector. Its "inner group" consisted of J. P. Morgan & Company, First National Bank, National City Bank, Guaranty Trust, and Bankers Trust. This group held 341 directorships in 112 corporations, including banks, insurance and transportation companies, public utilities, and industrials, with assets totaling $22 billion. Other investment banking houses, along with Chicago's three largest commercial banks, were allied with the "inner group," so that together these institutions were "the principal banking agencies through which the greater corporate enterprises of the United States obtain capital for their operations."

Finance capital began to be hemmed in by legal and institutional reforms after the Pujo Report, stretching from 1913 through 1935.[56] But its hegemony was leveling off well before 1913. The dominance of finance over industrial capital proved to be a temporary stage of capitalist development in the United States, as the seeds of a more advanced form of accumulation were being sown. Profound changes in markets and technologies, on both a national and international plane, shifted the competitive rules of the game in favor of agglomerations of capital embodying "industrial control." Here the primary role of those in charge is to promote the interests of the controlled entity itself, rather than to pursue an indeterminate set of goals that might include selling securities for speculative purposes, manipulating the price of the company's stock, and deploying the underlying assets for personal gain or ends unrelated to the firm's own industry.

The commanding position of the investment bankers began to weaken as corporate executives worked to achieve autonomy for their organization. The key was retained earnings—the internal funds at the disposal of management after it pays its wage bills, debt-service charges, and any other current expenses. Retained earnings in the corporate sector expanded, as the growth of the U.S. economy increased the size, the profits, and the financial strength of business firms, further reducing their dependence on bankers. Even for the railroads through 1900, the power of financiers lay in organizing communities of interest and overseeing them, not in defining strategic plans or actually running individual companies.[57]

Before the turn of the century the outlines of the corporate order we know today were becoming visible in the form of "managerial capitalism," or a universe of management-controlled, financially independent corporations whose major goal is steady enlargement of profits through growth of sales and increased market share.

Conclusion

"It is very doubtful if there are any successful business ventures within the range of the modern industries from which the monopoly element is wholly absent," Thorstein Veblen stated in 1904, immediately after the great merger wave but in words that could almost have been written ten years earlier.[58] Giant corporations were created because they offered a seemingly better means of reducing uncertainty and stabilizing profits in a new environment of nationwide markets and science-based technologies. To the business leaders of the time, the problem was seen as one of huge increases in fixed capacity and the difficulty of deploying the new methods of production profitably in a competitive market setting. Control of prices was essential along with control of other elements of the production process, especially in industries where vertical integration appeared feasible.

The root issue here is not "market failure" or "breakdown of competition." In the antebellum era, pure competition was rare in a world of disconnected local economies with small-scale producers who possessed strong, if localized, monopoly perquisites: "oligopoly preceded the rise of the large firm."[59] But after the Civil War, market-perfecting forces—more abundant flows of information and wider transactions ranges—were simultaneously becoming control mechanisms, the benefits of which are bound to be unevenly distributed. "Competition" and "monopoly" are not polar opposites but integral parts of one competitive process that leads to concentration of power resources in a few hands. Even without growth in the scale of operations, and even with classically competitive markets with price shading, competition weeds out many firms and leaves others in positions of greater leverage. In the world of 1875–1902, it produced national monopolies and oligopolies.

The new technologies may have been compatible with small production units and decentralized operations. The German electrical engineer and inventor Werner von Siemens believed in 1878 that "the electric motor will in course of time produce a complete revolution in our conditions of work, in favor of small-scale industry."[60] That romantic expectation was not fulfilled. By the time such technologies filtered down toward smaller firms, it was probably too late. Innovations take time to copy and digest, so that while most business units are trying to catch up with the new methods, the innovators may run off with a dominant share of the market.

The industrial structure that evolved after the Civil War harbored competitive pressures as intense as ever, but they now involved competing corporate giants that began by seizing positions of supremacy in their industries and, after a time of turmoil, exhibiting impressive staying power.

5

Investment, Growth, and Instability: Oligopoly and the Pursuit of Prosperity, 1900–1929

Over time, the interplay between accumulation and monopolization has produced an economy dominated by giant business firms—in manufacturing and mining, banking and insurance, transportation and regulated public utilities. Rooted in these sectors of the economy, the corporate business share of national income reached 53 percent in 1929, and it has continued to rise, past 59 percent in the late 1980s.[1] This increase has been accompanied, and promoted, by a shift in aggregate saving from private households and small firms toward the large corporation, mainly in the form of retained earnings but also depreciation allowances and employee contributions to company pension funds. Corporate retained earnings alone have risen steadily as a part of private sector income, from about 6 percent in the 1920s to 12 percent in the 1980s.[2] These are clear indications of the growth of corporate control over income generation. The means for preserving such control—increases in profits and in corporate saving—both flow out of successful investment.

But the principles that actually govern corporate investment must be specified, for they have produced a number of propensities and practices that affect the way the overall economy operates. The evolving accumulation process, in other words, creates new forms of production and distribution, and these changes are inevitably reflected in new microeconomic conditions. Throughout the U.S. economy, in manufacturing and nonmanufacturing alike, "the majority of the industries are noncompetitive in an important way. Specifically, they choose to operate at a point where marginal cost is well below price, a policy that makes sense only if firms influence prices through their volumes of production." The result is that "market power and excess capacity diminish the strength of the economy's drive to full employment."[3]

Thus, instead of focusing on the "microeconomic foundations of macroeconomics'' in the manner of the conventional analysis of recent years, students of the capitalist economy should instead be inquiring into the macroeconomic foundations of microeconomics.

The Oligopoly Firm:
Investment Behavior and Effects

The capitalist enterprise launches investment projects because it expects profits from them—otherwise, no investment. This rule has given rise to three investment characteristics in the age of the oligopolistic corporation. They are not simply three elements of a textbook "monopoly" situation, but symbols of an economy becoming monopolized, with powerful tendencies not present under atomistically competitive conditions. With the spread of corporate organization techniques to all sectors of the economy, oligopoly investment characteristics can be said to shape the rate and direction of economic change in the twentieth century. In fact, it seems safe to assume that of all the private business investment actually undertaken in the economy, the oligopolistic sector has accounted for most of it.[4]

1. *The markup or "the degree of monopoly."*[5] When a firm enjoys substantial market power, its pricing decision does not ordinarily reflect market demand. The large corporation chooses a percentage markup of prices over costs of production that will provide a target rate of profit to support some desired volume of investment. Product prices are set not strictly to maximize short-run profits but to finance the level of investment consistent with profitable growth, with profits and growth mutually interdependent. As prices are fixed, at least in the short run, quantity becomes the main regulative mechanism of the economy. Instead of responding to weakening demand by reducing prices, the corporation will normally scale back production, and new investment, to try to maintain prevailing profit margins. This does not mean that price competition has been extinguished; it still exists and can break out any time industrywide gluts appear or when new products throw market shares into a state of flux typically in younger industries. But as industries age, a planned oligopolistic price equilibrium develops, and oversupplies of goods lead to price shading through temporary discounts off list price and easier consumer credit.

2. *The finance or money-capital imperative.* Investment must be financed. "Savings" of real resources may be a precondition, but financing is needed to set the investment process in motion, as it does not happen automatically. Funds may come through retained profits or through borrowing from financial institutions. Loans must eventually be repaid, but nothing guarantees that the profits expected from the investment will be forthcoming. Thus, when a firm takes on liabilities to acquire assets, it is hoping it will be able to pay off those liabilities out of current

income or refinance them. In effect it is betting on a favorable outcome in an uncertain future.[6]

3. *Process innovation.* At times the monopolistic producer may hesitate to introduce new products for fear of spoiling the market, but it will rarely slow down its process innovation or its attempts to cut all costs of production. From historical experience, however, American entrepreneurs knew that the long-run trend of wages in particular was upward, and they knew even better that while capital equipment will not organize itself into unions or go on strike, workers can.[7] So from the start a recurrent reason for introducing new plants and machinery has been to reduce labor requirements. This labor-saving bias in the techniques used in U.S. industry has been found to be "pervasive" and "overwhelming."[8] Periodic labor shortages, as when immigration was halted after 1921, only intensified it. Moreover, capitalists may even choose methods of production that sacrifice immediate productivity gains for increased control over workers. As early as the 1830s there were examples of workplace reorganization aimed at "breaking the back of labor's resistance to the discipline of factory life" even at the cost of greater inefficiency, as one study of the Springfield, Massachusetts, Armory reveals.[9]

Pursuit of investment under these three conditions gives rise to *structural contradictions*. Actions designed to promote profitable investment undermine economic stability—and the investment that depends on it.

First, if any events lead a corporation to cut back production and investment but to hold the line on prices, weakness in the economy will develop. The problem is that under a regime of imperfect competition, the growth of a large-scale firm's sales is limited in a direct and recognizable way by market demand for its products. (For a "purely competitive" firm, by contrast, its output constitutes only a tiny portion of total industry supply and its output decisions are governed by market-determined prices beyond its control). Any expectation of merely a slower growth of demand, let alone an absolute decline, causes the oligopolistic firm to trim its output levels. Excess capacity will almost immediately begin to appear. In a competitive regime, underutilization of plant and equipment brings on price cutting and the demise of marginal firms. But under oligopoly the excess capacity cannot be competed away like this; in recessions total profits may shrink but excess capacity remains in place. Excess capacity becomes "a thermostatic device governing investment in the short run."[10]

Second, when a corporation takes on debt to acquire assets, its ability to meet its financial obligations can be impaired if the investment itself was a poor idea or the general economic situation deteriorates. During a boom, firms are convinced that "guessing right" will bring large profits, and such optimism often breeds excessive borrowing. Declining profit rates can also lead to heavier debt financing, as the internal funds corporations have for investment are reduced. Whatever the demand for credit, financial intermediaries rush to meet it. They devise new types of credit, usually riskier, to try to offset the diminishing opportunities for profitable investment in the economy's nonfinancial sector.[11] Before long the mood shifts toward doubt and caution, "upsetting the delicate balance of spontaneous optimism." Just ahead lie expectations of lower future income, a scramble to liquidate assets to raise cash for debt repayment, and cutbacks in investment. Financial instability is a natural consequence of "animal spirits" that override "strict mathematical expectation" built into conventional calculations of cost and revenue.[12] If consumers too finance major purchases by borrowing, then households become potential sources of trouble. The primary danger is that a recession will reduce the cash flows of households and businesses, making it harder to service their debts. A series of defaults would interrupt cash flows and profits to banks and other lending institutions, precipitating a crisis in the financial system.

Third, labor-saving measures reduce production costs for a firm, but they do more than that. Money wages constitute the major portion both of costs of production *and* consumer demand. Continuing efforts to cut the wage bill constrain consumption spending. The National Income and Product Accounts show that wages and salaries are equivalent to over 90 percent of consumption outlays and that consumption itself accounts for more than 80 percent of the national income. The Polish economist Michal Kalecki (1899–1970) constructed a macroeconomic model in which all wage and salary income is spent on consumer goods while all profits go to purchase capital goods. These simplifying assumptions illuminate the paradox of capitalist investment from the third angle.[13] One effect of investment is to introduce labor-saving techniques that limit the growth of consumer income, the other is to expand the capital stock. Even constant net investment will continually increase productive capacity, as new plant, machinery, and equipment are added to the stock of already usable capital. But it will only maintain and not increase the level of national income (since it would amount, say, to $50 billion year after year). Under such conditions aggregate demand would tend to be insufficient to warrant further investment. At the same time, Kalecki and his followers point out, capitalists are also striving to push up their share of national income—profits—and to cut the costs of new capital per unit of output, with the aid of the latest technologies. This too tends to throttle aggregate demand: profits tend to grow faster than investment outlets. In Keynesian terms, full employment savings can be maintained only if the economy can generate the investment to absorb them, but if the first outruns the second, stagnation becomes the norm.

There are, to be sure, several possible offsets to these structural contradictions. First, while investment adds to capacity, it also creates income when it is carried out—its dual role embodied in the Harrod-Domar model. A constant level of investment only adds to capacity, which may quickly become excess, while increasing levels of investment create income growth through the multiplier effect.[14] It is conceivable that investment could grow so as to generate the precise rise in aggregate demand needed to keep the economy's expanding capital stock fully utilized. Second, under certain political or demographic conditions, labor may be in short supply, either because it has somehow strengthened its bargaining power relative to capital or because a slowdown in population growth has reduced labor force growth. In this case competition in labor markets could keep wages increasing in line with productivity or even cause wages to rise enough to encroach upon the profit share of national income. Such an "economy of high wages" would be less likely to suffer from inadequate consumer demand relative to industrial capacity (although any squeeze on profits from rising costs could soon darken investment prospects). Third, while a firm may be threatened by the cyclical risks of investing too much, it can also be trapped by the competitive risks of investing too little. A company must protect its market position by renewing its plant and equipment to keep its product line competitive in price and design.

Though all these offsets are very real and have been evident at several stages of U.S. economic development, they do not automatically prevent a mismatch between the nation's productive capacity and the purchasing power to keep it utilized. There is, for example, no reason why the growth of demand that results from a given rate of investment should be exactly equal to the growth of capacity that results from that investment. Nor can anyone count on aggressive advances in wage rates or competitive investment surges automatically to counteract the constant drive of capital to amass greater profits and to cut all costs of production, investment included. And it must be remembered that all investment has a time horizon that requires long-term finance commitments, with the possibility that an unexpected drop in profits can cause a liquidity crisis that leaves firms unable to meet their interest and amortization payments, triggering a chain of bankruptcies that can turn a normal recession into something far more serious.

Instability is inherent in the capitalist investment process. Every aspect of investment makes for the possibility of cumulatively destabilizing forces, compounded every step of the way by "the state of long-term expectation."[15] Over the past century or more, expansionary forces have prevailed: critical-mass investment has generated three great waves of economic expansion. During such booms everything "looks right" for investment, in terms of sales volumes, capacity utilization, the costs of borrowing funds, and profitability. But little of it stemmed from the free market that the "new economic history," and so much of the "old," take for granted: powerful external stimuli were the chief causes. They came from new frontiers of investment opened up by "epoch-making innovations" like the railroad and the automobile.

But the basic problem never disappears. Sometimes capacity increases at very rapid rates, especially when the productivity of new capital goods is rising, at other times mass-purchasing power and final sales lag, and at still other times both phenomena occur. As a result, breakdowns of the investment-dependent system have been so severe that government has increasingly been called upon to guarantee stability not only through "regulation" but also by massive expenditures to prevent aggregate demand from collapsing as it did in the 1890s and the 1930s. The tension between forces making for expansion and contraction has not abated. Since 1929 it is easily discernible in the debate over the role of government in the economy, as well as in the business cycles that somehow keep happening.

From Instability to Settled Oligopoly, 1903-1920

The long depression of 1893-1897 marked the end of the Grand Traverse. Unemployment soared to 18 percent of the labor force in 1894 and remained near 15 percent through 1897.[16] Housing was badly hit, as the dropoff through 1897–1901 shows (Table 3.1), and it did not regain its 1889-90 level until 1904.[17] Railroad spending on fixed capital plunged so steeply that net investment was negative from 1895 through 1898.[18] It was a preview of the way the next wave of expansion would end thirty-one years later—and of the way depressed economic prospects would persist as though they were the new equilibrium conditions of capitalism.

Investment and economic activity picked up smartly in 1898 and unemployment sank below 4 percent of the labor force by 1902-03. Still there were widespread complaints by industrial spokesmen about excess capacity in the midst of prosperity. "We need to open our foreign markets in order to keep our machinery employed . . . [it] can produce in 6 months all we can consume in a year," was one typical complaint before the U.S. Industrial Commission in 1899 and 1900, during a time of vigorous economic growth.[19] The stock market slide of 1903 checked private investment, which fell about 6 percent that year, but expansion soon resumed and investment outlays rose nearly 30 percent over the next four years.[20] The panic of 1907, however, drove industrial stock prices down nearly 40 percent from July to November. It ushered in another extended period of sluggish growth in the economy. From 1907 through 1915, real GNP grew very slowly, at an average annual rate well below 2 percent per year.[21] Unemployment, around 3 percent in 1905-07, jumped back to 8 percent in 1908 and averaged 6.4 percent through 1915—figures that seem understated, particularly for the recovery years they include.[22]

These unemployment figures are symptomatic of excess capacity. In fact the unsatisfactory performance of the economy from 1907 until 1915 was a subject of debate at the time, with several economists attributing it to inelastic supplies of credit and calling for reform of the banking system (a call answered by creation of the Federal Reserve in 1913). But these monetary problems had long existed, whereas the business cycles of the period were exhibiting unusual characteristics. The two full cycles that covered June 1908 through December 1914 had contractions that averaged 23.5 months and expansions of only 15.5 months—almost exactly the opposite of the five previous cycles between May 1891 and June 1908.[23] A later landmark study of "economic tendencies" looked upon the years preceding the First World War as ones of "notable decline" in manufacturing costs—"the most conspicuous result of the improvements in manufacturing technique." "It would appear," concluded its author, "that increased industrial productivity did not result in any substantial addition to the real income of employed workers in general."[24] This suggests a tendency to divert productivity gains toward profits rather than wages, with an eventual dampening effect on economic activity.

Gross private fixed investment (new residential and business construction, plus producers equipment) stagnated from 1907 well into World War I, as the following figures (in billions of 1929 dollars) reveal:[25]

1907	$10.06	1912	$10.03
1908	8.49	1913	10.87
1909	9.75	1914	7.82
1910	9.96	1915	7.39
1911	8.87	1916	9.05

The 1907 level was not reattained until 1913, whereupon investment sagged again. From 1917 through 1921 the economy was further buffeted by the sudden diversion of labor and capital for the war mobilization and then by the steep recession of 1920–21. During these years gross private investment averaged only $7.58 billion per year, and not until late 1922 did private capital spending rates surpass the early 1913 high. The business component of gross private investment—spending for nonresidential construction and producers durables—was flat from 1908 through 1921.[26]

Business conditions themselves were depressed from late 1907 through the spring of 1915. The recovery of 1915–1918 was caused not by any revival of investment but by the frantic demand for war supplies emanating from France and Great Britain. U.S. sales of arms and ammunition, metals and machinery, horses, clothing, and food rose spectacularly, from $824 million annually in 1914 to $3.3 billion by 1916 (while commerce with Germany and Austria dwindled to a bare $1 million). By the time the United States entered into the conflict in April 1917, total U.S. merchandise exports had climbed from $2.3 billion to $6.2 billion per year and, more significantly, from 6 to 11 percent of the GNP, while imports remained around 5 percent.[27] It appears to have been the sharpest two- or three-year balance of trade swing in American history, bringing about a tremendous boom through the summer of 1918—and just in time.

Until the war the problem with the economy was not the "monetary disorders" over which contemporaries spilled rivers of ink but the weakness of investment in the new age of big business. Table 5.1 shows how investment was

Table 5.1

Gross Fixed Capital Formation, Rates of Increase, 1869–1931

	Percent increase, 1869–73 through 1897–1901	Percent increase, 1897–1901 through 1927–31
Gross investment	267.9%	130.5%
Gross producers durables	280.4	245.7
Total construction	264.0	93.6
Nonfarm residential	266.0	94.2
Business	258.7	38.5
Public nonmilitary	290.9	518.6

Source: See Table 3.1.

slowing down over the long term. If public investments are excluded from this table (by excluding the last column from Table 3.1), private capital formation increased 266.5 percent from 1869–73 through 1897–1901, but only 105.9 percent over the next three decades. Nor can this secular decline be attributed to a reduced rate of population growth, as Alvin Hansen (among others) suggested in 1939.[28] In 1929 dollars, gross private investment per head amounted to $45 in 1869–73, $91 in 1897–1901, and $115 in 1927–31.[29] Thus, while investment per head increased over the two three-decade periods, its rates of increase declined, from 102 percent to 26 percent—a faster drop than for absolute volumes of investment. In response, it could be said that slackening population growth reduces the need for home construction; and that category did grow less rapidly after 1900 than before (Table 5.1). But the larger component of private construction—business outlays for plants and offices—grew even less than residential construction from 1897–1901 through 1927–31.

Table 5.2 throws more light on these trends. Private fixed capital formation slowed progressively from every five-year period to the next from the late 1870s through the turn of the century. The recovery of 1899–1907 was led by renewed investment, at generally lower rates than during the first phase of the previous expansion (1882 through 1891). Another bout of stagnation followed, through the World War I decade. Table 5.2 (last column) also exposes the extent to which the new age of oligopoly was giving rise to the "replacement economy." Net investment, a measure of the actual expansion of the nation's capital stock after depreciation allowances, tended to decrease relative to gross investment outlays. The private sector was moving toward mere replacement of worn-out and obsolete structures and equipment, lest productive capacity overshoot consumer demand for the goods it could produce.

Table 5.2

Gross and Net Private Fixed Capital Formation, Annual Averages, 1877–1931 Billions of Dollars, 1929 Prices

	Gross investment	Percent change from preceding period	Net investment	Percent change from preceding period	Ratio, net to gross investment
1877–81	2.73		1.38		.51
1882–86	3.88	+42.1	2.00	+ 44.9	.52
1887–91	5.42	+39.7	2.89	+ 44.5	.53
1892–96	6.64	+22.5	3.42	+ 18.3	.52
1897–1901	6.78	+ 2.1	2.98	− 12.9	.44
1902–06	9.03	+33.2	4.46	+ 49.7	.49
1907–11	10.02	+11.0	4.42	− 0.9	.44
1912–16	9.83	− 1.9	3.19	− 27.8	.32
1917–21	9.39	− 4.5	1.43	− 55.2	.15
1922–26	14.62	+55.7	5.74	+301.4	.39
1927–31	13.96	− 4.5	4.33	− 24.6	.31

Source: Kuznets (1961), 576–78, 592–97.

The unsettled economic conditions between 1903 and the First World War also contributed to instability in the world of the giant enterprise. But that world itself continued to be inherently unstable in the wake of the merger wave of 1898–1902, which was followed by a unique period of antitrust activism on the part of the federal government.

The transition to the relatively stable corporate universe we know today was not easily accomplished. The new combinations formed by merger or consolidation were not uniformly successful—far from it. For one thing, the dominant firms' ability to enforce oligopolistic rules of the game would henceforth depend on keeping excess capacity from developing. For another, success was easier in technologically progressive industries that achieved genuine economies of scale by producing for national or world markets (steel, rubber, petroleum, chemicals, electrical manufactures, foods). In others big business could protect its domain by establishing a high-entry threshold of advertising and distribution costs, the methods employed by makers of cigarettes, breakfast cereals, and several household items.

In all, about half of the substantially sized combinations between 1888 and 1906 were successful. They established greater stability in sales than smaller firms, survived on their own or as parts of "rejuvenated companies," and continued to be profitable. Firms that achieved market power turned out to be significantly more successful by these measures.[30] Many others "rose like mushrooms in the night and disappeared almost as quickly."[31] These included the likes of American Bicycle, American Soda Fountain, U.S. Leather, United Button Company, and National Starch. Most of the trusts and combinations put together through the turn of the century aimed at guaranteeing profitable growth through vertical integration or substantial control over product markets, or both. Large-scale private capital was obviously groping its way toward a new distribution of economic power and testing the outer limits to industrial concentration in the brave new world of nationwide markets, high-speed transportation and communication, and science-based techniques.

The instability of this formative phase of oligopoly was aggravated by an unprecedented—and unrepeated—series of antitrust actions. Under President Theodore Roosevelt, 19 civil suits and 25 criminal suits were brought; his successor, William Howard Taft, initiated 78 more between 1909 and 1913. Following the Northern Securities case of 1904, the two major "trust busting" decisions of the Supreme Court were the 1911 breakups of the Standard Oil holding company and the American Tobacco Company, a single manufacturing concern. Both were judged to have used monopoly power intentionally to reduce competition, an "unreasonable" restraint of trade; they were dissolved into 34 and 16 parts respectively. Between 1911 and 1918 antitrust suits were also filed against International Harvester, U.S. Steel, Armour (acquired by Greyhound in 1970, sold to Conagra in 1983), Swift (acquired by Esmark in 1973, in turn acquired by Beatrice in 1984), and American Sugar Refining—all among the top ten industrial firms in 1909—as well as GE, Eastman Kodak, Corn Products, Du Pont, and American Can. Horizontal mergers by already-dominant firms seemed more likely than anything else to trigger antitrust action, although government policy may have looked less predictable to the empire builders of the time.

This period of economic and legal uncertainty, however, was actually solidifying the displacement of competitive markets by the constrained rivalry of increasingly stable oligopolies. In the legal sphere, the antitrust decisions of 1904-1911 served to reinforce the consolidation movement, as the judiciary allowed that not every restraint of trade was unlawful under the Sherman Act. Even though sheer size conferred market power, it did not *per se* transgress the law. This "rule of reason" (1911) was followed by the Clayton and Federal Trade Commission Acts of 1914. They prohibited several "unfair" and discriminatory trade practices, and they barred corporation executives from serving as directors of competing companies (interlocking directorates) and acquiring the stock of competing companies. Section 7 of the Clayton Act went beyond Sherman, outlawing mergers that "substantially lessen competition or tend to create a monopoly," so that federal action might "arrest . . . monopolies in their incipiency."

These decisions and laws were not only the high-water mark of antimonopoly policy; they simultaneously cooled anticorporate ire by convincing the public that their government was taking resolute action against "bad" trusts. The corollary was that "good" trusts did exist and should be left alone because they did not lessen competition or engage in predatory activity. U.S. Shoe Machinery and U.S. Steel were duly exonerated of antitrust violations in 1918–20, because they had not committed undesirable acts and had been losing ground to competitors (U.S. Steel's share declined from 65 percent of the nation's output in 1901 to 40 percent in 1920). Joe Bain, an authority on industrial organization, appraised "the total effects" of all antitrust prosecutions through 1915–20 as "not very great." The Sherman Act's ban on monopoly

> was not directed at the phenomenon of industrial concentration or market control . . . but rather at specific actions designed to exclude competitors or to restrain their ability to compete. . . . The courts showed no disposition, therefore, to apply the penalties of the Sherman Act to the already typical American case of a highly concentrated industry, the ruthless tactics of whose member firms were in the past, their purpose having been accomplished. . . . Concentration was accepted as a *fait accompli*. . . . The Sherman Act had lain idle when it might have been employed to prevent concentration; it now appeared that it could not be used to dissolve most well-established combinations.[32]

Across industry and finance, the movement toward oligopoly was powerful and, in practice, irreversible. In industries like oil, steel, sugar, and metal cans, monopolized in the "robber baron" era of 1865–1900, the market shares commanded by the "trusts" actually declined, as it did for Standard Oil and American Can. Smaller and more innovative firms often took business away from the oversized, conservative giants. "Big Steel," for example, was content with fat profit margins and a stable price environment and thus extended an umbrella over the industry, allowing a newcomer, Bethlehem Steel, to expand after 1913 through the introduction of new processes. But firms like Bethlehem were very large by the standards of three decades gone by. The smaller companies created in 1911 out of the dissolutions of Standard Oil and American Tobacco would have been seen as titans in the 1870s, and they quickly proved to be formidable oligopolistic competitors—Socony Mobil (now Mobil), Sinclair Oil (acquired by Arco in 1970), Texas Oil (now Texaco), American Tobacco (later American Brands), and Liggett and Myers (acquired by Grand Metropolitan, a British conglomerate, in 1980) all had assets of $150 million or more in 1919.[33]

By purely competitive norms, entry was becoming more difficult in a widening array of industries. The new oligopolies could be reasonably effective in stabilizing prices and muting the cutthroat competition that had proved so dangerous for large-scale business. Price leadership without formal collusion was becoming standard practice, but competition by other means was not eradicated. Big corporations continued to fight for market share by advertising, after-sale service, credit, and constant product innovation and differentiation. Profits also "resulted from continued cost cutting, improved administrative coordination, greater use of existing facilities, and expansion overseas."[34]

Indeed, just as small capital germinated giant enterprise, so national accumulation was beginning to overspill its home boundaries. This story is taken up in Chapter 8; here it suffices to say that as early as 1865, oil, the foundation of the best known trust, had already become the nation's sixth-ranking export and that in 1879 Rockefeller began extending his operations overseas to guarantee marketing channels and, after 1900, sources of supply. Ford, Singer Sewing Machine, and Eastman Kodak had two or more plants abroad by 1914, inaugurating the age of multinational enterprise that flourished after 1950. The vertical integration of the years before 1915–20 can best be understood as a reaching backward into raw materials, both domestic and foreign, and forward into development of a national and international marketing apparatus. Such efforts also erected barriers to entry and strengthened the positions of the largest firms.

By 1916–20 the era of corporate instability was drawing to a close. There appear to be two reasons. First, the gloomy economic climate of 1907–1915 was reversed by the export-led expansion of World War I, which was followed by a postwar boom lasting until early 1920. In the sixty-one months between December 1914 and January 1920, the economy underwent only one minor recession, from August 1918 to March 1919, even though business investment remained nearly stagnant the whole time. Second, forces rooted in competitive capitalism were producing on an aggregate level what they have been producing ever since in one new industry after another—a "shakeout" ushering in relative stability featured by an uneasy coexistence among oligopolistic rivals. They created barriers to entry that consolidated the positions of a few large firms no single one of which was strong or efficient enough to establish a pure seller's monopoly (one firm with 100 percent of the market).

In the corporate world, the turnover rate of the biggest firms, or exits by companies from the top 100 industrial corporations, started dropping substantially after 1910–15. "By the early twenties—certainly by 1923—the system had 'stabilized,' and relatively little change has occurred since then."[35] Corporations that emerged as industry leaders by 1920 continued to dominate over the next half-century and beyond. Exceptions were few—in textiles, furniture, drugs, and of course in brand-new industries like airlines and computers. In the majority the oligopolistic structure set in place by 1920 endures today. The names are familiar. Among the largest manufacturing companies in 1919 were Alcoa, Bethlehem Steel, Borden, Chrysler, Firestone, Ford, General Motors (GM), Goodyear, Gulf, International Paper, Mobil, R. J. Reynolds, Standard Oil of New Jersey (now Exxon), Union Carbide, Weyerhauser. Fifty-five others, several dating from 1875–1902 (see Table 4.1 and p. 59), survive today or else have been absorbed by other firms in mergers that perpetuated the lives of both. The same trends are evident in other sectors—telephone, gas, and electric utilities, life insurance companies, merchandising firms, and banks: of the largest in 1917–19, the majority continued among the top ten or fifteen into the 1970s.[36]

As companies grew in size, the individual or family control patterns of their youth inevitably changed. Permanence-oriented institutions began to replace indispensable individuals as commanders and principal stockholders, and rugged-individualist entrepreneurship gave way to managerial bureaucracies. Even the personal stamp of a Rockefeller, a Carnegie, or a James Duke on the 1875–1900 era is somewhat illusory, "for the businesses they began quickly outgrew their ability to control or manage them."[37] It is another facet of capitalism's superseding its own antecedent forms of accumulation, in this case as the scale of production and the complexities of technology grow and make arbitrary, "rule of thumb" decisionmaking unworkable.

As giant integrated firms moved toward domination of most industries vital to the growth and technological prowess of the economy, their chief executives were working out the structures and procedures to administer their enterprises more systematically. Thus, by 1910 nearly half of the prominent business leaders were products of the inside bureaucracy, as opposed to the founding family or outside legal or financial interests.[38] "Industrialists" would now be people who assumed no direct financial responsibility for their enterprises but who built organizations dedicated to planned, routinized profit growth. Names like Theodore Vail (AT&T), Alfred Sloan (GM), Gerard Swope (GE), David Sarnoff (RCA), and William Paley (CBS) were less recognizable than those of the buccaneers of 1870–1900 but far more representative of the new mode of corporatism.

The Second Merger Movement, 1916–1929

Renewed economic expansion during 1915–1920 created a favorable environment for the natural tendencies of capitalist enterprises to absorb other ones, and a new merger movement began around 1916. It abated during the recession of 1920–21 and peaked in the late 1920s, with the great bull market and the aura of prosperity it helped to spread. "From 1924 through 1929 stock prices increased greatly while industrial production increased only moderately. The merger series more closely followed stock prices."[39]

This movement grew out of a more permissive federal government attitude toward big business. Looking back on it in 1934, a leading trade association advisor, Charles Stevenson, stated that "practically, under the Harding, Coolidge, and Hoover Administrations industry enjoyed, to all intents and purposes, a moratorium from the Sherman Act, and, through the more or less effective trade associations which were developed in most of our industries, competition was, to a very considerable extent, controlled. The Department of Justice acted with great restraint and intelligence and only enforced the Sherman Act against those industries who violated the laws in a flagrant and unreasonable manner."[40]

Nor was there any inclination to close the loophole soon discovered in Section 7 of the 1914 Clayton Act: its restrictions applied to mergers made through the acquisition of another company's common stock, but not to purchase of its actual assets. Then, in the 1926 Thatcher case (*Thatcher Manufacturing Co. v. Federal Trade Commission*, 272 U.S. 554), the Supreme Court allowed a company to be free of Section 7 altogether if it purchased a competitor's stock to gain control and then liquidated it while retaining the acquired assets—so that the company could not be prosecuted "even though this [merger] was brought about through stock unlawfully held." Even this remarkable opinion failed to move Congress, and Section 7 became a dead letter until this gap was plugged by the Celler-Kefauver Amendment of 1950.

By the late 1920s most mergers appear to have been inspired by professional promoters and investment bankers, taking advantage of the feverish demand for corporate securities. "During 1928 and 1929 some investment houses employed men on commission who did nothing but search for potential mergers. . . . A group of businessmen and financiers in discussing this matter in the summer of 1928 agreed that nine of ten mergers had the investment banker at the core."[41] The increasingly promotional and financial basis of this merger movement indicates a surplus of funds seeking speculative profits, as opportunities for productive investment profitable enough for the corporate sector were waning. A study of 2,110 new security issues in the 1920s indicated that "roughly two-thirds . . . was not for new real investment but for financial purposes, analogous to those of investment trusts. . . . the increase in new capital issues after 1924 consisted wholly of 'non-productive' issues," mainly to effect mergers or modify the structure of industries for quick financial gain.[42] The Securities and Exchange Commission found that "from 1924–30, utility holding companies floated some $5 billion of securities, the great bulk of which went not to build or improve utility properties, but to purchase already outstanding voting securities of operating utility companies."[43]

Multifirm consolidations, the hallmark of the first merger movement, were far less common in the 1920s; merger via acquisition became the dominant form of combination. But new sectors were drawn into merger activity. Mergers among electricity and natural gas suppliers in the 1920s were so extensive as to raise the specter of a "power trust." More than 43 percent of all utility companies operating in 1922 disappeared into combinations by 1928;[44] many were put into "pyramid" holding companies, incredibly tangled networks of intercompany loans and debts, several of which collapsed after 1929.

Banks and retailing also became beehives of merger activity for the first time. In New York, the Chase Bank emerged as the world's largest in 1928 after a massive consolidation, and the California-based Bank of America soon had 500 branch offices across the state. Retail chains expanded faster than ever before. The nation's first chain, the Great Atlantic and Pacific Tea Company, founded in 1859, had 5,000 stores in 1922 and 17,600 by 1928. Frank W. Woolworth's variety chain began with 7 outlets in Pennsylvania in the 1880s, expanded to 318 by 1909, then passed the 1,500-mark by 1927. Sears Roebuck, begun as a Chicago mail-order house in 1887, had sales exceeding $240 million in 1925 ($70 million more than rival Montgomery Ward), but in that year Sears set out on a new path when it opened its first retail store in Chicago. By 1929 the company had 324 stores.[45] Success came not only from economies of central buying and mass distribution, but from an aggressive sales effort, mainly through periodical advertising, in the growing urban and suburban markets. And although improved management strengthened some of these enterprises, it was anything but fully responsible for their growth. Robert E. Wood, whose career with Sears stretched from 1924 through 1968 and who was president from 1928 to 1939, stated that "Sears made every mistake in the book of retailing except one—it catered to automobile traffic."[46]

In manufacturing and mining the pattern was also one of piecemeal acquisitions by the merger route rather than by consolidation. Compared to 1890–1902 there was a higher incidence of vertical integration and diversification in the form of product extension, involving firms that were making the same product or product line in different geographic areas. Apparently longer-run organizational improvements were insisted upon by at least some merger strategists.

Desire to avoid many of the postmerger problems and failures of the 1898–1902 wave often was the publicly stated rationale for the mergers of the 1920s, and some business historians point to managerial goals of operating economies and administrative coordination as the guiding force behind the second merger movement.[47] But efficiency improvements that reduce costs for large firms hardly erode market power and profitability. Then too, giant horizontal integrations, involving producers competing in the same geographic market, were now on record as being an unavoidable challenge to the antitrust laws—probably the only one in the 1920s. The fact is that the 1917–1929 movement was successful in enlarging market shares for several corporations in the active merger industries—food products, chemicals, primary metals, nonelectrical machinery, coal. In typical cases, mergers involving firms other than the recognized leader created a "number two firm." Bethlehem Steel combined with four of the top ten steel makers between 1916 and 1923; Continental Can absorbed 19 companies between 1927 and 1930. The Union Carbide and Carbon consolidation of 1917, the biggest since U.S. Steel in 1901, brought together two large chemical companies and several smaller ones, and the Allied Chemical and Dye consolidation of 1920 completed the oligopolistic structure of the twentieth-century chemical industry.

Other industrial firms that expanded through merger during the 1920s were the major petroleum companies, as well as GM, Chrysler, B. F. Goodrich, Caterpillar Tractor, United Aircraft, and General Mills. The first diversified food giant appeared in the 1920s, as General Foods Corporation (acquired by Philip Morris in 1985) put together a string of product-extension acquisitions, among them Maxwell House coffee, Sanka, Jello, and Bird's Eye. Borden too was a major food acquirer, as was National Dairy, which took over 360 firms between 1924 and 1929, including Kraft-Phoenix Cheese, itself a product of a 1928 merger of the two largest cheese producers with 40 percent of domestic sales. Such product-

extension mergers were not disturbed during the 1920s. They brought the acquiring firm "noncompeting" products with related production processes or marketing channels that could crisscross the country.

Overall, between 1925 and 1929 the 100 largest corporations' share of total
manufacturing assets rose from 34.5 to 38.2 percent (and to 42.2 percent in
1931). Nearly all the increase came from merger activity.[48]

The second merger movement cannot be divorced from the "new era" thinking that swept America in the 1920s. These were times when many believed that
business cycles were finally a relic of the past. In the *Ladies Home Journal* in
August 1929, GM Board Chairman John J. Raskob stated that "anyone not only
can be rich, but ought to be rich. . . . If a man saves $15 a week, and invests in
good common stocks . . . at the end of twenty years he will have at least $80,000
and an income from investments of around $400 a month. He will be rich."

Toward a "New Era" of Prosperity, 1917–1929

The recovery from the recession of January 1920-July 1921 brought "a prolonged investment boom."[49] During 1917–21, gross private fixed investment
averaged $7.58 billion per year in 1929 dollars, net investment only $0.47
billion. From this low level, the increases through 1926 were large, as the
following figures show:[50]

	Gross investment	Net investment
1922	$10.37	$3.01
1923	12.80	5.24
1924	13.34	5.38
1925	14.77	6.81
1926	15.91	7.36
1927	15.19	6.63
1928	14.90	5.98
1929	14.56	5.33

Yet these outlays dropped off after their 1926 peak; through 1929 gross investment declined 8.5 percent, net investment by 27.6 percent. These swings must be
kept in mind when evaluating the history of the "roaring twenties" economy.

What were the forces making for a sustained economic expansion that finally
pulled the nation out of the doldrums of 1907–1915? And why did they end in the
greatest economic calamity in American history?

The energy behind a vigorously growing market economy comes chiefly from
a core of dynamic young industries. Between 1917 and 1929 electrification and
automobiles provided the key investment outlets that came to fruition after World
War I. They overrode the depressive tendencies of the oligopolistic investment

mode, at least long enough to allow the economy to expand for several years without significant interruption. Business activity remained at high levels from late 1921 through mid 1929, with minor recessions in 1924 and 1927. Unemployment averaged 3.6 percent, as real gross investment and GNP in 1929 were both 40 percent higher than in 1922 and industrial production was 50 percent higher.[51] "It is important to remember that this record was achieved," R. A. Gordon points out, "without a high and rising level of military expenditures. We have not been able to do as well since then."[52]

The revolution that began with the mechanical generation of electricity in the early 1880s spread to the technological universe first through communication and lighting, then through local railway traction, finally through industry and agriculture. Gross investment in central electric power stations, electric streetcar railways, and telephone facilities was in its infancy in 1887–91, but ten years later it exceeded gross capital spending by railroads and surged well past it in the 1920s, as the following annual average figures (billions of 1929 dollars) show:[53]

	Railroads	Total electrical utility sector
1887–91	$0.57	$0.14
1897–1901	0.32	0.48
1907–11	1.10	0.74
1917–21	0.51	0.51
1927–31	0.73	1.22

During 1920–29, annual net investment in electric power stations alone averaged $367 million per year compared to $256 million for railroads.

Total electrical utility sector investment constituted 8.7 percent of gross private investment in 1927–31,[54] a significant figure even though well below the railroad share from the 1850s through the 1880s (see p. 32). To it, moreover, must be added the effects of electrification in industry and private households. These two sectors were by far the major consumers of the output of the electrical utility sector, which increased enormously between 1902 and 1929: total electricity output grew from 6 billion kilowatt hours to 118 billion, and electricity used per dollar of real GNP increased 8.1 times.[55]

The manufacturing sector was growing in importance between the 1890s and 1929; its share of national product increased and its share of net fixed capital formation rose from 31 to 38 percent.[56] This growth coincided with the extremely rapid electrification of plants and machinery in manufacturing. In 1904 the *Census of Manufactures* reported that "the use of electric motors is now so general that it is difficult to name any industry . . . to which this modern mechanism has not been applied. Practically all the newer factories and shops . . . constructed within the past five years, have an electrical drive either exclusively or for most purposes."[57] At that time, 10 percent of all primary power capacity in manufacturing was electric and 81 percent was steam-engine. By 1929 the electric proportion was 78 percent, the steam-engine share 22 percent.[58] Investment outlays connected with this electrification must have been substantial, especially for "unit drive" motors and for the redesign of older buildings to accommodate the more efficient organization of production flows. One persuasive clue is investment in producers durables, overwhelmingly machinery and equipment for manufacturing: between 1897–1901 and 1927–31, this component grew faster than any other private investment component (Tables 3.1 and 5.1). It also grew faster during the economy's slow years of 1907–1916—the decade of greatest advances in manufacturing electrification.[59]

Electrical appliances for the household also made their appearance. The range, iron, fan, clock, vacuum cleaner, and washing machine were all introduced before 1920, but (with the automobile) constituted "another outstanding change in demand . . . after 1922," associated with "the exercise of merchandising imagination and changes in the 'tempo' of living."[60] By then the principal new electrical appliance was the radio, accompanied by refrigerators, sewing machines, coffee makers, toasters, waffle irons, heaters, and heating pads. Retail sales of radios and parts climbed from $60 million in 1922 to $850 million in 1929, while all other electrical appliance sales exceeded $400 million.[61]

For all end uses as capital goods and consumer products, output of electrical machinery, appliances, and supplies increased 2.5 times between 1909 and 1919 and more than doubled again in the 1920s.[62] By 1929 this was the fifth-largest manufacturing industry (behind motor vehicles, nonelectrical machinery, iron and steel, printing and publishing), representing 5 percent of total manufacturing-sector value added.[63]

An estimate of the total electrical impact on the economy, for consumption and investment and gross output, would include the electric utility and electrical machinery industries, which sold their products to each other as well as to nearly every other part of the economy. Any such calculation would be hazardous in view of data limitations: input-output data for the 1920s are not sufficiently detailed, although they do show electric utilities serving thirty-eight of forty-one industries, with two of the three others (construction and petroleum-natural gas) probably relying on self-generated electricity.[64] But the foregoing account should leave little doubt about the importance of electrification through 1929.

Less doubt can exist about the automobile. Factory sales of passenger cars, trucks, and buses, barely 4,000 units in 1900, increased to 127,000 in 1909, 1.88 million in 1919, and 5.34 million in 1929. Total output from 1920 through 1929 was 35.7 million units, 87 percent of them passenger cars.[65] During the 1920s, the industry became the nation's leader in manufacturing. Motor vehicles furnished 6.3 percent of all value added in manufacturing in 1929, up from 4.6 percent in 1919 when it already ranked third.[66] The rising levels of output created backward linkages, or demands for new plants and equipment in other industries, like steel, nickel, lead, rubber, plate glass, and petroleum refining. For all these industries, motor vehicles were the biggest customer, with motor vehicle production itself absorbing 20 percent of all steel output, 75 percent of plate glass, and 80 percent of rubber. Automobiles and trucks transformed the petroleum industry from a producer of illuminants and lubricants into a supplier of gasoline.[67]

But that was only part of the history-making impact of the "insolent chariot." The best gauge of its cumulative effects on the economy is the stock of motor vehicles in use: the number rose from 312,000 in 1909 to 7.6 million in 1919 and 26.7 million in 1929, when there was one for every 4.6 persons. The result was a steady increase in employment in filling stations and garages, hot dog stands, billboards and road signs, truck and bus driving, and construction and repair of roads. Expansion in these activities meant new investments in buildings, equipment, and highways; and as personal living styles began to be affected, further rounds of investment were stimulated by the development of suburban communities.

In a static neoclassical economics setting, automobiles undoubtedly took an appreciable part of the incomes that would have been expended on other goods and services. The decline of the railroads under competition from motor vehicles was already evoking considerable comment in the 1920s. But in a real-world capitalist economy that tends to create pools of unemployed resources and simultaneously requires rapid growth to perpetuate itself, the accumulation possibilities opened up by steam power and railroads, and now by automobiles, invigorated the whole economic machine. As the 1920s drew to a close, 3.7 million jobs were directly created by the production and servicing of motor vehicles, a large figure in a total labor force of 46 to 49 million, and many more jobs were created indirectly, in highway construction and other activities.[68]

One example stands out with unwonted clarity. Tables 3.1 and 5.1 indicate that the only investment component that grew faster after 1897–1901 than before was the public one, and in the 1920s, more than half of it was for highways.[69] Funds for streets and roads became more readily available with the Federal Aid Road Act of 1916, amended by the Federal Highway Act of 1921. They required states to set up highway departments to plan road projects and submit to federal inspections to qualify for federal aid on a "matching funds" basis. Actual outlays, done almost entirely by state and local governments, passed the billion-dollar mark early in the decade and reached $1.82 billion by 1927—one-sixth of all government expenditures, federal, state, and local.[70] This too proved well timed. Government spending was coming to the aid of flagging private investment, although on a thoroughly insufficient scale for the years just ahead.

The End of the Boom: 1929 and All That

As the 1920s stretched on, the prolonged investment boom was sowing the seeds of its own demise, through its contributions to increasing productivity and inadequate consumer purchasing power. The years following the First World War were ones of record-breaking increases in efficiency, in output per worker and per unit of capital stock. The reasons are clear—electrification, automotive transport, and widespread mass-production innovations, with expanding markets and longer production runs bringing still greater economies of scale. The end of mass immigration in 1921 threatened to restrict the supply of labor and push up wage bills, leading employers to substitute machinery for labor at an even faster rate and to squeeze more production out of existing work forces through "human engineering" techniques. For this was also the age of the behaviorist-psychology school of management, an outgrowth of Taylorism, but emphasizing better worker morale as the way to improve productivity.[71]

For the overall private economy, the productivity of labor and capital underwent "a distinct change in trend about 1919."[72] Labor productivity, increasing about 1.6 percent per year from 1889 to 1919, rose at 2.3 percent annually during 1919 to 1957. Productivity advances were "much more marked" for output per unit of capital, almost tripling. The manufacturing sector had historically high gains in productivity in the 1920s. Output per labor-hour leaped 72 percent—the previous decade record had been 27 percent in the 1880s—and output per unit of capital rose 52 percent. The output-capital ratio in manufacturing and mining was actually reversed around World War I, falling before those years but rising in the 1920s. Capital in manufacturing industries grew only 3.2 percent in the 1920s, the lowest decade rate since industrialization began in the 1870s.[73] This increasing efficiency of capital goods was having a distinct impact on corporate investment policy. A 1929 questionnaire sent to "800 of the larger and more representative manufacturing concerns" disclosed a dramatic shortening of payoff horizons: 43.6 percent of the respondents required that new equipment should return its cost through production cost savings in two years or less, 76.9 percent required that it pay for itself in four years or less.[74]

The nation's productive capacity was expanding quickly in the wake of record gains in labor and capital productivity, but consumer demand could not seem to keep pace. The problem was keenly felt by industrialists and business economists. "Since 1920," observed one manufacturer in 1929, "it is pre-eminently the problem of marketing, and especially the creation of demand . . . which has held the attention of business executives." Professor Melvin Copeland of Harvard added that "producing capacity was awaiting opportunity for utilization which furnished a strong incentive to the exercise of merchandising imagination."[75]

These fears were not unfounded. Investment saturation was showing up in two bellwether sectors, automobiles and housing. Growth of passenger car sales was sharply reduced after 1923, as the market was moving from one of first-time purchasers to replacement buyers. Average annual automobile sales in millions rose as follows:

		Percentage increase over preceding period
1919–20	1.779	
1922–23	2.949	65.8%
1925–26	3.714	25.9
1928–29	4.115	10.8

The industry's capacity exceeded even the 1929 peak output of 4.455 million units, a number not surpassed until 1949. Conditions in residential housing were shakier. New housing starts rose from 247,000 in 1920 to a decade high of 937,000 in 1925, then declined to 509,000 in 1929. Between 1925 and 1929 residential housing expenditures dropped 37 percent. Still there were excess supplies.[76]

In manufacturing and mining as a whole, the rate of capacity utilization peaked during 1923.26 at 88 to 91 percent and then drifted downward.[77] For manufacturing, utilization rates during 1925.29 may have averaged as little as 80 percent, and in railroads there was "unutilized capital equipment of wholly exceptional dimensions."[78] Manufacturing employment dropped 3.6 percent from 1919–20 through 1928–29, as production increases came entirely from productivity improvements; jobs in transportation and public utilities were off 6.8 percent. Only the expansion of employment in trade, finance, real estate and other services (up 37.5 percent) and in government (up 26.6 percent) absorbed the growth in the labor force.[79] "It was, in fact, the timely development of 'mass services' which saved our country from a critical unemployment problem during recent years," the Committee on Recent Economic Changes stated in 1929, citing "travel, entertainment, education, insurance, communication; the facilities of hotels, restaurants, delicatessen stores, steam laundries, and public libraries, to mention but a few."[80]

Thus it seems likely that the accelerating gains in productivity caused potential output, or capacity, to rise faster than wages in many sectors, leading to inadequate consumer demand that could have been offset only by higher wages or lowered product prices for consumers. One of these two conditions was at least partially met: the real earnings of nonfarm employees rose substantially in the 1920s, by 26 to 28 percent, a higher rate than at any time in the previous three decades.[81] Also, unlike what happened during the Grand Traverse, the shares of national income of both employee compensation and labor as a whole edged up throughout the 1900–1929 period.[82]

But if real wages and labor income were rising during the 1920s, what was making the gap between consumer income and industrial capacity harder to close?

1. Income inequality was growing. Labor income as a whole may have grown faster than property income (profits, rents, interest), but labor income is a

heterogeneous aggregate that includes the earnings of the lowest-wage worker and highest-paid corporate president or banker. Distribution of that labor income became much more uneven during the 1920s. Between 1920 and 1929, real disposable income per person for the bottom 93 percent of the nonfarm population grew 6 percent, while for the top 7 percent it nearly doubled.[83] The trend was powerful enough to allow the top 5 percent of the total population to increase its share of disposable income from 24 to 34 percent. By 1929 the income distribution reached another "plateau of high inequality."[84] As a result, personal savings became more concentrated, with the 2.3 percent of families with incomes over $10,000 supplying more than two-thirds of all saving.[85] Concentration of savings in the high incomes constrained mass purchasing power, and it also fueled financial instability as the rich diverted portions of their increasing wealth to real estate and stock market speculation.

2. Government support of the macroeconomy was tapering off during the 1920s, at the same time that it was channeling income away from wage earners. As a proportion of the GNP, total public spending for all purposes dropped slightly between 1922 and 1927, from 11.9 to 11.2 percent.[86] This did represent a higher government share of GNP than during 1900–1915. But it came in part from a big increase in federal debt, from $2.9 billion in 1917 to $25.5 billion in 1919, to pay for American participation in the First World War. During the 1920s, interest on the public debt (federal, state, and local) was running about $1.4 billion annually, or the equivalent of 1.8 percent of GNP in 1922 and 1.4 percent in 1927. It constituted a regressive public expenditure, redistributing income from poorer households toward wealthier bondholders. Only highways and education were larger public expenditure items. Although the impact may have been only mildly regressive given the proportions of GNP involved, it was not counteracted by a progressive tax system. On the contrary, despite the enactment of the federal income tax in 1913, state and local property and sales taxes, which have always been regressive, provided over half of all public sector revenue in the 1920s. Federal income tax rates were cut for everybody during the decade, with the rich benefiting as much as the poor, far more in terms of total tax savings. The Revenue Acts of 1921 and 1926 actually shifted the tax burden away from upper-income groups.[87] Any stimulative effects coming from government spending itself were further weakened by federal budget surpluses, as Republican administrations reduced the federal debt from $25.5 billion in 1919 to $16.6 billion in 1930.

3. "Roaring twenties" prosperity was slow to reduce poverty, always a ceiling on capitalist expansion. "At 1929 prices," reported the Brookings Institution, "a family income of $2,000 may perhaps be regarded as sufficient to supply only basic necessities." In that year 12 million families—more than two in five—had incomes below $1,500. Nearly 20 million (71 percent) earned less than $2,500.[88] Economist Paul Nystrom of Columbia estimated that at the zenith of the boom 1 million Americans were public charges, another million were "unem-

ployable'' for reasons that today would be called job-search discouragement, and 7 to 8 million more straddled the borderline between starvation and accepting charity.[89] Aggravating matters were the dire conditions facing the nation's farmers, still over 20 percent of the labor force. As is well known, the Great Depression began for the agricultural sector in 1920–21.

4. Finally, one way out of this trap might have been to pass on productivity advances to consumers in the form of cheaper products. But this was becoming less possible. Industrial concentration increased during the 1920s as a result of the second merger movement. For the companies involved, "flexibility of price change was out of the question."[90] "Administered prices" guaranteed pricing stability for oligopolized industries but cyclical vulnerability for the macroeconomy: large price reductions would be forestalled by larger cutbacks in production and employment. From 1929 through 1932 prices in competitive industries fell 60 percent compared to only 15 percent in "the more concentrated industries"; and small price declines were associated with big production declines in motor vehicles, agricultural machinery, iron and steel (output down 74 to 84 percent), cement (down 55 percent), and tires (down 42 percent).[91] These forces must have been at work in the 1920s, exerting a negative "acceleration" effect on investment.

5. To these unfavorable real, or goods-markets, factors of the 1920s should be added the always-latent financial instability factor. The appearance of installment buying strengthened it. The automobile industry came to epitomize modern production and distribution of consumer durables, with

> deliberate product obsolescence, extensive advertising, and consumer finance. General Motors took the lead in all three; advertising, yearly model changes, trade-ins, and living in constant debt were thereby elevated to what many take to be the American way of life. They also postponed the day when the industry would find itself with chronic excess capacity.[92]

By the mid 1920s, three cars out of four were sold on credit. Household furniture, appliances, and even jewelry were increasingly sold on time.[93] While most people were at one moment or another mortgaging their future income through installment buying and charge accounts, total consumer debt outstanding (exclusive of home mortgages) in 1929 amounted to $7.1 billion, 20 percent of it for automobiles. This was equivalent to 8.5 percent of disposable income, compared with the 18 or 20 percent it would reach beginning in the 1960s.[94] But that "low" percentage conceals growing consumer sensitivity to credit conditions, and a convergence of consumption and investment as vectors of financial instability. When mortgages on homes are included, total personal debt grew considerably faster than disposable income after 1922, rising to the equivalent of 30 percent of disposable income in 1929. Further evidence of the potential instability of consumer demand is that during the 1920s debt-supported spending on both durables and housing not only increased relative to total consumer outlays but also began to fluctuate more erratically.[95]

Did these five investment and consumption-weakening forces cause, or preordain, the Great Depression? The answer must be no. The economy of the 1920s, even with hindsight, appeared to be headed less for an overwhelming disaster than for a characteristic recession. After all, during the 1920s real GNP grew at an impressive 4.0 to 4.2 percent per year on average.[96] Business profits were healthy to the end of the decade; the volume of profits expanded, and the rate of return on invested capital increased through 1926 and then leveled off at a rate comparable to that of other booms.[97] The main problem was overbuilt capacity in an array of industries and barriers to the expansion of wage income. As Gordon describes the situation, "it is difficult to conceive of any increase in *total* consumption that would have maintained investment in a number of areas at the rate that had been reached before the turning point." Under the conditions of the 1920s, nothing could have prevented a sag in investment in residential and commercial structures, automobiles, and other industries where "capacity . . . had been expanding at a rate that could not be maintained indefinitely."[98]

The expansion in industrial output in 1928 and 1929 was very large, a sign of cumulative increases in productivity and capacity.[99] Business inventories tripled from late 1928 through mid 1929. In June 1929 employment in large factories began to fall. Industrial production peaked in July. The downturn in business activity began in the next two months, *before* the stock market crash, as the nation's biggest industries, motor vehicles and iron and steel, scheduled cutbacks in output. By December industrial production was already 12 percent below its July level, and the Federal Reserve was urgently cutting interest rates and purchasing securities to increase the reserves of the banking system. Retail sales started declining in the last quarter of the year, with consumer spending off 5 percent from the third to the fourth quarter of 1929. Factory payrolls and freight-car loadings were also decreasing now.

All this time the economy was being undermined by two other forces. The first, as noted, was a gathering weakness in investment, especially in residential construction, which peaked in 1925 and then fell sharply through 1929. The other was the New York Stock Exchange. In early August 1929 the New York Federal Reserve raised its rediscount rate to dampen speculation, by increasing the cost of call money borrowed to buy stocks on margin, with little apparent effect. Share prices reached their great bull-market peak on September 3, 1929 and turned wobbly a few days later. In late October the market started plunging in earnest, to panic proportions on October 24 ("black Thursday") and to devastation on October 28 and 29, two days that erased 21 to 23 percent of the value of all stocks. It was the beginning of a long and excruciating slide that bottomed out on July 8, 1932 when stock values on average were 89 percent below their September 1929 heights. The stock market debacle shattered business confidence, ruined countless thousands of private investors, and wiped out holding company and investment trust structures by the score. It effectively compounded factors making for output and employment drops that would not by themselves have produced a prolonged and desperate economic crisis.

The fact is that the boom of the 1920s was no more distorted than many booms before and since; it was one of the most vigorous that private enterprise capitalism is capable of producing. But like its predecessors it took place in an unprotected economy. There was no government safety net under the legion of high-wire risk takers. The fall was all the more brutal because it had been preceded by ''new era'' psychology, one of those capitalist self-intoxication devices that give rise to massive overconfidence and a propensity to throw all caution to the winds. The crucial break occurred in the security markets rather than in the consumer goods or capital goods markets. The stock market crash of October 1929 hit the corporate economy at its weakest link—its fragile financial structure featured by the heavily indebted holding companies that controlled large segments of the utility, entertainment, and transportation industries. Interest on the bonds was paid out of the profits of the individual operating companies. Soon the decline in profits led to defaults on a number of bonds and a series of spectacular bankruptcies. Meanwhile, the Wall Street collapse was drastically raising the cost of issuing new corporate equity and closing off this source of cheap finance as a way out. It proved to be ''an exceptionally effective way of exploiting the weaknesses of the corporate structure.''[100]

Investment and consumption soon began to sink. As sales and prices fell, large corporations responded by reducing their outlays for inventory and capital goods and increasing their holdings of cash balances, withdrawing funds from the economy's spending stream.[101] Consumption dropped autonomously once the slump was under way: the drop in household spending was larger than can be explained by the fall in disposable income alone, probably because of pessimistic expectations about future personal wealth and income. By 1930 household net worth was in fact being eroded, by increasing indebtedness and the continuing drop in stock prices.[102] As unemployment shot past the 10 percent mark in the fall of 1930, consumers cut their spending even more for fear they would be next to lose their jobs—better to sock away some extra dollars now while it was still possible.

The financial system was pushed to the breaking point by misguided monetary and fiscal policies—an increase in interest rates in late 1931 (it was deemed necessary to protect the nation's gold reserve) and a large tax increase in June 1932. Not surprisingly, government policymakers understood the nature and extent of the economic cave-in no better than most economists or industrial leaders or anyone else. But financial institutions had already begun to totter well before these counterproductive government policies. Lending institutions started to feel the pressure in 1930, as the value of their assets was reduced by what were turning out to be bad (uncollectable) loans to stock traders, farmers, and other borrowers who faced declining prices or contracting markets for their goods. A wave of bank failures hit the Midwest and South in October 1930; two months later the Bank of the United States, a large private New York savings institution with 400,000 depositors, closed its doors. The following spring there was a second wave of bank failures. Millions of Americans who had regarded banks as the bedrock of their security only two years earlier now were withdrawing their savings in the form of cash or gold. In Europe a similar crisis was swiftly developing, and as Europeans demanded gold, banks all over the world had to call in loans and shrink deposits. A new wave of liquidations, international in scope, followed. In the summer of 1931, the jerry-built house of international credit, debt, and war reparations finally gave way, crushing the last hopes for a ''normal'' recovery.

The human dimensions of the worst depression in American history have been amply documented, if written words can convey the magnitude of the catastrophe. In sheer economic terms the cost is beyond the grasp of most people now alive. From 1929 to their lowest points of 1932–33, real GNP shrank 31 percent, industrial production 46 percent. Gross private fixed investment virtually collapsed, down 74 percent. The loss in real disposable income per head was 28 percent.[103]

Despite the efforts of Franklin Roosevelt's New Deal, real GNP did not regain its 1929 volume until 1939, when per capita income was still 7 percent below its 1929 level. Unemployment, reaching an estimated 25 percent of the labor force in 1933, averaged nearly 19 percent from 1931 through 1940 and never dipped below 10 percent until late 1941. The anemic nature of the recovery during the 1930s was a direct result of the inadequate increases in government support for the economy. Even though many New Deal programs seemed to be spendthrift by the standards of the day, the total public-sector deficit averaged only 2.5 percent of the GNP in 1934–37.[104] Only the Second World War ended the Great Depression. ''Rearmament'' commenced in June 1940 and over the next year, before the Japanese attack on Pearl Harbor, military spending jumped more than six-fold, to 11 percent of the GNP. It rose to 42 percent of GNP in 1943–44. Under this mighty stimulus, real national product increased 65 percent from 1940 through 1944, industrial production by 90 percent. So great was the expansion of the armed forces—to 12.1 million people by 1945—that the civilian labor force actually decreased and unemployment dropped to a historic low of 1.2 percent in 1944.

What had really happened between 1929 and 1933 is that the institutions of nineteenth-century free market growth broke down, beyond repair. Had the chain of circumstances been ''right,'' it could have occurred in 1920–21 or possibly 1907. The tumultuous passage from the depression of the 1930s to the total economic mobilization of the 1940s was the watershed in twentieth-century U.S. capitalism. After that, nothing in the macroeconomy would ever be the same;

6

Investment, Growth, and Instability: The Great Postwar Boom, 1945–1972

The 1940–1945 expansion wiped out the effects of the Great Depression so completely that it triggered a debate in corporate circles, in Congress, and among economists over the likelihood of renewed economic stagnation once wartime spending was terminated. The debate was overtaken by events. To general surprise, postwar "reconversion" went smoothly. Even though total government expenditures were reduced by the equivalent of 27 percent of GNP in less than a year, GNP regained its wartime peak by the end of 1946.[1] Consumer expenditures rose swiftly the moment hostilities, and rationing, ended in August 1945. Investment had to keep up, so total private spending jumped $40 billion from early 1945 to early 1946, about 20 percent of the annual level of GNP at the time.

But the early postwar prosperity soon gave way to sputtering economic growth—an unwelcome, if familiar, prospect. In this uncertain environment, students of the U.S. economy would not have believed that a long wave of economic expansion was about to begin. Yet throughout the postwar era, the economy has functioned far better than it did during previous decades. The eight postwar recessions through 1982 were significantly milder than the 21 between 1854 and 1938 (see Table 6.1). Unemployment averaged 5.4 percent of the labor force from 1945 through 1984, against 8.1 percent from 1900 through 1939. Fixed business investment, the economy's most volatile spending component, fluctuated less widely as well, as did growth in GNP.[2] One result was an 80 percent increase in real disposable income per capita from 1947–48 through 1972–73, surely equal to—or better than—any other quarter-century in U.S. history.[3] With it came a drastic improvement "in the average level of economic well-being," as "real consumption per capita increased by more than 80 percent . . . [and] the basic necessities of life—food, clothing, and shelter—commanded ever decreasing shares of the consumer budget."[4]

Table 6.1

Post-World War II Recessions: Measures of Severity

Cycle Peak to Trough	(duration in months)	Decline in real GNP	Decline in industrial production	Decline in business fixed investment	Peak unemployment rate	Manufacturing capacity utilization: lowest rate
Nov 1948-Oct 1949	(11)	2.0%	10.1%	16.8%	7.6%	72.4%
Jul 1953-May 1954	(10)	3.0	9.6	3.3	5.8	79.1
Aug 1957-Apr 1958	(8)	3.5	13.5	14.9	7.6	72.4
Apr 1960-Feb 1961	(10)	1.0	8.5	3.8	7.1	73.5
Dec 1969-Nov 1970	(11)	1.1	7.1	5.9	6.1	75.9
Nov 1973-Mar 1975	(16)	4.3	14.8	14.7	9.1	69.0
Jan 1980-Jul 1980	(6)	2.4	5.9	6.9	7.8	75.5
Jul 1981-Nov 1982	(16)	3.4	11.4	15.2	10.7	68.8

Sources: U.S. Department of Commerce (1986), 8-11; Board of Governors of the Federal Reserve System (1986), 171; and various issues of *Survey of Current Business* and *Federal Reserve Bulletin.*

Note: Between 1854 and 1938 there were twenty-one business cycles with expansion phases averaging twenty-six months and recessions averaging twenty-one months; for the eight recessions since World War II (through 1988), expansions averaged forty-five months, recessions eleven months. See Sherman and Evans (1984), 26, or U.S. Bureau of the Census (1987), 511.

Why did this superior economic performance take place in the quarter-century following the Second World War? And how was it limited by forces inherent in corporate capitalism?

The 1945–1949 Business Cycle
and Its Aftermath

The first postwar surge in consumption and investment came from a huge pent-up demand, following sixteen years of depression and wartime short-ages. Although the most glaring deficiency probably was in consumer durables, outlays for plant and equipment had been abnormally low for years. Financing of this demand spree came principally from a large pool of liquid assets accumulated during the war in the form of war bonds, but high profits had also reflated the retained earnings of corporations to use for investment. In addition, both consumers and businesses resumed borrowing after the war, and Congress cut taxes for both in 1946. The Federal Reserve helped too, following a policy of monetary ease throughout the period. Aggregate demand was further stimulated by sales to war-ravaged nations: merchandise exports spurted from 2.5 percent of GNP in 1945 to 6.8 percent in 1947, while import levels remained much lower (around 2.2 percent of GNP). "Perhaps at no time in our history," R. A. Gordon concluded, "were the forces tending to expand private investment as strong as they were after World War II."[5] The result was an inflationary boom that lasted thirty-seven months, October 1945 through November 1948.

These were extraordinarily favorable times for capitalist growth. Furthermore, unemployment rates were held down by the withdrawal of women from the labor force; their participation rates fell from the wartime peak of 36.3 percent in 1945 to 31.8 percent in 1946–48.[6] Still, the private sector generated an expansion less than a year longer than the average expansion phase of the 21 complete business cycles from 1854 through 1938. Production and employment growth ground to a halt by mid 1948, as wartime-induced bottlenecks in materials, housing, and finished goods (except automobiles) had been eliminated. The three-year boom had substantially expanded the stock of capital: from 1945 to 1949 producers durables increased by 49 percent, business structures by 8 percent, and residential housing by 7 percent.[7] Excess capacity began to develop, and private investment started falling in late 1948. As an eleven-month contraction unfolded (Table 6.1), the "deflationary forces all came from the private sector of the economy."[8]

The recession was relatively mild, as real GNP declined 2 percent (Table 6.1). But the drop in fixed business investment was large by subsequent postwar standards. Unemployment averaged 5.9 percent in 1949 and reached an uncomfortably high 7.2 percent in the first quarter of 1950. The ghosts of the Great Depression still could not be banished, despite the postwar prosperity. Considerable pessimism was expressed over the fact that the economy was nowhere near full employment by June 1950, when the Korean War broke out. The war itself proved to be the catalyst for a new political solution to an old economic dilemma—how to use selective government intervention to stabilize the private economy. For there is little doubt that the major growth stimulus for the American economy from 1950 through the early 1970s came from the public sector, not private investment.

In the view of Arthur Okun, liberal economist and chairman of the Council of Economic Advisers under President Lyndon Johnson, this expansion of government should be judged "not in dollars of real GNP, but in the very survival of United States capitalism." The policies that prevented an encore of the Great Depression were "made in Washington": the shift to a rising public sector share of GNP constituted "the largest single stabilizing development" in the postwar economy.[9] From 1945 through 1972 there was a historic reduction in business-cycle instability and in uncertainty for large corporations in their financial and investment planning. The more stable environment came from an enlargement of government, the one component of the economy that is relatively immune to cyclical swings in aggregate demand.[10] It was chiefly a product of two forces that complemented one another over most of the postwar period.

The first one was high levels of spending on goods and services by all levels of government (federal, state, and local). The spending was not (until the 1980s) financed by large budget deficits but by higher taxes on profits and nonwage incomes, in other words by taxation that was more progressive than before World War II.[11] Public expenditures of this magnitude increased aggregate demand for goods and services produced by the private sector without increasing its chronically excess productive capacity. The effect was a higher utilization of capacity and a permanent addition to the rate of investment as a consequence of the higher utilization. The second was the "automatic stabilizing" effects of progressive income taxes and government transfer payments (unemployment compensation, food stamps, and other welfare assistance), as during a recession household disposable income falls by less than GNP and consumption falls even less. Data from the recessions of 1948–49, 1953–54, 1957–58, 1960, and 1974–75 show that the fiscal stabilizers produced federal government deficits that offset 36 to 52 percent of the declines in GNP. The comparable figure for 1932 was about 6 percent.[12]

Table 6.2 shows that in 1929 all three levels of government absorbed less than 9 percent of the GNP in purchases of goods and services for their own uses. Through much of the postwar period the figure has hovered around 20 percent. Government purchases represent direct claims by the public sector on society's resources and output: labor, capital, and materials used to build a nuclear submarine, construct a high school, or staff a government agency are in effect denied to private industry. The other element of government spending, excluded from Table 6.2, is transfer payments, which involve no public claim on resources.

Table 6.2

Government Purchases of Goods and Services, Percentage Share of Gross National Product, Annual Averages, 1902–1987

	Total government purchases	Federal military	Federal nonmilitary	State and local
1902	6.7%		2.1%		4.6%
1913	7.0		2.3		4.7
1929	8.6		1.4		7.1
1933	14.8		3.9		10.9
1939–40	14.5	1.8%	4.1%	8.6
1946–49	13.1	5.3	2.0	5.8
1950–54	19.4	10.8	1.8	6.8
1955–59	19.5	9.7	1.5	8.3
1960–64	20.2	8.6	2.2	9.4
1965–69	21.3	8.3	2.3	10.6
1970–74	20.5	6.3	2.3	12.0
1975–79	19.5	5.1	2.4	12.0
1980–84	19.7	5.9	2.3	11.5
1985–87	20.5	6.5	2.1	11.9

Sources: U.S. Bureau of the Census (1975), 224, 1120-21, and U.S. President (1988), 248-49.

Note: Calculations are in current dollars. Detail may not add up to total because of rounding.

Government simply shifts income around by taxing one group of people and giving social security, food stamps, veterans benefits, or interest payments to another (although many people fall into both categories as taxpayers and transfer payment recipients). The growth of transfer payments is included in Table 6.3, which shows that aggregate government spending for all purposes has likewise risen dramatically relative to the pre–1940s era.

Table 6.2 tells us something more. Until the Second World War, state and local government (SLG) was two or three times larger than the federal government. But federal purchases then expanded faster, so that the federal government grew larger than SLG through the 1950s and 1960s. Military spending accounted for more than four-fifths of all federal purchases in this period (9.7 of a total federal GNP share of 11.2 percent during 1955–59, for example). During the sharp break-in-trend that occurred between the late 1940s and the early 1950s, when total government purchases jumped significantly as a share of GNP, the leading salient of change was military expenditure. Transfer payments, which are over-whelmingly federal, were shrinking at the time in relative importance (Table 6.3), as were federal nonmilitary purchases (public works and construction projects, national forests and parks, acquisition and disposal of agricultural com-

Table 6.3

Total Government Expenditures, Percentage Equivalence of Gross National Product, Annual Averages, 1902–1987

	Total government expenditures	Government purchases	Transfer payments
1902	7.3%	6.7%	0.6%
1913	7.6	7.0	0.6
1929	9.9	8.6	1.3
1933	19.1	14.8	4.3
1939–40	18.8	14.5	4.3
1946–49	20.8	13.1	7.7
1950–54	25.3	19.4	5.9
1955–59	25.9	19.5	6.4
1960–64	27.7	20.2	7.5
1965–69	29.3	21.3	8.0
1970–74	31.2	20.5	10.6
1975–79	31.9	19.5	12.4
1980–84	34.0	19.7	14.3
1985–87	34.9	20.5	14.5

Sources: U.S. Bureau of the Census (1975), 224, 1120-21, and U.S. President (1988), 248-49, 342.

Note: Calculations are in current dollars. Detail may not add up to total because of rounding.

modities, law enforcement, scientific and medical research, and other such programs); and "the momentum toward a welfare state gained during the great depression was largely, although not entirely, dissipated."[13]

It is a matter of record that military spending broke down the barriers to an expansion of government just when the dilemma for postwar U.S. capitalism was acute. The recession of 1948–49 was raising, once again, the fundamental question of the 1930s—whether private investment could be relied upon to provide steady economic growth and full employment. The need for government support for the economy was reemerging at a time when political reaction against the New Deal was at its height and resistance to practically all nonmilitary forms of state intervention was on the rebound. Under these circumstances it is not surprising that government and corporate leaders were attracted to military spending like moths to a light bulb. As early as 1948 military spending was being used as a sort of backhanded planning. In that year the Secretary of Defense announced in his annual report that "special measures were also taken to promote the President's program to stimulate industry in areas where unemployment exceeded 12 percent of the estimated labor force. The measures included the placement of military contracts in those areas wherever practicable."[14]

It did not take long for the idea to spread in "establishment" circles. Two months before the outbreak of the Korean War, *Business Week* declared in its "Washington Outlook" (April 15, 1950) that "pressure for more government spending is mounting. And the prospect is that Congress will give in. . . . The reason is a combination of concern over tense Russian relations, and a growing fear of a rising level of unemployment here at home." To this, *U.S. News and World Report* added (May 14, 1950) that "government planners figure that they have found the magic formula for almost endless good times. . . . Cold War is an automatic pump primer." The strategy was given intellectual support by a number of Keynesian economists, who contrasted the economic boom conditions of World War II with the naggingly high joblessness extending through the spring of 1950. Stepped-up arms spending, Harvard economist Sumner Slichter explained at the time, "increases the demand for goods, helps sustain a high level of employment, accelerates technical progress and thus helps the country to raise its standard of living."[15]

Views like these strongly influenced the April 1950 report of President Harry Truman's National Security Council, soon labelled NSC–68, "a reexamination of our objectives in peace and war and of the effect of these objectives on our strategic plans." Drafted after the first atomic test explosion by the Soviet Union but before the Korean War, NSC–68 called for a vast increase in arms outlays, from the 1950 level of $14 billion to $40 billion, and it embodied a new perception of the economic implications of military spending. Political and military concerns were the central justification for the proposed arms buildup, but Paul Nitze, overseer of the NSC–68 task force, thoroughly discussed the economic possibilities with Leon Keyserling, chairman of the Council of Economic Advisers, who expressed "full agreement" that military spending could indeed be good for the economy. Thus, military Keynesianism was "neither accidental nor ephemeral. It appealed powerfully to fears of recurring economic stagnation in the interwar years and to hopes for the full employment and prosperity of the war years."[16] It opted for a militarization of foreign policy and increased Pentagon budgets—"initiatives that were waiting for a crisis to justify them, rather than being direct responses to a sudden change in the global political military situation."[17]

The outbreak of hostilities in Korea in June 1950 provided the opportunity, although the conflict was civil in nature and the precise origins of the fighting unclear.[18] But the war made the connections between arms outlays and employment very clear. In June 1950 unemployment was still 5.2 percent, considered embarrassingly high at the time. Thereafter it dropped swiftly, to 3 percent by early 1951 and then to a post-Second World War low of 1.9 percent in August 1953. What had intervened was a massive escalation of military spending, from an annual rate of $14 billion in mid 1950 to $51 billion by early 1953, or from 5 to 14 percent of the GNP.

And once the war stimulus was ended, the economy reverted to slow growth.

The cutback in military procurement after the armistice of July 1953 touched off a ten-month recession (Table 6.1). The subsequent recovery flattened out in the closing months of 1955. During the expansion phase unemployment did not fall below 4 percent, and the growth in total output from late 1955 through the first half of 1957 was not large (only 2.3 percent).[19] This was the case even though military outlays were now climbing from their post-Korean War low of $38.5 billion in the last quarter of 1955 (9.2 percent of GNP) toward $46.3 billion in 1958 (10.1 percent of GNP). As one economic research institute observed, through 1957 "military demand has been the major and almost exclusive dynamic growth factor in recent years."[20]

Another recession, more severe, began in the summer of 1957, with real GNP falling 3.5 percent. The recovery from this one was even more disappointing, lasting only twenty-four months, April 1958 to April 1960. When it ended the unemployment rate remained stuck above 5 percent. A gap was opening up between the nation's growing productive capacity and total demand for goods and services, so that the economy was failing to generate full employment even at business cycle peaks. The persistent slack was attributable to a deficient growth of fixed business investment, as this record (in billions of 1982 dollars) shows:[21]

1955	$151.0	1959	$ 153.6
1956	160.4	1960	159.4
1957	161.1	1961	158.2
1958	143.9		

An extensive econometric study confirmed that "the sluggishness of business fixed investment was at the heart of the [aggregate] demand lag after 1957, given the fiscal and monetary policies of the period," and that without the ongoing stimulus of government spending the rate of economic growth would have been substantially lower than it was.[22]

The arms-dominated federal budget was bringing about a new structural relationship between government and the economy. "Interventionist government—that is, a fiscal policy with significant leverage on the economy—is largely the result of the rise of the arms economy."[23] As John Kenneth Galbraith has remarked, if an enlarged public sector "is the fulcrum of the regulation of [aggregate] demand, plainly military expenditures are the pivot on which the fulcrum rests."[24] Other government expenditures might well have served the same purpose, but the military spending preference became firmly established for two reasons—powerful opposition, economic and ideological, to any government programs that might compete with private capital or encroach upon its domain, and the external role that military spending immediately began to play in preserving the international capitalist system. During the 1950s and 1960s, as we shall see in Chapter 8, U.S. military supremacy and the "key currency" role of the dollar in international trade and finance were mutually supportive. Throughout the American sphere of influence, the dollar was accepted for all purposes, and its fixed rate in terms of all other currencies increasingly meant that it was overvalued on foreign exchange markets. As long as this situation lasted, it represented a subsidy from the rest of the world to the United States in the form of cheap imports, especially key industrial inputs of oil and ores.

Throughout the period arms spending remained the largest single controllable item in the arsenal of public planning devices. Furthermore, since the end of the first postwar business cycle expansion in late 1948, only increases in military spending have been able to push the official unemployment rate below the 4 percent "full employment" mark, in 1951–53 and 1966–69. The record-breaking, 105-month-long economic expansion from February 1961 to November 1969 was largely a result of arms spending. The Kennedy administration endorsed and practiced military Keynesianism, hiking Pentagon outlays from $45.3 billion in 1960 to $52.1 billion in 1962—15 percent in two years—and space expenditures from $400 million in 1960 to $5 billion in 1965. Substantial tax cuts in 1962 and 1964 further stimulated the economy. A special effort was made to revive investment through a 7 percent tax credit for businesses on purchases of machinery and equipment and through accelerated depreciation allowances—"a bribe to capital formation," Paul Samuelson labeled them.[25]

Nonetheless, the celebrated expansion would have ended in 1967 rather than 1969 without the $22 billion increase in expenditures for the Vietnam War from 1965 through 1967, when military spending jumped from 7.2 to 9 percent of the GNP. "Indeed," the government's chief statistician reported, "*all* the leading sector indexes began to decline in the first quarter of 1966."[26] As it was, the economy underwent a "minirecession" through most of 1967, with real fixed business investment dropping 3.8 percent—in the face of soaring arms spending. The Federal Reserve did contribute to the slowdown. Monetary policy turned restrictive in 1966, as the Fed tried to curb the inflationary forces unleashed by the escalation of Vietnam War spending, and the "credit crunch" of late summer helped bring on the minirecession.[27] But by the third quarter of 1966 the economy had been expanding nearly six years without interruption, and real fixed business investment was running 60 percent above its 1961 level.[28] The supply of plant and equipment available to private industry was probably greater than needed to meet consumer demand. In manufacturing, the productive capacity of the capital stock had grown considerably faster in the 1960s than during the 1950s.[29] After two decades of state-supported growth and other fiscal stimuli including tax cuts, the private economy was again exhibiting signs of lethargy.

The Course of Private Spending, 1947–1972

Any long stretch of capitalist growth must be related to expansion of markets and sustained increases in investment. One key development through the 1960s was the "Los Angelizing" of the American economy.[30] A few numbers will give an idea of the dimensions of the automobile-suburb symbiosis. From 1947 through 1960 the motor vehicle, petroleum, and rubber industries were responsible for one-third of all plant and equipment expenditures in manufacturing. Consumer outlays on automobiles and parts, gasoline, and oil rose from 6.5 percent of total expenditures to 9 percent during the same period.[31] By 1963–66 one of every six business enterprises was directly dependent on the manufacture, distribution, servicing, and use of motor vehicles; at least 13.5 million people, or 19 percent of total employment, worked in "highway transport industries."[32] Automobile registrations climbed from 25.8 million in 1945 to 61.7 million in 1960. Suburbanized population, adjusted for boundary changes due to metropolitan annexations, grew forty times as fast as central city population through 1960.[33] In the late 1980s the effects were still evident, as nine of the top 14 *Fortune* 500 largest industrial corporations in 1987, ranked by sales, were automobile or oil companies.

As the backlog of unrealized passenger car sales from the 1930s and early 1940s was exhausted by the time of the Korean War, the momentum behind Los Angelizing came from the cumulative impact of the Federal Highway Acts of 1944, 1956, and 1968. They opened the way to complete motorization and the crippling of surface mass transit. The 1944 Act promised federal monies for general highway construction and designated a 40,000-mile intercity highway network. The 1956 Act launched the Interstate Highway System, now to be "located in both rural and urban areas," and it set up the Highway Trust Fund to provide for 90 percent federal financing. In effect it wrote into law the 1932 National Highway Users Conference strategy of GM chairman Alfred P. Sloan to channel gasoline and other motor vehicle-related excise taxes exclusively into highway construction. It was amended by the 1968 Act, which added 1,500 miles to the interstate system. The U.S. Congress was never asked to finance this massive highway program out of general tax revenues—that would have been extremely difficult to accomplish. Instead, the methods adopted allowed $70 billion to be spent on the interstates without passing through the congressional appropriations process, as Congress surrendered control over the funds to the Bureau of Public Roads, while about 1 percent of that amount was allocated to rail transit.[34] This public "external economy" drastically lowered the risks to private investors in motels, shopping centers, sports complexes, residential housing estates, and suburban commercial and industrial zones.

It is hardly conceivable that the private sector alone could have financed Los Angelizing. Mainstream economists saw the process as a "reallocation of resources" by market forces rationally and efficiently responding to changing consumer demands. But this completely ignores the dynamics of the process, which grew out of an interplay between public and private decisions. A huge amount of investment was engaged in relocating rather than augmenting the supply of housing, commercial structures, and public infrastructure, and the relocation resulted in a massive destruction of central city capital stock. Consumer preferences for suburban sprawl and individualized transport—as opposed to clustered suburbanization compatible with a mix of rail, bus, and motor car transport—were strongly influenced by corporate initiatives. Between 1936 and 1950, National City Lines, a holding company sponsored and funded by GM, Firestone, and Standard Oil of California, bought out more than 100 electric surface-traction systems in 45 cities (including New York, Philadelphia, St. Louis, Salt Lake City, Tulsa, and Los Angeles) to be dismantled and replaced with GM buses. It was understood that the sale of automobiles, gasoline, and tires would benefit too. The project was generally successful. In 1949 GM and its partners were convicted in U.S. district court in Chicago of criminal conspiracy in this matter and fined $5,000.[35]

Full employment, and fears of renewed stagnation, appear to have been among the policy considerations behind the ambitious Interstate Highway System begun after the enabling legislation of June 1956. A U.S. Transportation Department official compiling a history of American road building has pointed out that "Ike was very much afraid of another Depression setting in after the Korean War."[36] One of the five authors of the House interstate highway bill in 1956, former Minnesota Congressman John Blatnik, added that the system "gave work all over the country. It put a nice solid floor across the whole economy in times of recession." In 1981 the Federal Highway Administration calculated $80 billion in total expenditures, and an anticipated $120 billion by 1992, with 300 million cubic yards of concrete, 1.5 billion pounds of dynamite, land acquisition equal to more than half the state of Connecticut, enough steel rods to reach the moon twenty-two times, and 2.4 billion hours of labor. The figures reflect only the direct first-round effects of the interstate program, not its multiplier effects on aggregate income and employment or the stimulus it exerted on supplier industries through its demands for their products.

Apart from the continued impact of motor vehicles, nothing since 1945 resembles earlier epoch-making innovations. But there have been new industries sparking investment and employment in other parts of the economy. In most of them, basic research and technological progress were closely linked to the expanding military sector. The major innovation in the 1950s was electronics, a heterogeneous industry that increased its output 15 percent per year. It was of critical importance in workplace automation, with the federal government providing the bulk of the research and development (R&D) dollars for military-oriented purposes. Infrared instrumentation, pressure and temperature measuring equipment, medical electronics, and thermoelectric energy conversion all benefited from military R&D. By the mid 1960s indirect and direct military demand accounted for as much as 70 percent of the total output of the electronics industry.[37] Feedbacks also developed between electronics and aircraft, the second growth industry of the 1950s. By 1960 aircraft became the fifth-largest manufacturing industry (behind electrical and nonelectrical machinery, motor vehicles, and steel in value added). Its annual investment outlays were 5.3 times larger than their 1947–49 level, and over 90 percent of its output went to the military. Synthetics (plastics and fibers) was another growth industry owing much of its development to military-related projects. Throughout the 1950s and 1960s, military-related R&D, including space, accounted for 40 to 50 percent of total public and private R&D spending and at least 85 percent of the federal government share.[38] Industrial chemicals and pharmaceuticals were the only growth leaders in the 1950s and 1960s that did not rely heavily on military orders or R&D.[39]

All this indicates that without public sector support, especially federal, private investment would have turned in a worse showing than it did in the 1950s and 1960s. The fact is that private investment simply did not stimulate the economy the way it did during the Grand Traverse or the 1920s. Between 1865 and the 1890s the investment share of GNP nearly doubled, and from the World War I years through 1926 gross private fixed investment again increased sharply as a proportion of GNP.[40] At no time during the post-World War II era did this happen. In 1948, gross fixed investment constituted 17.7 percent of GNP (in 1982 dollars), a level never again reached over the next four decades, during which the investment proportion of GNP stayed between 14.6 and 17.5 percent.[41]

Table 6.4 shows how the growth rate of investment outlays declined from the late 1940s through the mid 1960s. Business investment since the late 1940s must be judged as lackluster; only the long military-related expansion of the 1960s saved it from what might have turned into a serious slowdown resembling that of 1907 through 1915 or 1955 through 1961. This possibility is posed by the path it has traced since the late 1960s. From 1960–64 through 1965–69, the annual level of business investment jumped by $77.5 billion, and since then it has never come close to matching that achievement.

Personal consumption followed a steadier course than investment. Consumer spending fell 20 percent in real terms from 1929 to 1933, but it rose every year from 1947 to 1972.[42] The more moderate character of the postwar business cycle itself, along with generally lower unemployment, explains some of this stability, but not all of it and probably not the high levels of consumption that consistently took 90 to 92 percent of disposable income. The rapid growth of installment credit certainly helped to keep consumption on the rise. Starting in the late 1940s total installment debt (which excludes home mortgages) increased every year, except for a small dip during the 1957–58 recession, with automobile purchases accounting for about 40 percent of it.[43] Goods that people once treated as luxuries were increasingly viewed as necessities, and consumers began to use installment credit for a wider variety of purposes, including vacations. The ratio of installment debt to disposable income climbed in tandem, from 2 percent in 1945 to 11 percent in 1955 and 16 percent in 1972. By the mid 1980s it reached 20 percent, by far the highest level in the world.[44]

A further layer of indebtedness in the household sector is residential mortgages (excluding multifamily properties), which bulk considerably larger than

consumer installment debt. In 1972 it totalled $367 billion, 2.8 times as much as installment debt, a ratio maintained into the 1980s.[45] Thus, an upward trend in debt leveraging characterized American "high mass consumption": total household debt increased faster during 1947 to 1972 than business or government debt. In the late 1940s, mortgages and consumer debt together were equivalent to 7 percent of household net worth; that proportion rose to 16 percent in 1972 (nearly 20 percent by the mid 1980s). Personal interest payments as a share of disposable income rose steadily after the Korean War, from a low of 2.5 percent in 1953 to 8 percent in the mid 1980s.[46] Mounting debt charges (interest and repayment of principal) create a source of financial instability and raise the risk factor in any consumer-led prosperity. Declining national income and worsening employment prospects always cause consumers to retrench to pay off some of their debts. The higher the debt ratios the more likely this debt servicing could lead to reductions in spending for big-ticket items financed by credit, at the worst possible moment for the economy.

So while the economy performed better after the 1940s than before, the major structural change was not in its private sector institutions and goals; they appeared to be little different from what they had been since the onset of the corporate era. The big change, and the only structural change, was the greatly enlarged size and role of the state. Military spending led the way, but in the 1950s nonmilitary government programs began growing too. They shared with the military attributes of being business-supportive and posing no threat to corporate domination of investment priorities and resource allocation. Prominent among them was education, mainly an SLG function, which supplies employers with skilled labor and instills in young people values compatible with political stability and a free market economy.[47] In 1950 military spending amounted to $14.3 billion, SLG education $7.2 billion; in 1972 the totals were, respectively, $77.4 billion and $67.7 billion. Table 6.2 reflects the changes taking place. Education was by far the biggest component of SLG spending, averaging 37 percent of total SLG expenditures from 1950 into the 1980s. Highways were next, with about 16 percent. Together they drove total SLG purchases higher than total federal purchases by 1969–70 (11.4 percent of GNP compared with 10 percent).

Throughout the 1947–1972 period, but particularly in the 1960s, government activism increased as well, and it also contributed to greater private sector stability, in both an economic and social sense. Health and welfare, safety, environmental, and equal opportunity programs all expanded in scope, if irregularly, to meet perceived needs and political demands. These activities were carried out without a substantial increase in government employment, but federal spending on them did increase substantially, with most of the increase going to the aged, the disabled, and low-income women with children. Between 1960 and 1973 the proportion of the population living in poverty had been cut in half, from 22.2 to 11.1 percent, mainly because of the government assistance.[48] In addition, millions of elderly and poor were getting at least some medical care, and infant mortality had fallen significantly. Finally, the deterioration in the quality of air and water was halted in several areas, and reversed in a few. Government intervention, not private enterprise, was responsible for these gains too.

The Third Merger Movement, 1953-1969

Once postwar fears of a relapse into the stagnation of the 1930s were dispelled, a new merger movement began to stir. Corporate capitalism had virtually stared death in the face in the 1930s, and had not only lived to tell about it but was again prospering. Renewed confidence took hold and was fortified by the unparalleled supremacy of the United States in the world arena in the late 1940s and 1950s. These are the makings of an accumulation wave and a renewed release of competitive energies into productive and speculative activities alike. In the late 1890s and 1920s, an outburst of consolidations and mergers was one result, and it would have been surprising if something similar failed to occur at some point during the great postwar boom.

Still, doubts about the durability of the postwar boom remained, and the merger pace did not pick up until well after the recession of 1948-49. The subsequent movement began after the Korean War and crested in the late 1960s. Acquisition outlays rose from the equivalent of 1 or 2 percent of annual gross investment in manufacturing and mining in the early postwar years to a peak of 37 percent in 1967-69. Mergers completed by the 200 largest manufacturing firms appear to have increased their size and their power in individual product markets: in 1967-69 they acquired a total of 175 large firms (with assets of $10 million or more), representing 40 percent of all such acquisitions.[49] Thus, the third merger movement built upon the foundations of the first two by strengthening the forces making for concentration of economic power. Of the 100 largest manufacturing firms in 1955, as the third merger movement was beginning, 63 at some time in their history had made major acquisitions "markedly increasing" their size and leadership position in their industries.[50] By 1968, the third merger movement resulted in a further increase in aggregate concentration, as measured by the share of assets held by the largest manufacturing corporations. In the absence of these mergers concentration probably would have declined slightly.[51]

The third merger movement not only lasted longer than the first two; in the view of several industrial organization experts, it was given a special direction by the closing of the loopholes in Section 7 of the Clayton Act that had encouraged merger activity during the 1920s. The Celler-Kefauver Act of 1950 eliminated the necessity to prove intent to monopolize, and it prohibited mergers that "may substantially lessen competition . . . in any line of commerce," not only between merging firms. It set forth a criterion for judging market-share effects of combinations, a tool broad enough to encompass both vertical and horizontal mergers, it was hoped. The Act, and Supreme Court decisions that upheld it (against Bethlehem Steel in 1958, Brown Shoe in 1962, Von's Grocery Company in

1966), drew the line more boldly against straight horizontal mergers of any substantial size. But it probably had a rechanneling effect on the exuberance of aspiring empire builders in a period of capitalist expansion. Such energies, according to this view, were shifted away from the more traditional mergers targeted by Celler-Kefauver toward "diversification" of assets and earnings.

This perverse effect of a well-intentioned piece of antitrust legislation cannot be dismissed. But gigantic concentration-increasing mergers were already becoming rarer, as investment bankers and other promoters were much less in evidence. Thus, the third merger wave was distinguished by managerial initiative in pursuing mergers. The focus of these corporate entrepreneurial efforts was a specific type of diversification—the pure conglomerate merger. Here, managers diversify their companies by acquiring wholly unrelated businesses.

It was not a fortuitous development. The theory behind it, redolent of the contagious optimism of a new generation of risk takers, grew out of the science (so it was seen) of management expertise. Managerial functions and techniques were becoming professionalized and, therefore, transferable. A core executive staff could efficiently attend to capital budgeting, financial planning, and operations research and give its several divisions autonomy to compete in their own markets regardless of product line. This set of managerial complementarities would create "synergism": the whole conglomerate enterprise would be worth more than the sum of its parts. Additional strengths would come from reduced variance in combined profits over the course of a business cycle, greater latitude for allocating capital internally, and better opportunities for using loss write-offs and other tax savings to benefit all divisions in common. Furthermore, as the market placed higher values on the shares of the increasingly successful conglomerate, that company could pay for bargain-basement acquisitions with its own securities rather than cash. An "instantaneous merger profit" would result.[52]

That conglomerates should have expanded so quickly following the 1950 restrictions on traditional merger routes suggests surplus funds seeking outlets and a determination to increase corporate size and influence without much regard for niceties like economic fit or long-term rate of return. The nature of pure conglomeration—the merging of businesses with no apparent horizontally or vertically integrated ties—makes it unlikely that this burst of mergers had any genuine efficiency-enhancing aim or effect. The point is reinforced by the fact that during the conglomerate era acquisition targets were often well-managed, expanding firms that were more profitable than the acquiring firms themselves.[53]

Litton Industries is a quintessential case history. From 249th place in the *Fortune* 500 industrials in 1960 (ranked by sales), Litton rose to 39th in 1969 through 115 acquisitions like Monroe Calculating Machines, Landis Tools, Ingalls Shipbuilding, American Book Company, Emerton (household appliances), and Eureka Specialty Printing (trading stamps). Better known yet was Ling-Temco-Vought (LTV), which advanced from a small electronic company in 1958 to 14th on the *Fortune* 500 list in 1969, with total assets of $2.9 billion. Along the way it had merged with 32 companies that included Temco Aircraft, Chance Vought Aircraft, Greatamerica (a finance-transportation conglomerate), Wilson (meatpacking and sporting goods), and Jones and Laughlin Steel. Both LTV and Litton were the creations of "new men"—James Ling and Charles "Tex" Thornton—who entered business just after World War II at the periphery of the corporate establishment. "They started their own enterprises, often getting in on the ground floor of some of the new technologies like electronics or computers, took advantage of the military-powered expansion which began in 1948 . . . learned the ways of high finance and began to put together what later became the big conglomerates."[54]

Other firms that followed the Litton-LTV route were Tenneco, Teledyne, Occidental Petroleum, Gulf & Western, White Consolidated Industries, and International Telephone and Telegraph (ITT). All six made unrelated acquisitions totaling at least $1 billion in the 1960s. ITT, number nine on the 1969 *Fortune* list, absorbed 50 companies with combined assets of $3.7 billion in a variety of fields (hotels, insurance, rental cars, food processing and baking) and narrowly failed to pick off American Broadcasting Company in 1968.

Pure conglomerate mergers accounted for over one-third of the asset value of all mergers in the "go-go" boom of the late 1960s; diversification-type mergers, including pure conglomerates, made up around 60 percent. The rest were horizontal and vertical.[55] But the total diversification figure includes the newer type of product-extension mergers (companies whose products are not directly competitive but functionally related—detergent and liquid bleach, airlines and hotels) that were barely distinguishable in many instances from horizontal or vertical acquisitions. In addition, an impressive number of near-traditional mergers were carried out between 1959 and 1969, as the 40 percent remainder indicates. This result is one more sign of how, in the absence of vigorous antitrust actions that could destroy crucial business support for a national administration, antitrust policy sooner or later bends before corporate aggressiveness of purpose cloaked in new legal or organizational garments. Among the mergers carried out by older-line corporations were vertical ones by General Telephone and Electronics (Sylvania in 1959), Ford (Philco in 1961), and U.S. Plywood (Champion Paper in 1967), and horizontals by Union Oil of California (Pure Oil, 1965), Atlantic Refining (Richfield Oil, 1966), McDonnell Company (Douglas Aircraft, 1967), North American Aviation (Rockwell-Standard, 1967), Owens-Illinois (Lily-Tulip Cup, 1968), and Xerox (Scientific Data Systems, 1969). Several firms with well-established brand names were taken over—Planters Peanuts by Standard Brands, Minute Maid by Coca Cola, Pepperidge Farm by Campbell Soup (all in 1960), Canada Dry by Hunt Foods (1968).

But the pure conglomerate drive gave the third merger movement its distinctive flavor, and when it deflated the movement ended. In 1968–69, some 2,400 large firms per year were absorbed in mergers, but by 1971–72 the annual rate sank to 960. The November 1969-November 1970 recession exposed the weak foundations of several conglomerates, demonstrating that what goes up can come down even faster. As the highest-flying conglomerates were failing to convert their acquisitions into higher profits, their common stocks plummeted in price, badly damaging their merger potential. Litton had soared from $8 per share in 1960 to $104 in 1968, LTV from $20 in 1960 to $135 in 1968. By mid 1970 they stood at $16 and $7 respectively. The vaunted conglomerate "management" had flunked the test of translating financial and tax "gimmicks" into solid internal growth.

The final chapter of the conglomerate era was written in later years, with the selling off of assets to reduce top-heavy debt structures and to restore impaired operating efficiency levels for constituent companies. Between 1979 and 1985 ITT was restructured through the sale of 65 of its businesses with assets worth $1.2 billion, and was planning further divestitures. In 1986 LTV, its fortunes crushed by excessive debt and continued decline in the American steel industry, filed for bankruptcy. The *ex post* evaluations of conglomerate mergers show that they led to no net gains in efficiency, no overall redeployment of assets to more effective uses, no profitability improvements for the shareholders of the acquiring firms. The large number of divestments of companies acquired in this period, from 30 to 50 percent of the total, also bespeaks systematic failure. Ravenscraft and Scherer demonstrate that the third merger wave "led to efficiency losses substantially exceeding identifiable gains." The consequences for stockholders are harder to measure, given the problems of timing and variation in individual conglomerate performance records, but on balance it seems that "investors got less return on average with more risk."[56] This parallels another finding that between 1950 and 1972 large manufacturing companies acquired in conglomerate (and horizontal) mergers experienced substantial losses in market shares.[57]

Beginning in 1968 the Justice Department began to challenge conglomerate takeovers. It filed antitrust suits against both Litton and LTV, inducing LTV to divest itself of Braniff Airlines as a condition of its Jones and Laughlin deal, and it brought three separate actions against ITT. Early in 1969 Antitrust Department head Richard McLaren promised that he would go after "mergers of a somewhat 'purer' conglomerate nature than have been ruled on by the Supreme Court thus far," adding that the assault would not be limited to antitrust issues but would cover every ground the government could think of.[58] At the same time the House Antitrust Subcommittee opened hearings on the bid by Leasco Data Processing Equipment, an upstart New York City firm, to take over Chemical Bank of New York, an old member of the corporate elite. Committee chair Emmanuel Celler stated that in his forty-seven years in Congress he had never received so many demands—"unprecedented"—from business quarters for federal action against mergers.[59] His Senate counterpart, Philip Hart, noted ironically that many of the demands did not refer to "established conglomerates like General Electric, or RCA, or ITT. They are referring to the brand-new ones who are threatening the old-line companies."[60] Acquisitions by established firms were one thing; forays into the inner circle by *parvenu* outsiders, it appeared, were something else.

While the merger movement of the 1960s made its special contribution to American capitalism in the form of conglomerates, at bottom it was another manifestation of the optimism, the excesses, and the power plays that are integral parts of an accumulation wave. Even more significant in this respect is that during the wave of the 1950s and 1960s there was an unusually large increase in the "degree of monopoly" in U.S. industry—the ratio of profits to variable costs (wages and raw materials). "The rise in the degree of monopoly by 20 percent in the years 1947 to 1967 is completely without precedence."[61] Another analyst finds an even greater increase in the degree of monopoly, adding that "this pattern is clearly consistent with the development of managerialism, and is certainly suggestive of the need of large corporations to absorb rising profits into discretionary managerial expenditures."[62]

This period in American economic history offers a lesson in how the income and wealth-maximizing behavior of the corporate class leaves its mark on the statistical record. The organizational hierarchy always fulfills two functions for corporate executives—tighter control over the firm's operations and the flow of information relevant to them, and self-insertion into the firm's income stream for the financial benefit of the executives themselves. During times of robust expansion that have brought forth merger movements, the pecuniary gains of management usually swell.

For the great postwar boom, evidence of corporate self-enrichment comes from the sharp rise in inequality in the distribution of earned income (wages and salaries) between 1958 and 1970. It was driven by "rapid increases in the number of highly paid professional and managerial personnel," with "managers and officials" increasing their earnings faster than any other occupational category in the nonfarm sector.[63] Further evidence is the share of manufacturing-sector gross revenue captured by the managers. That share nearly doubled between 1947 and the 1970s, when it surpassed 25 percent, so that "substantially all of the output due to increased productivity was absorbed by the corporate bureaucracy." Accompanying this diversion of income were signs of deteriorating "entrepreneurial performance" and slackening productivity growth.[64] These signs indicate that the large pecuniary returns were not related to supply shortages of corporate managers or a greater demand for them because of their unique contributions to company productivity. They suggest instead that, as Veblen noted back in 1904, management has ample independent power, "exercises it freely," and can affect "the conjunctures of change [in which] their gain emerges."[65]

Conclusion

The true "American century" arrived between 1947 and 1972, the golden years of the postwar expansion. During this run, real GNP grew at a rate of 3.7 percent per year, real disposable income per person at 2.3 percent per year.[66] Civilian unemployment averaged 4.7 percent of the labor force, the lowest quarter-century average in the statistical series dating back to 1890, and its highest annual rate was 6.8 percent in 1958.[67] Corporate profitability, or rate of return to invested capital, rose substantially over most of the period, peaking in the mid 1960s.[68]

In these times the United States was the only superpower, and the rest of the capitalist world depended much more on the United States than vice versa. America's economic policies could be formulated almost in splendid isolation, to keep the GNP growing without any interruptions other than mild recessions. Corporations could raise wages and benefits annually, keep the industrial peace, pay the bill out of productivity increases, and pass off any added costs in higher product prices with little fear of losing customers to new oligopolistic rivals or foreign suppliers. Foreign-made goods were available, but largely for specialty and luxury markets. Neither foreign competition nor balance of international payment constraints intruded upon the American century in any serious way. The United States exported more merchandise than it imported, with unbroken trade surpluses through 1970 and net exports of goods and services well into the 1970s. International trade in goods and services represented only 5 percent of GNP, although the proportion reached 6.6 percent in 1972.[69]

If this was paradise, or even an approximation, it would soon be lost.

7

Investment, Growth, and Instability: Stagflation and the Corporate Counterattack, 1973–1988

The recovery from the recession of December 1969-November 1970 at first appeared normal, but it was soon marked by events that clashed with the usual profile of growth and prosperity. In 1971 a crisis broke out in the nation's foreign economic relations, culminating in the devaluation of the dollar, an abrupt move away from free trade through a surtax on imports, and controls placed on prices and wages for the first time since 1951. Early in 1973 the inflation rate began to accelerate; then the Organization of Petroleum Exporting Countries (OPEC) succeeded in quadrupling the price of oil during the winter of 1973–74. After thirty-six months the recovery stalled, and the economy fell into what by some measures was the worst recession since the 1930s (Table 6.1).

The events of 1971–1973 signalled the end of the postwar boom. They indicated that the underlying tendencies of stagnation were at once reinforced and diffused by a restructuring of America's economy, which was becoming effectively internationalized and far more vulnerable to external shocks. Only 5 or 6 percent of GNP was involved in foreign trade in the early 1970s; that proportion would double by the late 1980s.

From 1973 through 1987 real disposable income per head grew at 1.4 percent annually, well below the 2.3 percent rate of the boom years. The highest previous civilian unemployment had been 6.8 percent during 1958, but that rate now would be almost a luxury, as unemployment averaged 7.2 percent from 1973 through 1987. Clearly, the hard times that many Americans began to feel were no illusion.

113

Table 7.1

Components of Fixed Business Investment, Annual Averages, 1964–1986
Billions of Dollars, 1982 Prices

	1964–66	1971–73	1977–79	1984–86
Producers durable goods, total	$125.9	$173.7	$241.3	$301.6
Communications and high technology	15.3	25.6	50.0	124.0
Heavy industrial	43.5	55.7	67.8	63.8
Transportation	32.1	45.2	60.3	60.6
Construction, oilfield, mining	9.3	11.9	18.5	12.7
Agricultural	11.7	16.3	21.0	11.4
Service and other	14.1	18.9	23.7	29.2
Nonresidential structures, total	$ 99.5	$111.5	$119.1	$141.0
Industrial	19.0	12.4	15.6	12.9
Commercial	21.4	30.8	27.2	49.0
Public utilities	20.8	31.0	30.0	24.2
Oil drilling and mining, shafts and wells	15.3	13.2	25.9	32.9
Institutional*	18.0	17.2	11.5	17.4
Farm and other	5.0	6.8	9.0	4.5

Sources: U.S. Department of Commerce (1986), 231–35; Survey of Current Business, July 1987, 53–54.

Note: Because of rounding, detailed figures may not add up to total.

*Includes religious, educational, hospital, hotels, passenger terminals.

Aggregate Demand: Investment, Consumption, and the Public Sector

As the data in Table 6.4 indicate, the growth of private investment slowed considerably after 1972. Since the late 1960s business investment has been sustained only by purchases of communications and high-technology goods (office and store machinery including computers, communication equipment, scientific engineering equipment, photographic equipment) and by commercial construction in shopping malls and retail stores, fast-food restaurants, and office buildings. Table 7.1 reveals that communications and high technology accounted for 62 percent of the increase in producers durables between 1964–66 and 1984–86 and for all the increase after the late 1970s, as the other sources of investment demand slowed down, then actually decreased.Modern telecommunications are an outgrowth of technological advances in electronics. The introduction of electronic components in telecommunications equipment has made that equipment cheaper, smaller, and far more reliable. It has also improved computer systems and engineering and photographic equipment and led to their application in many industries and the armed forces. Government expenditures for military and space programs have helped the rapid progress in all these areas, when they have not been primarily responsible for it.[1]

Business construction reflects the same imbalance. Of the $41.5 billion increase over the entire period (Table 7.1), $27.6 billion was provided by the commercial sector alone; after 1977–79 this sector generated all the net increase, as the energy price-driven outlays in oil drilling and mining were not sufficient to offset declines in the other sectors. Construction of new factories, the backbone of American industrialism, decreased very sharply after the mid 1960s, as economic activity began to shift from capital-intensive manufacturing of mass consumption products toward higher-profit enclaves in the commercial sector— upscale retail trade, business and professional services, communications, real estate, and the ballooning financial and insurance industries. Funds flowed into commercial real estate largely from institutional investors such as pension funds and insurance companies; they increased the share of their portfolios invested in real estate in the search for higher returns and hedges against inflation.

Total plant and equipment expenditures in nonfarm business averaged $424.3 billion annually in 1984–86 (in 1982 dollars). Of this total, the commercial sector—wholesale and retail trade, finance, insurance, personal and business services, communication—was providing 42.1 percent, considerably more than any other sector. Manufacturing accounted for 35.3 percent of the total, with transportation, public utilities, and mining contributing the rest.[2]

Consumer spending continued to grow more steadily than private investment after 1972, but not so steadily as it had before. Total consumption expenditures in 1982 dollars increased every year without exception from 1947 through 1972, but during the recessions of 1973–75 and 1980 they fell sharply enough to cause consumption to decline on an annual basis in 1974 and 1980. From the third quarter of 1973 through the fourth quarter of 1974, total consumption in real terms dropped 1.8 percent and purchases of consumer durables 16 percent. Relatively large declines recurred from the fourth quarter of 1979 through mid 1980—2.2 percent for aggregate consumption, 14.4 percent for consumer durables.[3]

Apparently it has become harder to keep the great American consumption machine operating without missing a stroke. Increasingly, the required fuel has been deficit financing. Household debt grew much faster following the early 1970s than in preceding years; by the mid 1980s it represented 20 percent of household net worth against 16 percent in 1970, and was equal to 85 percent of personal disposable income against 68 percent in 1970.[4] This debt increase, pushed by aggressive marketing practices by the sellers of goods as well as by banks and finance companies, has gone to purchase houses, automobiles, and other consumer durables.

But since the late 1970s economic growth, and the private consumption that depends on it, have been propped up by a large increase in federal government deficit spending, so large that debt expansion has been outrunning GNP for all three borrowing sectors together—households, nonfinancial business, government. It marks a break with earlier decades, when the total debt-to-GNP ratio was relatively stable.[5] The following breakdown of aggregate credit market debt (for government and the private nonbank sector) in billions of current dollars tells the story:[6]

	Year-end 1976	Mid-year 1987
Households	$852	$2,705
Nonfinancial corporations	586	1,768
Farms and unincorporated businesses	323	1,094
Federal government	516	1,874
State and local government	234	535
Totals	$2,511	$7,976

These figures show an accelerating use of credit, with total debt up by 218 percent and the federal government leading the way with a 263 percent increase. During this period, current-dollar GNP grew only 140 percent ($1,871 to $4,485 billion). The result was a sharp rise in the proportion of the GNP that was debt-financed, to a level 60 percent above its long-term historical trend.[7] The big deficits of the Reagan years underwrote the increasing debt dependency that the above figures portray, with the federal government and the Federal Reserve as the spenders and lenders of last resort. That debt dependency compensates for a sluggish economy—for slower growth in real GNP and aggregate demand since 1972.

But a high-consuming capitalist economy cannot live by debt alone. It has been getting by with more than a little help from its friends—in the public sector. And here, military spending continues to be the only virtually unchallenged public program to prevent aggregate demand from collapsing as it did after 1929.

Since 1947 the military share of GNP has averaged 7.5 percent.[8] The official figures, however, understate the totality of military spending. They exclude military-related expenditures of the Central Intelligence Agency, National Aeronautics and Space Administration, Department of Energy, National Oceanic and Atmospheric Administration, Coast Guard and Maritime Administration, Army Corps of Engineers, and U.S. Information Agency, as well as export sales of military equipment and the impact aid program that assists school districts where military bases are located. A single example is compelling: the Energy Department has become heavily militarized, with two-thirds of its 1987 budget of $12.5 billion formally allocated to nuclear weapons production, and part of the other third to civilian research actually furthering the Strategic Defense Initiative ("star wars") program.[9] One estimate for 1980 is that while official military spending accounted for 5.2 percent of GNP, 9.5 percent of GNP was really tied up with military-generated or derived programs.[10]

Military spending underwent a relative decline from the 1950s through 1975–79 (Table 6.2). At times it has even destabilized the economy, when it was sharply increased for hot wars in 1950–52 and 1965–68 and then curtailed, as in 1954–55 and 1970–71. Each major military adventure gave rise to a reluctance to increase taxes to pay for it and an inflationary boom, followed by a recession. Military production has also drawn resources, including sophisticated R&D talent, away from some industries, although as a whole commercial R&D expenditures have grown most rapidly when defense and space research was expanding. Heavy military spending, Seymour Melman and others have argued, has "depleted" U.S. society and undermined its ability to produce goods that can hold their own in world markets.[11] While Pentagon orders and R&D support have strengthened America's most internationally competitive industries, including aircraft and engines, computers, scientific instruments, communications equipment, and laser technology, there are signs that military projects have become more narrowly specialized, with less spin-off for the decisive consumer industries. A crossover may have been reached in the early 1980s, when the spillovers from the civilian sector to the military began to exceed the flow from the military to the civilian.[12]

Nonetheless, the lure of military Keynesianism has continued. In 1974 the Ford administration added over $1 billion to the Pentagon budget as "an element of economic stimulus" for a weakening economy.[13] Economists familiar with Pentagon politics confirmed that "the defense budget is being used as an economic instrument," even as the official military share of GNP was dropping to 4.9 percent in the late 1970s.[14] The Reagan administration not only reversed the relative slide of military spending but touted its "substantially beneficial effect on the economy," as Defense Secretary Caspar Weinberger told the House Appropriations Committee on February 24, 1982. Weinberger's self-serving remarks were superfluous, because the huge increases in military dollars under Reagan were solidifying what was already a powerful constituency built up behind every weapons program. Rockwell International, prime contractor for the B-1 bomber, informed Congress in 1982 that components would be purchased from companies in 48 of the 50 states. It got the support of liberal Democrats like Senators Alan Cranston of California and Howard Metzenbaum of Ohio, whose states stood to gain thousands of jobs. The Pershing II and Cruise missiles had 147 prime contractors and major subcontractors in 31 states.[15] The Reagan "star wars" program attracted "representatives of dozens of companies and universities" to the Pentagon in 1985 for a share of the research bonanza, estimated to be worth $30 billion from 1985 through 1990.[16] "Why," a leading investment newsletter asked rhetorically, will dovish politicians and academics alike "support patently aggressive weapons . . . even strategic nuclear weapons? The answer, rarely mentioned, is simply—jobs."[17] "Congress," Republican Senator

Ted Stevens of Alaska commented, "has made the defense bill a jobs bill."[18]

Military spending has not been "necessary" for the U.S. economy in the strict sense of the word. Other government programs would have been just as stimulative and infinitely more desirable for society as a whole. But military spending possesses highly functional characteristics for American capitalism.[19] In 1977, when official military spending constituted 5.1 percent of GNP (the lowest since 1948 except for 4.9 percent in 1978–79), the Pentagon made direct purchases from 69 of the nation's 77 major industries and 340 of their 515 subgroups.[20] Electronics, aircraft, shipbuilding, and communications equipment have been heavily dependent on military sales, while computer networking and computer graphics have been further outgrowths of the military's needs. Profits on military work have run higher than in civilian markets, notably for the prime weapons contractors whose return on equity averaged twice that of other manufacturing corporations in the 1980s.[21] Opportunities for profiteering and fraud are also greater in the incestuous Pentagon-military contractor relationship. In 1985 the Pentagon's inspector general announced that 45 of the nation's 100 largest military contractors were under criminal investigation: "We stole it fair and square" is how one official described the attitude of the arms industry.[22] A year later, the President's Blue Ribbon Commission on Defense Management, chaired by former Deputy Defense Secretary David Packard, recommended sweeping changes in the $130 billion-a-year weapons acquisition process to reduce waste and discourage overstatement of costs. It was the thirty-sixth in a series of military management reports dating back to 1945. Few of the proposed reforms have ever been adopted.[23]

Then in June 1988 the biggest Pentagon scandal in history was uncovered, involving "hundreds" of Defense Department officials, military contractors, consultants, and members of Congress. The sale of secret information on multi-billion-dollar contracts, manipulation of bid specifications to steer business to particular suppliers, and collusive bidding were among the illegal activities. "It involves people enriching themselves on proprietary information, and the scope is beyond the wildest imagination," declared Senator Charles Grassley (Republican, Iowa).[24] Others might have found it less incredible. President Reagan's $2 trillion military buildup, combined with a disdain of controls that were lax to begin with, fostered corruption on a scale to match the lavishing of resources on the Pentagon.

Military output does not interfere with or saturate private demand. Pentagon dollars jeopardize no business interests because they go to private firms, providing support rather than competition. The same cannot be said for low-cost housing, Amtrak and mass transit, public recreational and wilderness projects, and many social services like legal aid for poor households. A sizable expansion in areas like these would have disrupting effects on private production and on free labor markets. It would also demonstrate that the public sector can provide certain goods and services more effectively than private profit-seeking companies—a "bad example" to be blocked at all cost.

Most significantly, military spending reproduces the oligopolistic structure of the corporate economy, as it consolidates the power of some of the largest firms in concentrated sectors of the economy. The "defense sector" of private industry looks much like any other industry dominated by big business: among its familiar features are monopolistic power and private planning of output levels and prices, high market shares and excess profits. With success also comes longevity. "Turn-over rates among the top 50 prime contractors for the Department of Defense have been low for at least twenty years. New entry into the market is impeded by the need both for technological expertise to qualify as bidder and for the ability to deal with government regulations."[25] These firms are fully integrated into the corporate economy. In 1987, 33 of the top 50 military contractors (in dollar value of prime contract awards) were among the top 100 *Fortune*-ranked industrial companies, and of the other 17, ten made the *Fortune* 500 and two more were major corporations not classified as industrials (Pan Am and GTE). Conversely, of the top 50 *Fortune* industrials, 27 were among the 100 largest military contractors and two more (Du Pont and Unisys) were among the top nuclear weapons contractors.[26]

Spending by state and local government (SLG) exceeded net federal purchases by 1969–70 (Table 6.2). By 1986.87, SLG, with education the largest component, was accounting for 12.0 percent of GNP, compared with the federal government share of 8.6. Starting in the late 1960s (Table 6.3), a group of federal transfer expenditures grew much more rapidly than both federal and SLG purchases: income security, social security, and medicare collectively surpassed $400 billion by 1986.87. The surge in transfer payments was caused by a commitment to supporting private incomes to stabilize the economy and prevent a replay of 1929–1933. In the late 1970s, however, a strong attack was mounted against the "welfare state." But in 1983, even after the cutbacks in federal programs by the Carter and Reagan administrations, nearly three of every ten Americans lived in a household receiving direct federal benefits through social security, medicare, veterans pensions and allowances, as well as food stamps and other means-tested programs.[27] This persistent citizen demand for economic security might be contrasted with the steady shrinkage in the relative size of the federal government measured by its share of GNP and the resources used to produce it—from a postwar peak of 12.6 percent of GNP in 1950–54 to 8.2 percent in 1980–84 (Table 6.2). And that declining federal base was again being dominated by military spending, which took 86 percent of federal purchases in 1950–54, only 68 percent by 1975–79, but 77 percent in 1986.87.

The Faltering Economy and the Curb on Government

Table 7.2 offers another perspective on trends in the postwar U.S. economy, contrasting its performance before and after the early 1970s. Growth rates for all

Table 7.2

Macroeconomic Performance Indicators, Annual Percentage Growth Rates, 1947–1987

	1947–48 through 1972–73	1972–73 through 1986–87
Gross national product	3.7%	2.5%
Consumption	3.7	3.0
Gross fixed investment	3.7	2.3
Fixed business investment	3.5	2.8
Residential construction	3.9	1.2
Government purchases of goods and services	4.5	2.2
Federal government	3.6	2.5
State and local	5.3	2.0
Industrial production	4.6	2.4
Employment in nonagricultural private industries	2.1	2.1

Source: U.S. President (1988), 250–51, 296–97, 302.

Note: All calculations except for industrial production and employment are in 1982 dollars.

key macrovariables fell significantly after 1972–73, except for total private employment. The basic problem for the economy was slackening growth of demand, or GNP.

Private investment has suffered no breakdown on the order of 1929–1933, but, as Tables 6.4 and 7.2 indicate, it has tended to slow down and to reach successively lower growth peaks during business expansions. Fixed business investment dropped off less than GNP, industrial output, and residential housing. But this statistic represents gross investment, covering replacement of worn out and obsolete plant and equipment and net additions to business's capital stock for any needs that might arise. Furthermore, capital spending by business has repeatedly been the target of public policy inducements in the form of tax concessions—corporate tax cuts, investment credits, and accelerated depreciation write-offs in 1962, 1971, and 1981. They reduced corporate tax payments from 22.8 percent of total federal receipts in 1960–62 to 9.6 percent in 1983–85.[28] And even with these government incentives, business investment tends toward instability and deceleration.

The relatively respectable performance of fixed business investment after 1972–73 owes something to the dramatic increases in the costs of energy. The great relative price change gave rise to a replacement cycle, with the need to transform much industrial capital from an energy-intensive to an energy-economizing mode. The data in Table 7.1 support this hypothesis, with producers durables outlays increasing 74 percent between 1971–73 and 1984–86 and business construction growing only 26 percent. Making the existing capital stock more energy-efficient implies greater volumes of investment without adding much to productive capacity. Once the replacement cycle was completed, however, continued growth in business investment began to recreate excess capacity, even during the peak years of utilization associated with business cycle expansions:[29]

| | Capacity utilization | |
	Total industry	Manufacturing
1966–68	88.5%	88.3%
1972–74	85.2	84.1
1978–80	83.6	82.7
1985–87	80.2	80.3

The most striking figures in Table 7.2 are the decreases in government support for the economy after 1972. The plunge in SLG spending is extraordinary, especially since SLG was the leading sector in the U.S. economy during the heyday of the postwar boom by virtue of its rapid expansion after 1955 (Table 6.2). The relentless attacks on "big government" by a resurgent right wing, anchored in the Republican party but well represented among Democrats, have borne their bitter fruit—a reduction of the amounts of public spending necessary to generate sufficient aggregate demand to keep the economy operating at a high level of employment and output. The laboratory test is the great postwar boom: in the absence of the rapid growth of government spending from 1947–48 to 1972–73, the economy would probably have exhibited the same stagnationist tendencies evident since 1973. With reduced growth of both investment and government spending, it is not surprising that the overall economy—GNP—has turned in such a poor performance since the early 1970s.

The most tangible aspect of the decline in the nonmilitary public sector is the decrepit state of America's infrastructure—its rail and mass transit systems, streets and highways, bridges, ports and airports, its waste disposal and water treatment facilities, its national forests, parks, and recreation areas. The cutbacks began during the presidency of Jimmy Carter, and starting in 1981 publicity was given to a problem that was assuming enormous proportions.[30] Net public investment tumbled, in 1982 dollars, from $62.8 billion in 1964 to $11.5 billion in 1984. As a percentage of GNP, it fell from 2.3 percent in the late 1960s to 0.4 percent in 1980–84. By 1987 a debilitating impact on business investment and private sector efficiency was observed, with research suggesting that, dollar for dollar, the productivity of public capital is greater than that of private capital.[31] But at least through 1988 the spark of recognition was extinguished by the Reagan administration, with budget cuts that not only made "rebuilding America" unthinkable but wreaked havoc on existing programs however impoverished.

Signs of inadequacy were also evident in the nation's housing stock, as the sagging course of residential construction indicates (Tables 6.4 and 7.2). This sector was battered by spiraling interest rates in the late 1960s and especially from 1978 through 1982, when new construction plunged 41 percent in real terms.[32] By 1980 an estimated 7.3 million households (of 80.8 million in all) were spending more than half their income for housing, and six million were living in "physically inadequate housing." A typical new house was within the means of two-thirds of all families in the 1950s, spending 25 percent of their income or less; by 1981 that proportion had fallen below one-fifth.[33] The percentage of households owning their own homes had risen from 44 percent in 1940 to 65 percent in 1980, but then, for the first time since the Second World War, it began to drop, below 64 in 1987. Homeless people numbered two to three million, due mainly to shortages of low-cost housing, chronic unemployment, and lack of services for the mentally ill.[34]

As is evident in Table 7.2, only private employment grew at the same rate over the whole postwar period. But the growth after 1972–73 came almost entirely from the service sector: employment growth in goods-producing industries has been virtually zero.[35] The new service sector jobs started forcing large numbers of people seeking full-time work to accept part-time. From 1979 through 1987, 14 percent of the total increase in civilian employment came from people working less than thirty-five hours per week "for economic reasons"—that is, involuntarily. Another 13 percent came from "voluntary" part-time employment.[36] Many of these "voluntary" part-timers, however, are not unwilling but unable to obtain full-time jobs because they are limited by physical or mental disabilities, lack of affordable child care, or inadequate transportation. Thus, "involuntary part-time work represents the fastest growing employment arrangement during the 1980s."[37]

The economy's performance has not been strong enough to hold unemployment at bay. Civilian unemployment officially averaged 4.5 percent in the 1950s, 4.8 percent in the 1960s, 6.2 percent in the 1970s, and 7.7 percent during 1980–87. The unemployment rise was exacerbated during the 1970s by a rapid expansion in the labor force caused by the coming of working age of the "baby boom" generation (born during the high birthrate years 1944–1960). Table 7.3 shows that labor force growth peaked in 1975–79 at 99.2 million, a record-high 13.9 percent increase over the 1970–74 total. Table 7.3 also reveals, however, that all measures of unemployment increased more than the labor force did over most of the postwar era, whether the labor force was growing slowly or rapidly. This was particularly true after 1965–69. Nor can the higher unemployment be blamed on the rise in the labor force share of women and youth who supposedly have higher rates of unemployment: shifts in the demographic composition of the work force account for "only a small part of the worsening joblessness of the 1970s and early 1980s."[38]

Table 7.3

Labor Force and Unemployment Growth, Annual Averages, 1950 through 1984 In Thousands

	Civilian labor force*	Total unemployment	Duration of unemployment	
			15–26 weeks	27 weeks and over
1950–54	62,604	2,518	273	195
1955–59	66,902	3,361	448	409
1960–64	71,125	4,067	558	576
1965–69	77,409	2,973	292	211
1970–74	87,113	4,702	551	409
1975–79	99,231	6,933	941	952
1980–84	110,182	9,169	1,328	1,590
Percent changes				
1950–54 through 1960–64	+13.6%	+61.5%	+104.4%	+195.4%
1960–64 through 1970–74	+22.5	+15.6	– 1.3	– 29.0
1970–74 through 1980–84	+26.5	+95.0	+141.0	+288.8

Source: U.S. President (1988), 284, 294.

*Persons 16 years of age and over.

Until the deficit spending-fed expansion of the mid 1980s, only the prolonged boom of 1961–1969 held unemployment in check—temporarily. Especially disturbing is the virtual explosion of "long duration" unemployment (fifteen to twenty-six weeks) and "very long duration" unemployment, during every period of worsening joblessness (Table 7.3). The impact of joblessness falls most heavily on lower-income people. In 1982–83, when overall unemployment averaged a postwar record 9.7 percent, the rate for operators, fabricators, and laborers was 16.2 percent and for black males 20.2 percent; for managers and professionals it was 3.3 percent.[39]

Such statistics, dismal as they are, understate the extent and impact of unemployment because they omit 1) workers on involuntary part-time schedules, and 2) workers who have become so despairing at their inability to find or keep jobs that they give up the search—"discouraged workers." An exceedingly conservative adjustment of the official unemployment rate would add only the second category, "persons not in the labor force who want a job but think they cannot find work." Including these discouraged workers, enumerated since 1967, increases the official rate as follows (annual averages):[40]

	Official unemployment rate	Official rate plus discouraged workers
1967–69	3.6%	4.5%
1970–74	5.4	6.4
1975–79	7.0	7.9
1980–84	8.3	9.4
1985–87	6.8	7.7

Still these figures understate true unemployment, which should include involuntary part-time workers. The Bureau of Labor Statistics "labor force time lost" statistic estimates this latter category, in terms of aggregate hours lost by the unemployed and persons on part-time for economic reasons as a percent of potentially available labor force hours. This correction increases the official rate about as much as the addition of discouraged workers does: the 1980–84 official rate of 8.3 percent becomes 9.4 percent by the "labor force time lost" measure.[41] When adjusted for both discouraged workers and involuntary part-timers, the official unemployment of 8.3 percent for 1980–84 becomes 10.5 percent—meaning that the official rate understates true unemployment by at least one-fourth.

All these shortfalls in national product, investment, and employment are associated with the residual effects of cyclical instability. Recurrence of economic slumps darkens the investment outlook and makes firms wary of rehiring laid-off workers. Of the eight postwar recessions through 1982 (Table 6.1), the last three, since the early 1970s, were the most cumulatively damaging, with longer average durations (12.7 months) and steeper drops in GNP (3.4 percent) and fixed business investment (12.3 percent). The withdrawal of public sector support for the economy (Table 7.2) certainly contributed to this unsatisfactory performance.

But why withdraw something that on balance is beneficial to the economy, as government spending has been since the late 1940s?

What seems to mainstream economists like an enigma or a misjudgment is neither. Rather, it is proof that economics and politics are never independent but are organically interrelated. In American society, investment and consumption flow in directions largely determined by corporate decisionmaking centers, and the market economy gives rise to a definite set of institutions and values that, in turn, constrain the solutions mainstream economists can put forward. Thus, the economy may well have performed far better with an ongoing fiscal and monetary stimulus than it did in "the good old days," but that stimulus can nonetheless be eliminated or curbed for political reasons. This would occur when the constituency favoring full employment and government intervention is overpowered by a superior force—corporate capital intent on doing whatever it thinks it must do to preserve its freedom of action.

The more astute members of the capitalist class may be well aware of the potential costs of high unemployment, excess capacity, and a recession that could spin further downward and set off a financial breakdown. The priority, however, is to maintain control over the profit-making environment and to keep unwelcome incursions into it bottled up. Prices and wages, labor discipline, technological change, product development and marketing, and industrial location all are determinants of profit and as such must be controlled or predominantly influenced by corporate capital. At the same time, aggregate demand must be bolstered by government macropolicies and institutions. But when the two collide, aggregate demand and full employment must give way, at least for what the policymakers trust will be a short run.

Stagflation and the Assault on the Social Wage

The impact of external events on an economy may be stimulative or depressive. The opening of new markets abroad or inflows of foreign capital can increase a country's income, while cheaper foreign goods or price increases for raw material imports can be disruptive. External shocks can be doubly damaging if they force, or promote, domestic policies that complement the stagnationist tendencies of the corporate economy.[42] Here the basic instability of capitalism reappears as an economic policy problem.

Many economists explain the end of the postwar boom by pointing to the "supply shocks" of the 1970s—the OPEC oil price increases of 1973–74 and 1979, worldwide shortages of other commodities as a result of crop failures, and two official devaluations of the dollar in 1971 and 1973. These combined to produce "double-digit inflation" between 1973 and 1981. In the late 1970s another supply shock came from the rise in real interest rates, which aggravated stagflation even while it represented an effort by the central banking authorities to stop inflation. But these dislocations, important as they were, served to obscure the reappearance of capitalism's old nemesis once the unusual stimulus of the 1960s began to fade. The problem was that in the 1970s these tendencies re-emerged in a setting of new constraints.

1. The exogenous shocks themselves tended to push up the inflation rate at any given level of output and employment. The Phillips curve trade-off, positing an inverse relationship between inflation and unemployment, deteriorated after 1972, so that halting inflation through standard Keynesian demand management (tight money or fiscal austerity) became costlier in terms of employment losses. Conversely, any attempt by government to stimulate the economy through expansive fiscal and monetary means was likely to touch off hotter inflation than in the 1950s and 1960s. This came on top of a mild inflationary bias already built into the system through a government spending floor.

2. The rate of profit to corporate business sank after the mid 1960s. By itself this was not an unprecedented event—what was unusual was the profit bulge of the mid 1960s, the peak of an inverted U.[43] The profitability decline of the 1970s was the result of two developments. First, business productivity was adversely affected by the escalating costs of energy and by the very policies implemented to fight inflation.[44] If, for example, energy is 5 percent of total costs and profits 5 percent, a doubling of energy prices will not only wipe out profits, it will drive up the costs of using energy-intensive plant and equipment (designed to run on low-cost energy). And if tight money and fiscal austerity create slack in the economy, output will grow more slowly, further impeding gains in productivity—and profits. Second, rising labor compensation conspired with lower productivity growth to depress profitability. The cost pressures hardly came from stronger labor bargaining power, which was under intense corporate attack by the late 1970s, but from increases in the social wage—employers' contributions for social security, health and disability, pensions, and other fringe benefits. From 1965 through 1979, these "supplements to wages and salaries," paid by employers, increased much faster than money wages and corporate profits, and from 6 percent of national income to 12 percent. Thus, with productivity growth falling off, corporate profits were squeezed by the expanding social wage. In effect, firms could not reduce wages fast enough to compensate for stagnating productivity.[45] Another profit-restoring road seems to have been closed off, at least temporarily: a slowing in the pace of innovation and a failure to take advantage of new technologies also contributed to the lag in productivity.[46]

The expansion of the service sector, with output per worker said to be lower than in manufacturing, was often cited as a major reason for the declining growth of productivity in the overall economy. But services is a heterogeneous sector, with some industries that are capital-intensive or technology-intensive (communications, banking, pipeline and electric utility systems, transportation).[47] Again the question is why in the services, as in the administrative echelons of goods-producing industries, "rapid electronics innovation and rapid adoption of the new [computer] equipment seem to have led to only a minor productivity payoff."[48]

3. The "social structure of accumulation" that had grown up in the postwar period was based on a "limited capital-labor accord," permitting annual pay and benefit increases for labor through wage-productivity agreements and commensurate increases in product prices by corporations.[49] It assured both parties that a good part of aggregate income growth would be channeled back into wages, in turn linked to corporate prosperity through high mass consumption and easy consumer credit. It also sanctioned government support of aggregate demand through military spending and tax breaks for corporate investment, as well as welfare-state protection for wage earners against the extremes of free market insecurity.

These arrangements constituted "our three-part system [of] income transfers for the poor, direct or indirect government jobs for the middle class, and little or no taxation for wealthy capitalists."[50] From the start, however, they represented a potential interference with the decisionmaking rights of management. Matters came to a head once inflation accelerated, placing on the public agenda discussions about formal wage-price "guideposts" or mandatory price controls. The Nixon "new economic policy" price freeze of August 1971 to February 1973, even though benefiting business by allowing productivity gains to spill over into profits once wage rates were frozen, seemed like an ominous portent of things to come from a less sympathetic future administration. In this riskier political and economic setting, the business community was becoming less inclined to take government assertiveness and the uneasy entente with organized labor as "givens."

4. The political reformism that bloomed in the 1960s was influenced by participatory democracy ideals, stressing local control over government and corporate decisions. Public accountability for corporate and state action was seen by growing numbers of citizens as a right rather than a "good deed" to be bestowed by higher powers. These "movements" were diverse but showed themselves as forces to be reckoned with in consumer and environmental affairs. Their crowning achievement was the pan-industry regulatory agencies of 1970–73—the National Highway Traffic Safety Administration, Environmental Protection Agency, Consumer Product Safety Commission, Occupational Health and Safety Administration, and Equal Employment Opportunity Commission. (The last one was established in 1964 but did not become effective until 1972 amendments to the law.) Covering industry and trade as a whole, all were less subject to domination by special interest groups than the older industry-specific regulatory agencies (Interstate Commerce Commission and Civil Aeronautics Board, for example). The new "social" regulatory bodies deal with acts that affect third

parties and came into being against considerable business resistance.[51]

5. For the United States, freedom of maneuver in the international economy had been taken for granted. A stable climate for production, trade, and investment all over the world left the United States free to take almost any economic actions it desired abroad or at home. But this freedom had always depended upon limited competition from imports in the U.S. domestic market, docile cooperation by foreign sellers of raw materials, especially petroleum, in setting market prices and quantities, and universal acceptance of the dollar as "key currency" for world trade, removing the United States from the discipline imposed on any other nation running large balance of payments deficits. By the late 1960s, these interdependent conditions began to unravel, with the rise in relative prices of U.S. raw material imports and the emergence of newly industrializing competitor nations in Pacific Asia. Then came merchandise trade deficits for the United States starting in 1971, along with the end of the privileged reserve currency status of the dollar with the devaluations of 1971 and 1973.

The impasse of American capitalism in the 1970s was defined by the tightening of all these constraints—accelerating inflation led by energy and food prices, expectations of annual wage and benefit increases in the face of pressure on corporate profitability, more frequent intervention by government in ways that threatened freedom of action by business, an emerging import penetration of consumer goods markets, and the seemingly sudden loss of international hegemony symbolized by military defeat in Vietnam in 1975 in the longest, costliest, and least successful of a series of postwar interventions against the socialist and communist left all over the world.

It was in this context that economic policy caused, or contributed to, the worst economic growth and employment record of the postwar period. The two deepest business slumps took place in 1973–75 and 1981–82, and the longest stretch of economic stagnation ran from 1979 through early 1983 when the economy registered zero net growth (in 1982 dollars, GNP amounted to $3.19 trillion in 1979, $3.17 trillion in 1982, and never surpassed $3.26 trillion during the four-year period). Tight monetary policy, with compressed supplies of money and credit and the highest interest rates since the Civil War, was the chief culprit in bringing on the back-to-back recessions (Table 6.1) that guaranteed four years of no growth. Monetary restraint had been brought into play to fight inflation from June 1973 through the fall of 1974. It was resumed in late 1978 and escalated in October 1979 with the arrival of Paul Volcker as head of the Federal Reserve System, despite the predictable economic devastation it wrought.

These decisions were political: they were seen as a last-ditch effort to regain control over everything that had seemed to go awry since 1972. Professor William Fellner, a member of the Nixon-Ford Council of Economic Advisers, stated that in 1973–74 administration policymakers were willing to risk a recession by unflinching use of tight monetary and fiscal policies to break the wage-price spiral: "The feeling was that if we don't get inflation under control, then the system is lost."[52] Quickly the fight against inflation broadened into war on the network of social institutions that had taken shape since the 1940s under the wing of an expanding federal government. The campaign to "whip inflation now" (1973) was invoked to justify government budget austerity and slashes in programs that would have seemed inconceivable as late as 1970, even in a nation where public services have been relatively modest. Fiscal and monetary policies, which are supposed to combat inflation and unemployment evenhandedly depending on the phase of the business cycle, were monopolized by the "anti-inflation" forces, with a resulting increase in joblessness that would have been feared by both Democrats and Republicans as political suicide a decade earlier. The lowest annual unemployment rate after 1974 was 5.8 percent in 1979. It should be recalled that the 5.5 percent rate of 1959–60 was seized upon by presidential candidate John F. Kennedy and the Democrats as proof of economic policy failure by the Eisenhower administration.

The losses inflicted upon millions of people in the name of inflation control were accompanied by an effort to redefine "full employment." In the 1960s, a 3 or 4 percent unemployment rate was considered to represent full employment. Now it was suggested that 6 or even 7 percent unemployment was the lowest that could be achieved without overheating the economy and accelerating inflation.[53] Corporate business exhibited a new aggressiveness, ascribing its own problems to a "capital shortage," "regulatory burdens," and "uncompetitive wage costs," with the federal government and organized labor held responsible.[54] An atmosphere of crisis was nurtured by corporate America, the business press, and the right wing of the Republican party, whose simplistic staples of economic thinking have always been attractive to most of the business community.[55] The mood complemented the drive to "restore America's greatness" abroad after the Vietnam defeat and the Iranian hostage affair in 1980. Here the chosen solution was increases in military spending to counter a widely publicized, and wantonly exaggerated, "Soviet military buildup."[56]

Since the mid 1950s all recessions have to some degree been policy-engineered. In an era of bigger government, labor unions, and expectations of annually rising wages, recessions more than ever are functional for capitalism—up to a point. The 1974–75 recession, wrote the chief economics correspondent of the *The New York Times*,

> like several of its predecessors . . . did a good deal of curative work for the American economy, it's widely agreed. Banks are much more liquid with fewer loans and more Treasury securities. Corporations reduced their short-term debt, slimmed their labor forces and opened the way to better productivity. Consumers have greatly increased their savings relative to their debts.[57]

In 1979, at the brink of four years of economic stagnation, *New York Times* columnist Leonard Silk stated that while "inflation remains the agony of the day

. . . for financial markets the good news, to rewrite Herbert Hoover, is that recession is just around the corner."[58]

The "curative work" accomplished by a recession is wide-ranging and is not limited to relieving a profit squeeze on business by rising wages under conditions of full employment, even if, as is not always the case, full employment brings a profit squeeze.[59] A recession can be instrumental in reducing inflation, assuring adequate supplies of compliant labor, and checking speculative financings and shortages of supplies that imperil coordinated expansion of a market economy. By easing imbalances created by capital itself, a recession can restore conditions for profitability or a less trouble-wracked expansion by deflating overvalued financial assets. Some corporations and banks pay a heavy price (although small businesses and farms always pay a heavier one), but the necessary work gets done. Government's role in this process is to allow a recession but to stop it short of catastrophe. It is anything but clear that such fine calculations will always be accurate enough to execute a "managed" recession.

Recessions are an exercise in political economy—the economics of capitalist instability, the politics of capitalist self-preservation. In 1943 Kalecki forecast such a future for public policy in the makings of a "political business cycle."[60] There are times when accumulation cannot go on because of real or imagined threats to business freedom of action and profits, the two usually seen as identical in import. A higher priority, at once economic and political, is served. Until the late 1960s, lower levels of unemployment than before the Second World War, sustained by the "limited capital-labor accord" and American international hegemony, maintained the workers' share of income in the face of the tendencies of oligopoly to create extra profits. As these arrangements broke down, a new political climate was forged to accommodate higher unemployment and to splinter the bargaining power of workers. Restoration of U.S. military "credibility" after the Vietnam fiasco completed the "Reagan revolution" that had actually begun in the mid 1970s.

The contradiction is that if corporate America succeeds in driving up profits to whatever level it can achieve, it will strengthen the forces that hobble economic growth. With oligopolistic resistance to price cutting, and with generous markup targets still the preferred pricing tool, the adjustment must come through lagging wage and salary income and lower capacity utilization. In the absence of new autonomous investment demands or substantial increases in the wage share of national income, renewed stagnation will lie ahead.

In the Reagan era this tendency was counteracted by federal budget deficits embodying the most aggressively expansionary fiscal policy of any administration since World War II. The increases in military spending and the cuts in personal and corporate income taxes produced federal deficits averaging nearly 5 percent of GNP during the nonrecession years 1983–86. Deficits of this size have alarmed many economists, most plausibly because the United States became dependent on foreign savings to finance them. But such deficits do stimulate the private economy. With demand for new capital goods chronically soft, the deficits absorb excess private savings that business firms do not need for investment. Then, as the federal government undertakes deficit spending, it pumps up aggregate demand and rebuilds corporate-sector internal funds (after-tax profits plus depreciation reserves). In effect the deficits end up in the liquid assets and net worth of corporations. Despite the depth of the 1973–75 and 1981–82 recessions, business internal funds never significantly declined. With government deficits on the rise, "[gross] business profits, correctly defined, were sustained and increased even as the country was in a severe recession!"[61]

Meanwhile, the assault on the social wage met with considerable success. The rollback of welfare state entitlements was accompanied by the most direct attack on organized labor since the 1920s. The key event was the breaking of the Professional Air Traffic Controllers strike in August 1981, when President Reagan summarily fired all 11,000 members. Union membership had already been falling, from its 1951–58 peak of 33.4 percent of total nonagricultural employment to 25 percent in the mid 1970s, but by the late 1980s it dropped below 18 percent.[62] Hourly pay concessions, "give backs" of health and safety regulations, and two-tier wage systems further fragmented the bargaining power of union and nonunion labor. Unemployment amplified the effects of the cuts in government income-support programs and wage-benefit packages. It worked the other way too: by 1988 fewer than 32 percent of the jobless were collecting unemployment insurance, by far the lowest level in the program's fifty-three-year history. As recently as 1975–76 the proportion had been 70 percent.[63]

The brunt of the blow fell on workers in the nonfarm private sector, as these average gross weekly earnings show (annual averages in 1977 dollars):[64]

1950–54	$139.41
1960–64	171.58
1970–74	192.88
1980–84	171.00
1985–87	170.26

Only intensified labor effort, principally in the form of the two-worker household and deeper indebtedness, enabled many Americans to cope. A middle-class standard of living was becoming harder to preserve. Between 1973 and 1988, real income fell for all families except those in the top fifth of the income distribution. Families in the poorest fifth saw their real incomes drop 32.3 percent, those in the second fifth, 18.4 percent. The top fifth had a small advance in their average real incomes, but only the top tenth enjoyed any substantial increase.[65]

It appears that a modest and irregular decrease in income inequality from 1947 through 1970 was reversed, as "a dramatic increase in inequality began in the late 1970s."[66] What happened may be judged by the data in Table 7.4. While the bottom 60 percent of all families lost ground from 1975 through 1987, only the

Table 7.4

Percentage Distribution of Aggregate Money Income by Family Percentiles, 1975–1987

	1975	1981	1987
Lowest fifth	5.4%	5.1%	4.6%
Fourth fifth	11.8	11.6	10.8
Middle fifth	17.6	17.5	16.8
Second fifth	24.1	24.3	24.0
Top fifth	41.1	41.6	43.7
Top 5 percent	15.5	15.3	17.0

Sources: U.S. Bureau of the Census (1987), 428, and U.S. Bureau of the Census, *Current Population Reports*, series P-60, various issues.

Note: Detail for fifths may not add up to 100 percent because of rounding.

top 20 percent gained throughout the period. The greatest gains for upper-income families came after 1981, during the Reagan years, with the top twentieth increasing its income share fastest of all.

By the end of the 1980s, prospects for a "high wage economy," combining full employment, buoyant consumer purchasing power, and business firms efficient enough to pay high wages and still make profits, were becoming more remote.

Reaganomics and the Fourth Merger Movement

"In 1981, when I first assumed the duties of the Presidency, our Nation was suffering from declining productivity and the highest inflation in the postwar period—the legacy of years of government overspending, overtaxing, and over-regulation. We bent all of our efforts to correct these problems."[67] Such was President Reagan's lament for the 1970s. His remedies came in the form of deep cuts in social programs, accompanied by personal and corporate tax reductions favoring upper-income households and by huge increases in military spending. The net effect was the biggest federal budget deficits in peacetime history.

"Economic recovery" was slow in coming, stopped in its tracks by the tight money policies and historically high interest rates of 1978 through 1982. After four years of policy-induced stagnation and postwar record unemployment, inflation began to subside, although part of that success came by chance, from a 25 to 30 percent fall in prices of fuel oil and other energy sources between 1982 and 1986.[68] The monetary chokehold was finally loosened, and growing federal deficits helped promote an economic expansion from early 1983 through 1988. Military outlays, 5.2 percent of GNP in 1980, climbed to 6.7 percent in mid 1986 (as officially measured). "Defense spending increases probably provided the greatest momentum to growth in recent years," stated the chief economist for U.S. studies at Wharton Econometrics in 1985. "About 15 to 20 percent of the employment gains we've seen in the past three years are directly or indirectly due to defense spending."[69] The new "supply-side" economics turned out to be the strongest dose yet of military Keynesianism. The only difference this time was that as deficit spending encouraged consumption to race ahead of domestic output, imports filled the gap and foreign savings financed both the budget and trade deficits. That was the "new" feature of supply-side economics—foreigners supplied the goods and the funds.

By contrast, regressive tax legislation and assaults on labor were nothing new in U.S. history, but now they were reinforced by "deregulation"—the decontrol of regulated industries and the gutting of regulatory agencies that protect workers and consumers.

Both deregulation policies were launched during the Carter years, but the Reagan administration pursued them with incomparably greater zeal. From the start, the Environmental Protection Agency, National Labor Relations Board, Occupational Safety and Health Administration, and all other regulatory bodies were subject to large cutbacks in funding and the appointment of chairpersons who refused to carry out the legislated duties of their agencies.[70] Deregulation of industries began in 1978 with the airlines and natural gas, followed by trucking and the banking system. The telephone industry, regulated in 1910 (see p. 46), was deregulated in 1984 with the breakup of the Bell system. Replacement of the leaden hand of government regulation by the invisible hand of the free market was supposed to spur competition and productivity and reduce prices. While some of these benefits did materialize, they were undermined as these industries congealed into oligopoly through the familiar shakeout cycle.[71]

AT&T's old long-distance network gave it a competitive edge, and for its rivals, like MCI Communications, it posed a barrier far more daunting than the deregulators had believed (they held that monopolized industries would become "contestable" once regulatory barriers were removed and entrants were allowed to shed unprofitable markets). In commercial airlines, the many new carriers that rushed into the industry after 1978 never captured more than 5 percent of the market. Cutthroat price wars brought on financial distress, the failure of Air Florida, Pacific Express, and other marginal firms, and a series of mergers in 1985–87. A handful of airlines tightened its grip on the lucrative routes, abandoning others and subsidizing large population-center traffic by raising fares on runs between smaller cities. "The long march toward oligopoly that began with deregulation in 1978 is accelerating," one Wall Street analyst stated in 1985. By 1987 the six largest carriers controlled 85 percent of the market versus 73 percent in 1978 and were increasing fares across the board.[72]

Despite the economic and political stimuli furnished by Reagan, the expansion that began in early 1983 was not vigorous; after 1984 real GNP grew only 2.8

percent per year. But Reagan's probusiness policies were arousing the "animal spirits" of capitalists, who had felt themselves under siege in the 1970s. The result, as in similar circumstances in the past, was renewed merger activity. From 1970 through 1977, according to figures from W. T. Grimm of Chicago, the value of all mergers and acquisitions had averaged $16 billion per year. The total rose to $39 billion per year in 1978–79, then jumped to $70 billion in 1981–83 and $177 billion in 1985–87.[73]

In its first stages this merger movement was touched off by "Q ratio" thinking. The ratio compares the stock market price of a company's assets to the cost of replacing them. If Q is less than one numerically, the assets are being market-valued at less than their underlying worth. With the double-digit inflation of the 1970s and the long slump of stock markets, Q ratios fell to near-historic lows, making it cheaper to buy a ready-made operating entity than to expand facilities or set up a new company.[74] Oil profits from the OPEC price hikes of the 1970s played a pivotal role. They led cash-rich oil companies to hunt for opportunities in other fields, and they made all but the largest oil companies attractive targets for major corporations like U.S. Steel or Du Pont, with large cash reserves and sluggish growth. Of the ten largest mergers from 1979 through the first quarter of 1984, seven involved oil companies as buyer or seller (five as buyer), topped by the record-shattering $13.4 billion takeover of Gulf by Standard Oil of California (Table 7.5).

As double-digit inflation waned, falling below 4 percent in 1982, a decline in interest rates and the new Reagan-era tax bonanzas fueled an increase in liquidity, a sharp stock market upturn, and a "merger mania." As in the 1920s, mergers spread beyond the goods-producing sector into retailing and finance. In another echo of the 1920s, the most hectic phase of this merger movement occurred during a major bull market, stretching from August 1982 to August 1987, and it received a boost from the *laissez faire* attitude of the executive branch toward big business, including a permissive antitrust stance. This was confirmed (if that were necessary) by the Reagan administration's opposition to a 1985 Federal Reserve proposal to limit the use of low quality "junk bonds" to finance corporate takeovers. The Justice Department's own Antitrust Division criticized the Fed's initiative, declaring that it "would destroy the market for corporate control, which disciplines inefficient management and enables stockholders to maximize return on their investment."[75]

Table 7.5 shows that the post–1978 mergers were a mixture of conglomerate (USX-Marathon, for example), vertical (Du Pont-Conoco), and horizontal (the first and second largest). For the first time in a U.S. merger movement, foreigners were important participants (British Petroleum-Standard Oil, Unilever-Chesebrough), another manifestation of the global changes in market structures in the 1980s. British firms, long the leaders in foreign investment in the United States, acquired at least 140 American enterprises worth $19 billion in 1987 alone.[76] The food giants, whose merger activities have been continuous since the

Table 7.5

The Twenty-five Largest Nonbank Mergers by Current Dollar Value, 1979–1987

Buyer	Seller	Dollar value (billions)	Year
Standard Oil of California	Gulf Oil	$13.4	1984
Texaco	Getty Oil	10.1	1984
DuPont	Conoco	8.0	1981
British Petroleum	Standard Oil of Ohio	7.6	1987
U.S. Steel (now USX)	Marathon Oil	6.6	1981
General Electric	RCA	6.4	1986
Mobil	Superior Oil	5.7	1984
Philip Morris	General Foods	5.6	1985
General Motors	Hughes Aircraft	5.0	1985
R. J. Reynolds	Nabisco	4.9	1985
Allied Corp.	Signal Companies	4.5	1985
Burroughs	Sperry	4.4	1986
Société Nationale Elf Aquitaine	Texasgulf Inc.	4.3	1981
Connecticut General	Insurance Company of North America	4.2	1981
Occidental Petroleum	Cities Service	4.1	1982
USX	Texas Oil & Gas	4.1	1985
Shell Oil	Belridge Oil	3.7	1979
Baxter Travenol	American Hospital Supply	3.7	1985
Campeau	Allied Stores	3.5	1986
Capital Cities Communications	American Broadcasting Co.	3.5	1985
Unilever	Chesebrough-Ponds	3.1	1987
Occidental Petroleum	Midcon Corp.	3.0	1985
Nestlé	Carnation	2.9	1984
Hoechst	Celanese	2.7	1987
Monsanto	G. D. Searle	2.7	1985

Sources: "The Top 200 Deals," *Business Week*, April 15, 1988; "The Top 200 Deals," *Business Week*, April 17, 1987; and other sources.

1920s, were major players. Beatrice Companies, which included Tropicana Orange Juice, La Choy Chinese Foods, and Samsonite Luggage, paid $2.5 billion in 1984 to buy Esmark, which itself had absorbed Playtex, Max Factor, Swift, Avis, and STP Oil Treatment in the 1970s. In 1986, Beatrice went private in a $6.2 billion leveraged buyout of its outstanding common stock, in which the goal was to sell off divisions of the company to finance the buyout and generate large profits as well. (The hoped-for gains proved elusive, largely because of the "overconfidence and hubris" of the investment bankers who masterminded the deal.[77]) In 1983, CPC International acquired C.F. Mueller, thus becoming the biggest U.S. pasta maker; and Pillsbury, which had taken over Burger King in 1967, added Häagen Dazs, and was itself taken over in 1988 by Grand Metropolitan. General Foods acquired Entenmann's baked goods and Ronzoni pasta in 1983 and then was itself bought by Philip Morris in 1985. Three years later Philip Morris acquired Kraft for $12.6 billion, creating the world's biggest food company and representing the second largest dollar-value takeover in history.

Fast foods and beer have figured in mergers for many years. Pepsico bought Frito-Lay in 1965, Rheingold Beer in 1972, Pizza Hut in 1977, Taco Bell in 1978, and Kentucky Fried Chicken in 1986, with the last vaulting it into second place in the fast-food industry behind McDonald's. Philip Morris acquired Miller Brewing Company in 1970 and infused it with cigarette profits to challenge industry leader Anheuser Busch (Budweiser). It proved to be a classic case of conglomerate cross-subsidizing with predatory overtones. (Cross-subsidization means subsidizing another division's sales made at a loss in competitive markets.) Miller, with only 4 percent of the market in 1970, was promoted not only by low pricing but by large product differentiation outlays, and it did not become profitable for nearly a decade. The result of the Miller-Budweiser battle was brand proliferation and advertising that drove scores of smaller brewers out of business. Fewer than 40 independents existed in the late 1980s, compared with 125 in 1967 and 404 in 1947. Miller and Anheuser controlled over 60 percent of the domestic market.[78]

In retailing, a number of department stores were bought out by others.[79] The financial sector became a merger focus with the breaching of the old interstate regulatory barriers, facilitated by the Depository Institutions Deregulation and Monetary Control Act of 1980 and the Garn-St Germain Depository Institutions Act of 1982. They authorized interest-bearing checking accounts for all depository financial institutions, decontrolled interest rates and prices of bank services, and permitted emergency mergers between commercial and savings banks across state lines. By 1985–86, bank deals accounted for the greatest number of mergers in any sector.[80]

Several nonbank corporations attempted to become "financial supermarkets." In 1981 Prudential, the biggest insurance company, took over Bache, a large securities brokerage house; and Sears Roebuck bought both Dean Witter Reynolds, the fifth-ranking securities company, and Coldwell Banker, the largest real estate brokerage, an industry in which concentration also increased in the late 1970s.[81] American Express purchased Shearson Loeb Rhoades, a major Wall Street firm. In 1984 American Express added another, Lehman Bros. Kuhn Loeb, becoming the financial services conglomerate of Shearson Lehman, which then took over E. F. Hutton in 1987.

The outstanding feature of the mergers of the 1980s was the hostile tender-offer, with the acquirer bypassing the management of the company by going directly to the stockholders to buy their shares. Acquirers, whether corporate raiders like Carl Icahn, T. Boone Pickens, and James Goldsmith, or old-line investment banking firms, obtained the necessary funds through new borrowing on a scale never matched in any earlier merger movement. With credit from bank loans or sale of junk bonds, or with investment bankers contributing their own capital (''merchant banking''), acquirers could target almost any corporation for takeover, regardless of size. The junk bond innovation in 1983 was the breakthrough, enabling raiders to finance takeover bids and putting very large corporations within their reach. Thus, whole companies came to be regarded as everyday commodities for purchase and resale, a unique feature of the fourth merger movement.

As in the first two merger movements (but not in the conglomerate era), investment banks and other financial institutions played a major promotional as well as a support role. Drexel Burnham Lambert became an investment banking giant as a result of its role in developing the junk bond and the mechanics of takeovers utilizing junk bonds. Others, particularly Kohlberg, Kravis, Roberts, became specialists in leveraged buyouts. Here investment bankers and managers use vast amounts of borrowed money, and a dash of their own funds, to buy a company's stock from its public shareholders and take it private; usually the aim is to break up the company and sell off its assets for a ''quick killing.'' Kohlberg Kravis made large profits for its partners and backers from its 1986 buyouts of Safeway Stores ($4.2 billion) and Owens-Illinois ($3.7 billion), but meager gains from its Beatrice deal. In 1988 it broke all records with a $25 billion buyout of RJR Nabisco, after a bidding war involving three financial groups fighting for the right to make millions in profits, not by creating anything but by taking apart one of the nation's largest corporations. (RJR Nabisco, it might be noted, had been put together only three years earlier, in a merger hailed at the time as beneficial to both companies.) In other buyouts, the managers themselves take the company private and retain control, as in the $3.6 billion R. H. Macy management buyout in 1985. In all, there were more than 700 leveraged buyouts from 1983 through 1988 worth $200 billion. Companies so restructured end up carrying less equity (common stock) and far higher levels of debt, making them more vulnerable to an economic setback. In a recession a corporation can suspend dividends to preserve cash flow—but not interest payments due on its bonds. The massive substitution of debt for equity, Galbraith observed in 1988, ''is one of the inbuilt destructive features of capitalism.''

In a bull market atmosphere, financial and promotional innovations have always been associated with large insider-banker profits. In 1986, the peak year of the merger wave, the ten highest-paid Wall Street professionals made an average of $68 million per person, an increase of $18 million over 1985. On the list of the highest-paid Wall Streeters were top executives of all the major investment banking houses including Goldman Sachs, First Boston, Shearson Lehman Bros., Morgan Stanley, Bear Stearns, and Salomon.[82] Once again, financial-sector profits were fattened by illegal activities. In the 1930s, several Wall Street operators (including former New York Stock Exchange president Richard Whitney) were prosecuted for rigging securities markets and for misappropriating clients' funds over a period back to the 1920s. Starting in mid 1986, a series of "insider trading" scandals broke out, leading to the imprisonment of speculator Ivan Boesky and, in 1988, to a guilty plea by Drexel Burnham for six securities law violations, including supplying false information to clients and tricking a corporation into being taken over, with a penalty of $650 million in criminal fines. And as always, such cases probably represent the tip of a large iceberg.

"Efficient market" economists argue that corporations can grow fat and inefficient, so that the new-style "market for corporate control" can displace entrenched managers whose interests may differ from those of owners seeking enhanced values for their shareholdings.[83] The result will be companies with more effectively deployed assets and an improved marketplace performance. Managerial underachievement was a fact of corporate life in the 1970s and 1980s, and several of these takeovers probably will result in leaner companies and more efficient production. But as a general outcome, this seems unlikely. "Deal mania, a late–1980s version of Monopoly played in fast forward," grew out of objective conditions—the psychological climate created by a probusiness administration, the great bull market of 1982–1987, abundant liquidity and the resort to debt financing, and the continued slowdown in real GNP growth.[84] Under these conditions, "corporate restructuring" is more attractive than directly productive activities because it generates faster profits. Speculative financial operations harm the nation's output potential by diverting effort, talent, and money away from substantive organizational concerns. But if such operations were stopped, the resources involved would not necessarily flow into productive investment, especially in a period of lagging aggregate demand and excess capacity—and intensifying foreign competition. The contradiction is expressed in this plaintive *Business Week* editorial (August 10, 1981), written well before the merger climax of 1985–87:

> What is hard to understand is why these companies with huge cash or borrowing resources and unrestrainable urges to grow cannot or will not grow their businesses internally, developing new products and upgrading manufacturing facilities. Last year, for example, RCA—once a premier high-technology company—explained [to us] that it did not have the $200 million necessary to

develop a videocassette recorder of its own, even though recorders have turned out to be the fastest-growing appliances of the decade. But RCA had no difficulty borrowing $1.2 billion to buy a lackluster finance company.

Any belief that mergers, buyouts, spinoffs, and recapitalizations represent a rational marketplace adjustment to the need for a more streamlined corporate sector should be dispelled by the "track record." Since the first merger movement of 1890–1902, the success rate for combinations of all types has been about half. And those that survive hardly do so by virtue of consistently superior efficiency.[85] There is little reason to think that, when the long-run returns on the megamergers of the 1980s come in, they will be different. One study, covering 1950 through 1986, discloses that 33 companies, "many of which have reputations for good management," on average divested more than half of all their acquisitions. "The track record in unrelated [conglomerate] acquisitions is even worse—the average divestment rate is a startling 74 percent." The results "give a stark indication of the failure of corporate strategies. . . . Only the lawyers, investment bankers, and original sellers have prospered in most of these acquisitions, not the shareholders."[86]

On October 16 and 19, 1987 the value of shares on the New York Stock Exchange plunged 25 percent, the greatest two-day loss in U.S. history. In the past, crashes of this magnitude have wiped out the ingredients for merger movements—a contagious euphoria, a conviction that share prices will keep rising, and a pool of liquid funds ready to be tapped for speculative purposes. The real economy was less fragile than in 1929, and this time the Federal Reserve moved even faster to flood Wall Street with liquidity to keep securities markets functioning. But financial crashes always cause seismic shifts in expectations. The consequences of October 1987 would not be seen for some time, symbolic as they were of serious economic and financial disorder, much of it associated with America's budget and trade deficits. "Dramatic breaks are not necessarily the most important aspects of an unraveling crisis. Much more significant is the slow and protracted deterioration of financial and economic affairs."[87]

Conclusion

Events since 1972 do nothing to dispel the view that the chronic problem of capitalism is insufficient private-sector aggregate demand to keep production and employment growing.

> Throughout the entire industrial phase of U.S. economic history the system has operated below its potential, with full employment obtaining only in brief spans surrounding cyclical peaks. . . . The decade of the 1970s thus reveals the face of long-run stagnation, unleashed by the demise of the state and local stimulus together with the failure of the federal government to compensate for this demise.[88]

It is true that there was a change in the structure of the world economy that began in the 1960s and became obvious in 1972–73. "Supply shocks" raised production costs and impaired existing industrial capacity in the United States (and elsewhere), so that Keynesian demand stimulation would have produced only a marginal output and employment increase, but probably a significant rise in inflation. But this constituted no reason to reject Keynesian economics, as conservatives (and many neoliberals) so quickly proclaimed it did. All economists agree that any decrease in productive capacity tends to cause a rise in prices and a fall in the quantity of output. The *response* to the supply shocks of the 1970s actually validated Keynesian theory, as tight fiscal and monetary policies depressed economic activity, generated persistent unemployment, and further discouraged the investments needed to get out of the trap. This period, moreover, was also marked by growing competition among capitalist nations, creating an oversupply of capital stock on a world scale in textiles, steel, motor vehicles, shipbuilding, and other industries. Even during the 1970s, the old excess capacity dilemma was at work—and expanding to global dimensions, with companies in North America, Europe, and Asia fighting for the same markets.

The Reagan years proved that "the Keynesian tools of fiscal policy—government expenditures and taxes . . . are still powerful instruments to influence the course of the economy."[89] The military-related character of the Reagan expansion also makes it similar to the expansions of the early 1950s and 1960s. The deficit-fed upswing that began early in 1983 pushed unemployment under 5.5 percent in 1988. But for the typical wage-income household the benefits were few, as average real weekly earnings remained 14 percent below their 1972–73 peak. The squeeze on working people was tightened by a redistribution of income toward the well-to-do, one of the objectives of Reaganomics. If another objective was to rechannel income toward corporate profits to increase investment rates, it failed. Real business investment, which fell from 1980 to 1983, snapped back from the long slump by jumping 17.7 percent in 1984 and 6.8 percent in 1985. It then stagnated again, declining in 1986 and increasing a bare 1 percent in 1987, so that its growth during the 1980s was below even the reduced trend rate of the post–1972 period.[90]

The corporate response to the disappearance of a captive domestic market with easy profits compounds the underlying problem of stagnation. It has involved a reallocation of profits and managerial resources toward unproductive activities in finance and insurance, real estate, and business services (advertising, legal, and other). The mergers and leveraged buyouts of the 1980s are an excellent example. Unproductive activities produce nothing that creates new capital, develops new technologies, or improves human skills. They serve only to preserve and extend the existing claims to income and wealth. The paradox of late capitalism may be that sluggish aggregate demand diverts resources into unproductive activity—undermining real capital accumulation and economic growth.[91]

The new dimension in the capitalist investment process since 1972 is the international. Increasing foreign competition and a greater mobility of capital on a global scale led corporate business to intensify cost-cutting efforts or to shift production abroad. Once foreign firms began to approach U.S. productivity levels, it became more difficult for American firms to keep paying higher wages and maintain the target profit rates they had come to regard as their birthrights. An assault on the social wage became inevitable.

The crusade against "big government" might be likened to the arrival in town of a new fire chief who immediately orders the removal of all fire hydrants. In the absence of demand-sustaining expenditures by government, "the economy would have exhibited much more severe chronic stagnation than it actually did."[92] The automatic fiscal stabilizers responsible for the milder character of postwar recessions (see p. 96) were weakened by the Reagan tax reforms and welfare program reductions. The Reagan cutbacks in spending on education, the environment, and public infrastructure were bound to be harmful to future economic productivity and growth. They demonstrate what were the real goals of Reaganomics, namely, to service the wealthy and the corporate economy, and to take Rambo-style vengeance on all those people and institutions responsible for the "ills" of the 1960s—defeat in Vietnam and an intolerable expansion of nonmilitary government.

8

Foreign Trade and Foreign Investment: The Road to Hegemony and Back, 1880–1988

For a century now the behavior of U.S.-based business organizations in the international economy has followed the same pattern evident in their domestic activities—a drive for control over the economic environment by internalizing capital market functions in firms that presumably specialize in the production and distribution of goods and services. Rather than operating exclusively through impersonal, competitive product markets, U.S. corporations have used their own funds and techniques to draw parts of foreign economies into their own profit-making orbits. Since the late nineteenth century, this set of motivations, unique to American capitalism, has hardly wavered. It has been promoted in the international arena by the U.S. government, as private interests were forced to rely on state action to counteract the risk and instability produced by the free market.

"One of the greatest paradoxes of recent times," Harvard economist John Williams wrote after World War II, "is that, while since 1914 the world has been in a state of profound and continuous disturbance, formal international trade theory has continued to emphasize equilibrating tendencies."[1] As it happened, a period of relative stability, based on American economic and military supremacy, was just then beginning—but, as Williams seemed to predict, that supremacy soon began to sow the seeds of its own undoing. By the 1980s the United States, a capital exporter over most of the twentieth century, became a huge net borrower, with its economy thirsting for debt financing, its federal budget wallowing in red ink, and its trade balance chalking up record deficits. The tableau started to resemble that of a poorly managed third world economy living beyond its means and usually eliciting solemn admonitions from Washington. Under these new conditions, the old American propensity for unilateral economic action could only cause greater instability, with possibly devastating consequences.

The Emergence of the Yankee Colossus, 1880–1929

No assessment of the international political economy is possible without a historical understanding of the rise of American hegemony and its ebbing after the mid 1960s. The unusual feature of this history is the concurrent appearance of "big business" and the "age of imperialism." In no other capitalist nation, with the possible exception of Germany, did these two phases of Western industrialization so wholly coincide.

The United States was drawn into the developing international economy from the start of the industrial revolution. From 1790 through 1860 net foreign capital invested in the United States grew from $70 million to $390 million.[2] The British were by far the biggest lenders; in the early years, the mercantile credit they supplied to American exporters and importers nurtured the foreign commerce of the United States, as well as its infant banking system. Federal government securities became a favorite of all foreign investors. Later, in the 1830s and 1850s, heavy U.S. borrowing was connected with major expansions of the interregional transportation net. Foreign investments underwrote more than a third of the total construction costs of canals, perhaps as much as 60 percent between 1834 and 1844. In the 1850s foreign funds helped build the railroads; by mid-decade foreigners already owned more than one-fourth of American railroad bonds. Foreign inflows into such key sectors of the economy must have contributed substantially to U.S. economic growth, even though they never financed more than 5 or 6 percent of domestic investment in the antebellum years (see p. 30). During bursts of economic growth, foreign capital helped to accommodate the needs of rapidly expanding sectors in an age when domestic savings were small and hard to mobilize.

Early foreign trade may be analyzed in similar terms of small numbers but strategic impact. In the U.S. economy, merchandise exports were a modest proportion of the GNP throughout the nineteenth century, varying between 6 and 8 percent. The trend in the import ratio was downward, from 10 percent of GNP in 1819–20 to about 5 percent at the end of the century. Only the farm sector was becoming more dependent on foreign markets; exports increased from 12 percent of value added in agriculture in the 1850s to 25 percent in 1890–99.[3] The export stimulus to the economy was offset by the growth of primary commodity imports (coffee, olive and coconut oils, tropical fruits and fibers, hides and skins, raw silks, rubber, tin, nickel, and copper). It was further reduced by the declining relative weight of agriculture in the overall economy as manufacturing became more and more important for U.S. economic growth after 1840.

This hardly means, however, that export-import flows were "unimportant" or "statistically insignificant" for America's growth, at any time in its history. Sometimes this kind of simplistic bookkeeping is utilized to ridicule the "Marxist approach," by minimizing the influence of external economic interests on U.S. foreign policy. Adding up the "balance sheet of imperialism" tells us little about the impact of incremental sales—foreign or domestic—on investment and output decisions or the way they shape the world view of decisionmakers in any profit-seeking enterprise in the economy.[4] In agriculture, for example, exports were more important for some crops than for others and became essential when their output was expanding most rapidly. Between 1850 and 1900 per capita production of food, feed grains, and livestock accelerated, while per capita domestic consumption remained about the same. Nearly three-quarters of the output growth of these industries was destined for foreign markets. The same was true for cotton and tobacco in the antebellum period; exports absorbed large proportions of increases in output and bolstered prices that might otherwise have dropped sharply.[5] These facts about the formative years of U.S. economic growth must be kept in mind when appraising the events that followed the Civil War.

While exports were vital to the agricultural sector and helped sustain prices for some major commodities, the transformation of America's role in the international economy did not occur until foreign trade and foreign investment were strategically integrated. This process began with the explosive growth of the managerial corporation after 1880 and the historic swing in the U.S. balance of payments position in the 1890s.

In the industrial sector (as seen in Chapter 4) the number and size of nation-wide companies increased, through vertical and horizontal combinations, to what seemed to be a paroxysm of mergers between 1898 and 1902. Successful entrants in the early twentieth century were themselves multiplant firms, few in number relative to the total business population, and henceforth possessed of well-entrenched oligopoly power. This stability in the corporate sector remains the most conspicuous aspect of the organizational revolution that began a century ago.

The other critical development of the late nineteenth century was the transition of the United States from a "mature debtor," a nation that borrows more from foreigners than it invests abroad, toward an "immature creditor." Beginning in 1876 American merchandise exports overtook imports on a permanent basis, except for 1888 and 1893, as nonfood manufactures began to displace older exports like raw materials and foodstuffs. Figures in Table 8.1 show how the United States achieved surpluses of merchandise exports over imports in the late 1870s.This first stage of trade surpluses was made possible in part by the depressed state of the economy, which reduced import levels during the longest business cycle contraction in U.S. history (1873–79).

From 1880 to 1913, U.S. merchandise exports nearly tripled in value; manufactures jumped from 15 to 33 percent of total exports, led by cash registers and typewriters, shoe machinery and leather products, sewing machines, electrical machinery, railroad equipment, refined petroleum, agricultural implements, and iron and steel products, including ingots, bars, rods, and rails. During this period America's share of world exports of manufactured goods climbed from approximately 4 to 13 percent.[6] The flow of U.S. manufactures to Europe and other parts of the world was described by contemporaries as constituting a "commercial

Table 8.1

U.S. International Balance of Payments, Merchandise and Current Accounts, Annual Averages, 1870–1914
Millions of Current Dollars

	Merchandise trade balance	Current Account balance
1870–74	− 18.8	−138.0
1875–79	+204.2	+ 88.6
1880–84	+159.0	+ 25.0
1885–89	+ 47.6	−122.8
1890–94	+140.0	− 56.2
1895–99	+385.0	+182.0
1900–04	+592.2	+364.4
1905–09	+546.0	+268.6
1910–14	+578.0	+201.4

Source: U.S. Bureau of the Census (1975), 864–65, 867–68.

Note: Merchandise trade balance equals exports of goods minus imports of goods. Current account includes merchandise trade, "invisibles" (income on foreign investments, tourist expenditures, transportation charges, insurance, and other services), and unilateral transfers, largely remittances from immigrants in the United States to relatives abroad.

invasion." In 1895 it was noted that even in British colonies "the markets are flooded with all descriptions of American manufactures," driving out British goods with "what amounts to quite an alarming promise of success."[7] It gave notice that the U.S. "comparative advantage" was very quickly shifting from agriculture to manufacturing.

Yet the United States continued to be a debtor (or net borrower) on international asset account, so that its merchandise export surpluses were offset by an outflow of interest and dividend payments on foreign investments in the United States. By 1896, however, the merchandise export surplus swelled sufficiently to carry the entire current account along with it. As Table 8.1 indicates, total export earnings now began permanently to exceed the cost of merchandise imports, service charges on accumulated liabilities, tourist expenditures by Americans abroad, net payments for foreign shipping, insurance, and banking services, and remittances from immigrants in the United States to family and friends back home. America's net current earnings in turn were used to finance U.S. private long-term investments in other countries, a clear sign that by the mid 1890s the century-old pattern of Americans importing foreign capital was near its end. Although total indebtedness to foreigners continued to rise until 1914, U.S. funds began to flow abroad in substantial amounts in the years just before 1900, as Table 8.2 indicates. From 1897 to 1914 American foreign long-term investments

Table 8.2

International Investment Position of the United States, 1869–1987
Billions of Current Dollars

	Foreign investments in United States				U.S. investments abroad				Net
	Direct	Portfolio	Short-term*	Total	Direct	Portfolio	Short-term*	Total	
1869	$1.4		$ 0.2	$ 1.6		$ 0.1		$ 0.1	$− 1.5
1897	3.1		0.3	3.4	$ 0.6	0.1		0.7	− 2.7
1908	6.4			6.4	1.6	0.9		2.5	− 3.9
1914	1.3	5.4	0.5	7.2	2.7	0.8	$ 1.5	5.0	− 2.2
1919	0.9	1.6	0.8	3.3	3.9	2.6	3.2	9.7	+ 6.4
1930	1.4	4.3	2.7	8.4	8.0	7.2	6.3	21.5	+ 13.1
1940	2.9	5.2	5.4	13.5	7.3	4.0	23.0	34.3	+ 20.8
1950	3.4	4.6	9.6	17.6	11.8	5.7	36.9	54.4	+ 36.8
1960	6.9	11.5	22.4	40.8	31.9	12.6	41.1	85.6	+ 44.8
1970	13.3	35.4	58.0	106.7	75.5	26.8	63.2	165.5	+ 58.8
1980	83.0	104.5	313.3	500.8	215.4	64.6	327.1	607.1	+106.3
1987	261.9	1274.1		1536.0	308.8	859.0		1167.8	−368.2

Sources: Lewis (1938), 445; U.S. Bureau of the Census (1975), 868–69; U.S. President (1988), 369; *Survey of Current Business*, June 1988, 77.

*Includes U.S. government liabilities and credits respectively.

leaped from $685 million to $3.5 billion.

The final shift of the United States from an international debtor to creditor occurred swiftly, as a result of World War I. Table 8.2 shows that between 1914 and 1919 U.S. foreign loans and investments nearly doubled, to $6.5 billion, while long-term holdings of U.S. securities by foreigners shrank from $6.7 to $2.5 billion. Europeans, mainly the British, liquidated more than $4 billion of American bonds and stocks and borrowed heavily from New York banks to purchase war materials from U.S. suppliers. By 1929 private U.S. foreign investments reached $15.4 billion, almost triple the value of foreign investments in the United States.[8] During the 1920s New York effectively replaced London as the leading financial center, and the Yankee colossus stood as the world's prime economic power.

Projecting Oligopoly Abroad:
The Rise of Direct Investment

Since the 1880s the imperatives of corporate control over markets, raw materials, and technical knowledge have dominated U.S. economic growth and instability. The integrating element in the revolutionary changes of 1880–1914 was the giant corporation. It spun a seamless web of oligopoly, commodity export, foreign investment, and internationalized marketing, the essential features of which have never changed. And it had economic and political ramifications that still pervade U.S. international policies.

On a macroeconomic plane, firms in countries that enjoy a surplus on current account will tend to have profits available to invest abroad. This begins to explain why American firms started exporting capital in the 1890s. It was the budding new structure of industry that provided the real impetus to "go abroad," however. In 1867 Singer Sewing Machine, already a large company by the standards of the day, was not only exporting its wares, but had salaried representatives abroad and was producing in Scotland. Starting in the 1870s companies like Colt Arms, Babcock and Wilcox, National Cash Register, Eastman Kodak, Standard Oil, American Tobacco, Westinghouse, International Paper, and the major New York insurance companies (New York Life, Equitable, Mutual) sought to strengthen their grip on existing export markets or to penetrate new ones afar.[9] It was not long before they too sensed the need, and opportunity, to set up overseas production and sales facilities to accomplish these goals more efficiently.

Another incentive to sell and invest abroad was the widely shared feeling—a reaction to the severe depression of 1893–97—that the nation's prosperity "depends largely upon ability to sell surplus products in foreign markets at remunerative prices," in the words of Secretary of the Treasury John Carlisle in 1894. Producers of locomotives, freight and street-railway cars, farm machinery, drugs and chemicals stated that the key to full employment and high wages was the exporting of "half of our product." Milling industry representatives added that "we do not believe that over 50 percent of the wheat produced in this country can be absorbed in our domestic markets."[10] It has been argued that such beliefs were false, and that growth of domestic demand and import substitution at home meant that there was little surplus production desperately seeking export markets. Even if true, this is probably irrelevant. What counts for oligopolists is growth of sales from all markets and a controlled pricing and cost structure, with satisfactory profits. Besides, one might think that conviction, even if mistaken, provides a reliable guide to the formulation and execution of supportive public policy.

Whatever the mix of reasons, and all seem to have been important, the basic goals of transnational expansion were taking shape—to secure market outlets and gain footholds in potential future markets anywhere they could be found. The turn toward foreign investment originated in industries that were highly concentrated in structure and ruled over by a handful of very large firms. It was the microeconomic complement to the enlargement of business profits and the success of manufactured exports—direct foreign investment by the corporate, or nonatomistic, firm.

From the early days of their foreign investment efforts, Americans demonstrated a preference for *direct investment*, which brings ownership of real assets abroad, through the building of new production or marketing facilities or the acquisition of such assets ready-made from their owners. Its form is the branch plant or subsidiary that permits extension of American technology and management techniques. (A "branch" is part of the home corporation transplanted abroad; a "subsidiary" is a separate corporate entity. Both are considered foreign "affiliates.") *Portfolio investment*, by contrast, includes the purchase of foreign corporate or government bonds, or minority shareholdings of their stock, with income and possible capital appreciation—not control—as the objective. Portfolio transfers and commodity trade are supposed to be the engines of international exchange in a purely competitive economic order. U.S. business rejected this model from the start.

The unique nature of this overseas presence must be emphasized: the United States began exporting capital overwhelmingly in the form of private direct investment, involving control over foreign operations, even while it was still a net borrower of portfolio capital, through the first decade of the twentieth century. During 1896–1908 around 80 percent of all U.S. investment abroad was of the direct variety, and in 1914 direct investment constituted over 75 percent of the total. By contrast, about 80 percent of long-term foreign investment in the United States was portfolio in 1914, as was true over the preceding half-century or more.[11] No other capitalist nation had ever made foreign investment and on-site operating control so symbiotic, not even Great Britain during its golden years of empire. "The migration of British capital . . . fostered the growth of a rentier governing class, whose economic interests lay outside the community [Britain] in which they lived and exerted influence."[12] In British overseas investment to

1914, "holdings of common stock were small." For France and Germany, the other major imperial powers, substantially more than half of all foreign investment comprised holdings of other governments' bonds.[13]

Then, as now, trade and investment were interrelated. Increased demand for American exports increased the funds available for U.S. investments abroad; the result was a steady growth in America's foreign holdings. In turn, the flow of capital roughly corresponded to the changing pattern of exports, because long-term investments, or extensions of credit, were necessary to open up markets and enable foreigners to buy American goods. The Latin American case is illustrative. Direct U.S. investment in Latin America was the largest component of America's external economic expansion through 1929, well ahead of Canada and Europe (Table 8.3). It made up 46 to 50 percent of total U.S. direct investment between 1897 and 1929 and multiplied twelve times, with heaviest placements in Mexico, Cuba, Central America, Venezuela, and Chile.[14] As U.S. investment in Latin America was building up, so were U.S. exports: that region took 11 percent of all U.S. overseas sales in 1890 and 19 percent in 1929, second only to Europe as an export customer of the United States. Close behind was Canada, which purchased 5 percent of U.S. exports in 1890 and 18 percent in 1929 and likewise was a major recipient—the largest single one—of American capital flows (Table 8.3).[15]

All told, accumulated U.S. foreign investment in 1929 accounted at most for 5.5 percent of all U.S. private investment at home and abroad, and only 2.6 percent on a net basis (private holdings abroad less foreign investment in the United States).[16] But $15.4 billion worth of total long-term holdings abroad— $17.0 billion including short-term investments—represented very large aggregates for the investing community, and it would seem presumptuous to discount them as unimportant compared to abstract "total investment" or "GNP" statistics that cannot be expected to count for much in the everyday business plans of firms struggling to survive and expand (and survival often hinges on continued expansion of operations and earnings anywhere possible, if only for defensive reasons). Thus, from the beginnings in the 1890s the critical factor was the vista that foreign opportunities opened up. Foreign business or investment may have been statistically peripheral to domestic investment through the first quarter of the twentieth century. "What is more important," writes Mira Wilkins in her study of the topic, "is that foreign business was *not* peripheral in terms of the aspirations of the nation's key industrial leaders."[17]

The underlying reason for the direct investment strategy was not a growing American involvement in foreign commerce. At no time were exports of goods or capital so quantitatively important to the United States as they were to its competitors. In 1913, exports represented about 6 percent of America's GNP, against 17 to 25 percent for France, Germany, Britain, and Canada.[18] U.S. business took a commanding lead in overseas direct investment, while still a debtor nation, because of its experience with its home market. In 1870 the United States already

Table 8.3

U.S. Direct Foreign Investment by Geographic Area, Total and Percentage Distribution, 1929–1987

	1929	1950	1968	1987
Total (billions of current dollars)	$ 7.5	$11.8	$65.0	$308.8
Percentage distribution				
Canada	26.7%	30.4%	30.1%	18.4%
Latin America	46.7	37.7	17.0	13.7
Europe	18.0	14.7	29.9	48.2
Japan	N.A.*	N.A.*	1.8	4.6
All Other	8.6	17.2	21.2	15.1

Sources: U.S. Bureau of the Census (1975), 870; *Survey of Current Business*, August 1988, 42, 65.
*N.A. = not available.

had the largest GNP and internal market of any nation, and only Great Britain could boast of a higher per capita income level. In the 1890s the American economy was big enough to breed giant corporations with substantial research and marketing potential, which naturally encouraged the process of product differentiation and oligopolistic market control. By 1913 the United States was far and away the world's foremost industrial producer and generated a GNP nearly as large as the combined GNPs of Britain, Germany, and France and a per capita output 22 percent greater than second-place Britain. The effect of demands generated by a huge, vigorously expanding domestic market, and of relatively high wage costs, was an environment for business that differed fundamentally from Europe's.

It caused departure from anything left of a business system composed of atomistic competitors. Even in industries based on older consumption goods, new means of mass-production were calling for reliable and manageable mass distribution channels. This learning process, once mastered, led to varying combinations of administrative efficiency and market power. The barriers to entry posed by decreasing unit costs of production and distribution and by national organizations of managers, buyers, salesmen, and service personnel made oligopoly advantages cumulative—and were as global in their implications as they were national. The world was becoming their "oyster," so long as they could reasonably well control it.

Conceivably, any of the activities associated with direct investment might have been carried out by other means. French, Brazilian, Canadian, or other foreign firms can obtain technical know-how or managerial skills by several routes that do not involve an organic tie with, say, a U.S. company—by hiring individual experts, purchasing technologies and equipment, and entering into licensing agreements or joint projects with American-based firms. If the foreign firms need to import funds, portfolio capital can be attracted; from the vantage point of the capital-exporting nation, its portfolio placements will flow from low toward high interest rate countries. It would come to own more foreign assets but not control them. In any case, in a world of perfect competition, capital would be allocated through impersonal financial markets, not by business enterprises that produce and market goods and services.[19]

Thus, for direct investment to blossom as it did nine decades ago, markets had to be "imperfect." Only such markets are compatible with "trickle-down marketing" or an international "demonstration effect" through product differentiation, where the full panoply of corporate planning, control over strategic techniques, heavy cash outlays for market development, and high-pressure salesmanship can be brought into play. U.S. foreign economic expansion grew out of the corporate learning experience at home—out of the struggle to secure oligopoly profits in a context in which profits are influenced by several factors in addition to efficiency in production and distribution.[20]

Controlling Overseas Domains:
Foreign and Domestic Means

But the looming question was how to control the process without the kind of active government help alien to the American business tradition, as it was romanticized by the corporate class itself. The adaptations that followed in the government sector shaped the contours and compulsions of U.S. foreign economic policy for a century to come. The 1890s, a decade of economic troubles, ended the disinterested attitude of many business leaders toward public policy. They now found themselves coping with new economic dilemmas without the benefit of the kind of government bureaucracies that had long existed in France and Britain. At this point ideology gave way to pragmatism, and government was called to the rescue.

Between 1887 and 1918 the U.S. Congress first created public bureaucratic power to try to rationalize the crisis-prone economy and curb ruinous price competition. The new wave began with the Interstate Commerce Act in 1887 (see pp. 45–46) and crested with the Federal Reserve Act of 1913 and the Federal Trade Commission and Clayton Acts of 1914. Gabriel Kolko calls these "political efforts to regulate the economy . . . a situation in which business interests increasingly relegated economic problems to the political arena for solutions."[21] The federal government, adds Cochran, "became a mediator between railroads and shippers, bankers and reserves of cash, big companies and their suppliers or competitors, and a regulator of a few business practices."[22] The change, although modest by European standards, was a virtual upheaval in a country many of whose citizens had come to regard their governments as corrupt and inefficient and hence as bodies whose activities should be limited.

In foreign economic relations, the National Association of Manufacturers, founded in 1895, asked the federal government for aid to exporters, reform of the consular service, revival of a subsidized merchant marine, uniform freight rates, and a Nicaraguan canal. "In fact, almost every aim of the Association prior to 1902 required federal intervention or aid."[23] Between 1890 and 1897 U.S. tariffs were hiked to levels surpassed only by the 1930 Smoot-Hawley rates. Meanwhile, trade associations, chambers of commerce, and other voluntary organizations sent representatives to the Far East to scour for markets. The establishment of the Department of Commerce in 1903 was a response to business demands for better domestic and foreign services. By World War I, U.S. Department of Commerce representatives were sending back scores of detailed reports on overseas trade conditions and, specifically, on the opportunities for market entry by U.S. firms. Corporations exerted pressure to relax federal antitrust enforcement and to authorize combined efforts by firms in marketing their goods abroad. The plea was answered in 1918 by the Webb-Pomerene Act, which amended the Clayton Act to permit cooperation and price fixing among firms in the export trade.

Military force was the natural complement to "political capitalism." Seizure of the remains of the Spanish empire was accomplished by "a splendid little war" in 1898. Two years later the United States dispatched 2,500 soldiers to join an international (European) "rescue" expedition to put down the Boxer Rebellion, a Chinese uprising against foreign intrusions in Chinese internal affairs. The Open Door to China and "dollar diplomacy" were securely in place by 1903. The main policy of the State and Navy Departments was to keep the Caribbean as a protected U.S. enclave and to replace European with American investment in the independent islands and surrounding nations. This required policing the financial policies of these governments to make sure that any defaults on bonds or abrogation of foreign concessions would be met by U.S. and not European intervention. From 1895 through 1929 the United States mounted 44 military actions and operations in Latin America, most frequently in Central America and the Caribbean area, without declarations of war.[24]

The overriding goal of U.S. foreign policy was set—to maximize the power and profitability of American capitalism in the global economy as it was perceived at the time. In his annual message of December 3, 1912, President William Howard Taft spoke of the bonds between America's new "position as a world power" and promotion of its economic interests, in describing the new diplomacy as "an effort frankly directed to the increase of American trade upon the axiomatic principle that the Government of the United States shall extend all proper support to every legitimate and beneficial American enterprise abroad." This "fundamental" policy "should be raised high above the conflict of partisanship and wholly dissociated from differences as to domestic policy. In its foreign affairs the United States should present to the world a united front."

Out of this economic view of international relations flowed noneconomic phenomena that would henceforth dominate public debate over foreign policy. But the desires and anticipations of business investors, on whom the entire society and government ultimately depend for creation of income and employment, would really shape the public agenda. In its conduct of foreign relations the State Department accordingly broadened its definition of the scope of "the national interest" and relied more and more on armed force to realize the nation's swelling ambitions. Soon it looked upon U.S. business interests in Latin America, and elsewhere, as allies in political control. Together corporations and the state could expel rival influence, forge closer economic ties between foreign theaters of operations and the United States, and promote "political stability" abroad. This was understood to consist of a stable environment for free-wheeling trade and investment activities anywhere in the world they might seem feasible.

Europeans, no strangers to imperialism, were still taken aback by this display of apparent unity and enthusiasm in a socially heterogeneous nation. Impatient aggressiveness of purpose, that hallmark of U.S. foreign policy, must also be attributed to the timing of America's coming of age. When Britannia ruled the waves, there were no other industrialized nations. From the outset the United States faced sterner competitive challenges from other imperialist powers. Britain wielded supremacy during a century of "peace" (1815–1914); the United States rose to power in a time of economic turbulence and, soon, two world wars.

The World the Dollar Built:
The Climax of U.S. Power, 1944–1971

The Second World War thrust the United States into a position of supremacy probably unparalleled in history. When it ended, America's enemies were crushed, its allies economically prostrate. The advent of "the American century" meant business as usual for the oligopoly sector of the economy, however. All that had really changed was the external setting—incomparably more favorable now. Overseas economic expansion could be pursued with a virtual absence of foreign competition and an urgent demand for all kinds of U.S. goods and techniques. It was underwritten by global U.S. military power and the "key currency" status of the dollar established at Bretton Woods, New Hampshire, in July 1944: all participating nations agreed to peg their currencies at par values to the dollar, which alone was fixed in terms of gold at $35 per ounce.

In the cold war atmosphere of the late 1940s, Pax Americana was extended in two ways.[25] The first began in 1947 with Marshall Plan aid to Western Europe. This program helped calm fears of a slump in U.S. exports and a return to something like the Great Depression, but it also represented the use of economic means to tie together the Western world (two years later Japan too) through restoration of liberalized international trade and capital flows. By now another lesson of the 1930s was being absorbed: no major free market country alone could achieve sustained economic growth in a stagnant or even slowly growing world economy. Specifically, the Marshall Plan was launched to strengthen the production capacity and financial markets of key European countries and to thwart the growth of indigenous socialism or communism. Almost $9 billion was channeled into Britain, France, Belgium, the Netherlands, Italy, West Germany, and Greece. Most of these funds necessarily went to buy exports from the United States. Another *quid pro quo* was that the United States would gain entry into formerly protected foreign and colonial markets (like those of the British Commonwealth) and would sacrifice "declining industries" at home to the forces of the international market (although in the late 1940s these domestic costs of free trade posed no active threat in the minds of U.S. policymakers).

The second extension of Pax Americana came through the North Atlantic Treaty Organization (NATO) in 1949 and, later, several more military pacts that positioned U.S. armed forces around the world for possible intervention against socialist and communist threats to the international capitalist system and its outposts in the Middle East, Asia, and Latin America. Rearmament also served the important purpose of ideological mobilization against any left-wing politics within Western Europe. The United States became the world policeman of capitalism, a role that entailed high foreign military expenditures and other costs that eventually helped undermine the key currency status of the dollar.

But from the start there were corresponding economic, as well as political, benefits. One was virtual domination of foreign sources of critical raw materials. This contributed to favorable terms of trade, as measured by the ratio of average export prices to average import prices. The higher the ratio, the greater the purchasing power of a country's exports and the more cheaply it can obtain imports. For the United States, the average price of exports to imports rose a substantial 18 percent from 1950–51 through 1969–70.[26] This terms-of-trade improvement had two important effects for the corporate sector. It increased profitability, and it made imports of key intermediate inputs (petroleum, bauxite, tin, nickel, copper, lead) cheaper, helping to keep down the cost of consumer goods—and the wage bill.

Another economic benefit of Pax Americana was to lower the risk on expected returns from overseas investment for large U.S. industrial, financial, and service corporations. Direct foreign investment remained the cutting edge, climbing from a cumulative total of $12 billion in 1950 to nearly $76 billion in 1970 (Table 8.2). In the postwar period it accounted for 70 percent of all long-term U.S. capital exports (with the rest portfolio). Profits derived from these investments must also be considered in any cost-benefit analysis of U.S. military spending abroad. In the early 1950s foreign operations supplied 7 to 11 percent of total after-tax corporate profits; this proportion then rose steadily, averaging 13 percent in the 1960s and 21 percent in the 1970s.[27] For the financial sector, the foreign link was just as significant. By 1970, from 26 to 46 percent of all deposits of the eight biggest New York banks lay outside U.S. borders.[28]

Numbers like these also suggest that, with U.S. multinational corporations

Table 8.4

**Percentage Shares of World Exports of Manufactured Goods,
United States and U.S. Multinational Corporations
1957–1984**

	United States, national total	U.S. multinationals, world total	Foreign affiliates of U.S. multinationals
1957	22.7%	N.A.*	5.8%
1966	17.5	17.7%	8.2
1977	13.3	17.6	9.7
1984	14.0	18.1	10.3

Source: Lipsey and Kravis (1987), 151.
*N.A. = not available.

(MNCs) expanding in size and scope, a growing proportion of production by U.S. corporations for world markets was taking place outside the United States. Table 8.4 provides data on the changes in progress. Exports of manufactures from firms located in the United States itself peaked in 1953, when those exports constituted 29 percent of the world's total.[29] By the early 1970s the U.S. share of total world manufactured exports fell to about 15 percent. But exports from foreign-located affiliates of U.S. MNCs were climbing steadily, from 5.8 percent of the world total in 1957 to about 9 percent in the early 1970s.

In the post-World War II era, U.S. firms generally went abroad to capture new markets and exploit existing ones, not to hire low-wage labor, which is not necessarily the most productive labor. The exceptions were a few labor-intensive industries like textiles and electronics, in which low wages were desirable and kept within bounds by model "free world" governments that repressed trade unions (South Korea, Malaysia, Singapore, Taiwan, the Philippines, the Dominican Republic). Foreign investment trends confirm the fact that footholds in higher-income countries were still the chief goal. With the dollar fixed in value as the world's key currency through the 1950s and 1960s, U.S. companies found that their exports tended to be expensive for foreign consumers, but that it was comparatively cheap to buy or build a factory and marketing facilities in a foreign country. The increasingly overvalued dollar shifted attention away from U.S.-based exports and reinforced the direct investment-overseas production habit.

With the birth of the Common Market in 1957, aimed at cutting trade and investment barriers among France, Italy, West Germany, Belgium, the Netherlands and Luxembourg, American firms rushed to get inside this tariff-free market by organizing subsidiaries and branches, as they had long been doing in Canada. Thus, direct U.S. investment in petroleum, mining, and primary commodities, largely in third world nations, dropped in relative importance. It made up 38.3 percent of all such assets in 1950–51 and 35.8 percent in 1969–70. In the late 1960s, three-fifths of all U.S. direct holdings were situated in Western Europe and Canada because of the superior market opportunities (Table 8.3). Canada remained the largest single host country, with 30.1 percent of all U.S. direct investment. The American presence completed "the recolonization of Canada," the leading example of the transition from British to U.S. control over significant portions of a country's industry and trade.[30]

Just as the great postwar domestic boom in the United States crested in the late 1960s, so did American domination of the international economy. Apart from the $10.1 billion merchandise trade surplus in 1947, largely a result of the war damage in Europe and Japan, U.S. surpluses peaked in 1964 at $6.8 billion. The trade balance remained positive, though declining, through 1970 when it amounted to $2.6 billion. The highest ratio of foreign direct investments to all U.S. corporate assets was reached in the early 1970s, and the 1972 direct total of $89.9 billion was six times the amount of direct investment by foreigners in the United States, the largest multiple of the postwar period.[31]

The End of Bretton Woods
and the Empire in Decline

The effective end of this liberal trade and investment era came in 1971. In that year the United States ran a merchandise trade deficit of $2.3 billion, its first since 1893. It marked a new phase in the deterioration of the U.S. balance of payments, and it certified the collapse of the dollar as key currency between 1968 and 1971. All monetary and commercial systems represent the institutionalization of power relationships, and the world the dollar built was no different. Two formal dollar devaluations, in December 1971 and February 1973, destroyed the officially privileged status of the dollar. They put everyone on notice that henceforth the dollar would neither be backed by some immutable gold value nor redeemable in gold for central bank settlements; nor would the dollar be buffered, by its own government or rescue squads sponsored by the International Monetary Fund, against foreign exchange speculation. In accepting dollars, foreign firms, citizens, or governments would now be incurring as much fluctuation risk as with other "mortal" currencies.

The decline of the American empire was the product of several forces. European and Japanese recovery from the Second World War inevitably ended the bumper export surpluses the United States enjoyed through 1960–64, its last days as the world's chief supplier of manufactured goods, as its trade surpluses began to shrink, then disappear (Table 8.5).Meanwhile, continued foreign investing by American corporations and, above all, military spending abroad threw the rest of the balance of payments irreversibly into deficit. From 1960 through 1970 net military spending abroad consistently accounted for 87 percent of the overall

Table 8.5

U.S. Merchandise Trade and Current Account Balances, Annual Averages (Billions of Current Dollars), and Export-Import Shares of GNP, Annual Averages, 1946–1987

	Merchandise trade balance	Current account balance	Exports, percent of GNP	Imports, percent of GNP
1946–49	+ $6.9	+ $4.3	7.2%	3.7%
1950–54	+ 2.1	− 2.8	5.3	4.5
1955–59	+ 3.7	+ 1.5	5.5	4.6
1960–64	+ 5.4	+ 4.3	5.9	4.6
1965–69	+ 2.8	+ 2.4	6.1	5.3
1970–74	− 2.1	+ 0.8	7.9	7.1
1975–79	− 18.6	− 1.7	10.4	9.6
1980–84	− 53.9	− 30.6	11.4	11.2
1985–87	−141.9	−139.5	9.2	11.6

Source: U.S. President (1988), 248–49, 364.

Note: Current account balance includes net military transactions. Export and import shares of GNP are exports and imports of both goods and services.

U.S. balance of payments deficits.[32] More than anything else it was military overextension in Vietnam that signalled the unwillingness of U.S. administrations, both Democratic and Republican, to control their now-spiraling balance of payments deficits. It convinced foreign bankers that, so long as the 1944 Bretton Woods system of international finance lasted, they would be left "holding the bag" of unrestrained increases in supplies of dollars. With the dollar's key currency status, the United States could buy foreign goods or assets without exporting an equivalent value of its own goods, because European or Japanese sellers had to retain the dollars they were being paid as part of their own money supply—their official international reserves. Thus, foreign government holders of short-term dollars found themselves with but two choices. One was to tolerate heavier inflows of dollars and thereby help to finance the Vietnam war, American takeovers of industries in their own countries, and possibly inflation too as the dollars expanded their own monetary base. The other was to get rid of these dollars by cashing them in for gold from Fort Knox.

Richard Nixon's own answer was not long in coming: when you're losing, change the rules of the game. On August 15, 1971, with no advance warning to any government, friendly or otherwise, he unilaterally slammed shut the U.S. gold window against foreign central banks, terminating dollar convertibility into gold and unhinging the exchange-parity rate of the monetary unit that had been the world's sole international reserve currency since the Bretton Woods agreements of 1944. Not only did President Nixon overturn the existing international monetary system. Equally fateful was his decision to impose a temporary surtax of 10 percent on imports, a signal that from now on the United States would discard free trade whenever its usefulness seemed outmoded for American purposes.

The passage from "dollar gap," which lasted until 1958–59, to "dollar glut" may seem swift in retrospect, but profound structural changes in the world economy were eroding American economic and financial strength and would have confronted Nixon's successors with a similar sort of international crisis. In contrast with the early postwar period, the weakening U.S. economy was becoming less able to provide the solid foundation for the international reign of the dollar. Reform of the International Monetary Fund system had been openly discussed starting in 1959–60, and American dominion over the international market economy would not last very much longer. Not only did the postwar recovery of Western Europe and Japan undermine America's economic supremacy; but also, beginning in the 1970s, the growth of lower-cost production activities in newer Asian countries, especially the "four tigers" (South Korea, Taiwan, Hong Kong, Singapore), began to affect world markets. In 1950 the United States turned out half of gross world product, but this fell to 22 percent by 1980–82. America's GNP comprised 61 percent of the total for the major industrial capitalist nations in 1950 (North America, Western Europe, Japan, Australia), only 38 percent in the early 1980s. The U.S. share of world exports of manufactured goods dropped from its postwar high of 29 percent in 1953 to 13 percent in the early 1980s.[33] Of the top 200 industrial corporations in the world in 1960 in gross sales, 127 were American; in 1986 only 90 were. Their portion of world sales of the top 200 slid from 73 to 42 percent over this quarter-century.[34]

Since its first merchandise trade deficit of this century occurred in 1971, the United States has exported more goods than it imported only in 1973 and 1975. In a sense a "mature creditor" country like the United States of the 1960s and 1970s is expected to run merchandise trade deficits. Such deficits should be roughly offset by foreign income U.S. companies earn from selling services abroad (now chiefly banking and real estate, insurance, advertising, film rentals, telecommunications, accounting, data processing) and by income from overseas investments (profits, dividends, interest, royalties and license fees). But this balance on overall current account, in almost constant surplus for the United States after 1895, also began to deteriorate, as Table 8.5 shows. In the twelve years from 1977 through 1988, it was in deficit ten times. The merchandise trade deficit simply became too big to be paid for by "invisible" services to foreigners, exactly the opposite of what took place between 1896 and 1914. This will become truer still as Asian and European countries increase their high-technology capacities and chip away at the American lead in world sales of telecommunication and computer services.

These trade and current account statistics are symptoms of how a hegemonic impulse tends to outlast its occasioning circumstances and the means for preserving it. In the heady days of the 1950s and 1960s, foreign imports in American markets were sparse—more like novelties—and U.S. firms singlemindedly produced differentiated, brand-name goods for a "high mass consumption" economy that yielded abundant short-run profits. American consumer goods, it was assumed, would be made available to the rest of the "free world," and the flexible U.S. form of corporate organization, which supposedly permitted individual initiative, innovative teamwork, and decentralized decisionmaking, would have to be copied as well if other peoples wanted to shape their own destinies (in the image of the United States).[35] With this degree of complacency, it should come as no surprise that a more-than-cyclical rise in imported consumer goods was one reason for the persistent trade deficits of the 1970s and 1980s.

The automobile industry became the symbol of the changing postwar era, and it serves as a model for the entrepreneurial-breakdown theory of U.S. industrial slippage.[36] By 1987–88 GM, Ford, and Chrysler were claiming only 65 percent of all domestic sales, a market share that would have been lower in the absence of "voluntary restraints" on imports of Japanese cars negotiated with Tokyo. But there was an even broader invasion of products from abroad, as foreign machine tools, textiles and apparel, shoes, consumer electronics and communications equipment seized from 30 to 70 percent of their respective U.S. markets by the mid 1980s, and foreign-made steel and lumber products took 20 to 30 percent. In 1987, imported goods supplied 23 percent of American domestic goods consumption, up from 9 percent in 1970. Also, from 1965 through 1980 seven of America's ten leading high tech-oriented industries, including pharmaceuticals, electrical equipment, and professional and scientific instruments, lost ground in world markets.[37]

Deep-seated problems were emerging, symptomatic of an imperial decline that usually brings with it a seemingly sudden loss of productivity leadership. Ambitious competitor nations, with exceptional productivity growth in their export sectors, seize such opportunities. Pacific Basin countries benefited this way after 1965, and they wiped out some portion of the old U.S. export surpluses irrecoverably. The implication is that a substantial drop in the real foreign exchange rate of the dollar would now be needed to achieve a new trade balance.

Contributing further to this decline in U.S. exports relative to imports has been the restructuring of world production patterns by MNCs, with U.S. companies in the forefront. While the American share of world exports of manufactures was falling, the American MNC share was not. Table 8.4 shows that the share of these MNCs in world export markets, from all their worldwide operations, held steady at 17 to 18 percent. The MNCs increased their exports from facilities outside the geographic United States, in both developed and less-developed countries, to account for more than 10 percent of world exports by the mid 1980s. It became common practice for American MNCs to fill foreign, and some U.S., orders from their overseas factories rather than from their U.S.-based facilities. Another statistic shows the cumulative impact on U.S. exports from MNC restructuring of global production. In 1957 foreign affiliates of American MNCs were supplying 17.6 percent of the exports of manufactures by all U.S. firms at home and abroad; in 1984 that proportion stood at 41 percent.[38] For U.S. corporations, foreign direct investment was providing an escape from constraints at home. But any escape could be short-run, as the transfer of production abroad may transform the excess capacity tendencies of corporate oligopoly into global ones.[39]

These developments indicate how U.S. MNCs have been in the forefront of the internationalization of production, cutting back domestic operations which are not, by their standards, sufficiently profitable and shifting the activities abroad. If such foreign production could be brought back to the United States, the nation's exports would double, according to some Commerce Department projections.[40] This might happen in a counterfactual world without MNCs—a particularly vivid staging of Hamlet without the Prince of Denmark. Meanwhile, in the real world of late capitalism, it implies the need for a still greater depreciation of the dollar to increase U.S. exports by a given amount and bring U.S. trade into balance again.

Trade and Investment in the 1980s: The Costs of Reaganomics

Despite such structural changes, it might be argued that the foreign commerce of the United States has not crashed. There was, after all, no way that the United States could have maintained as dominant a position in world trade in the 1980s as in the 1950–1965 period. In fact, in manufactured exports, the United States held its ground relative to the European Economic Community (EC) after 1971, and its export share losses in key industries were no worse than those of West Germany, Britain, the Netherlands, and Canada.[41] Furthermore, the export performance of the United States was obscured for a time by the 1973 and 1979 OPEC price rises, which drove the bill for U.S. oil imports from $4.7 billion in 1972 to $79.3 billion in 1980, so that the cost of these imports was greater than the total merchandise trade deficit in every year from 1973 through 1982. (In 1982, for instance, imported oil cost $61.3 billion, while the trade deficit amounted to $36.4 billion.) All this time the United States was doing well on nonpetroleum trade, with net foreign sales of agricultural produce, aircraft, computers and office machines, construction equipment, electrical and industrial machinery, and chemical products. These figures show how U.S. nonagricultural exports fared compared to nonpetroleum imports (annual averages, billions of current dollars):[42]

	Nonagricultural exports	Nonpetroleum imports	Ratio of exports to imports
1972–73	$46.7	$56.6	.83
1980–81	187.6	178.9	1.05
1985–86	191.9	311.1	.62

The underlying trend was toward positive U.S. trade balances in research-intensive products and in chemicals, machinery, and transport equipment, where the comparative advantage of U.S. firms appears to reside. Obviously, this trend was stopped cold in the 1980s.

The dramatic deterioration in the export performance of the United States as a geographical entity in the 1980s was largely a macroeconomic phenomenon, having to do with price levels and world demand. From 1979 through 1982, interest rates soared in the United States, with the arrival of Paul Volcker at the helm of the Federal Reserve and the shift toward a much tighter monetary policy with hikes in the discount rate the Fed charges member banks on loans of reserves. The average prime rate charged on loans by banks was an already high 9 percent in 1978, but in 1981 it reached nearly 19 percent.[43] Monetary policy was tightened in other industrialized countries too, but foreign central banks did not permit interest rates to rise as much as in the United States.

When the Fed relaxed its tight money policies in mid 1982 and allowed interest rates to fall, foreign central banks did the same, so that real U.S. interest rates remained higher than foreign rates through 1985–86. The result was an inflow of funds to the United States seeking higher returns and an increase in foreign demand for dollars to purchase U.S. assets, pushing up the value of the dollar. From 1980 through early 1985 the trade-weighted value of the dollar on foreign exchange markets rose by about 60 percent;[44] this means that on average it took 60 percent more foreign currency of the major U.S. trading partners to buy a dollar. The effect was to make U.S. exports much more expensive and imports cheaper. The ensuing drop in exports relative to imports was aggravated by faster growth of aggregate demand in the United States, sucking in imports in greater quantities; meanwhile the major U.S. trading partners were growing barely half as fast, further depressing demand for American exports. During the recovery years of the mid 1980s, increases in American GNP accounted for 70 percent of world demand growth in industrial nations, nearly twice as much as in previous postwar recoveries.[45]

Together, exchange rate appreciation and demand growth explain the bulk of the U.S. trade deficits in the 1980s.[46] They were direct results of American monetary and fiscal policies. The tight money policy of the Federal Reserve from 1979 through 1982 kept interest rates higher than they otherwise would have been at all stages of the business cycle, and the Reaganomics of huge federal budget deficits generated more rapid growth in national income and consumer spending than was occurring in the economies of the major American trading partners. From 1980–81 through 1985–86, total U.S. merchandise exports, in current dollars, grew less than 5 percent, while total imports jumped 37 percent— even though petroleum imports dropped almost by half.[47] The figures above, covering nonagricultural exports and nonpetroleum imports, reflect this balance of trade debacle.

But this domestic policy-centered explanation of the mounting U.S. trade deficits through the 1980s must not obscure the basic issue. The great monetarist experiment of 1979–82, and the Reaganomics of enormous increases in military spending coupled with a three-stage income tax cut, were both grossly unilateral acts in an international context of receding American power. Like the corporations' assumption of permanent economic superiority based on easy monopolization of the U.S. home market until the 1970s, such monetary and fiscal acts by U.S. administrations were relics of a bygone era, when the United States could contain, or compel acceptance of, the ripple effects of its own decisions. From 1979 through 1984 the United States was nakedly forcing its economic policies and priorities on the rest of the world. But this time it succeeded in causing major problems for U.S. foreign policy—as well as for its own economic health.

From 1985 through 1988 the trade-weighted dollar fell back, roughly to 1980 exchange rate levels, but the U.S. trade deficit nonetheless continued to grow (Table 8.5). Readjustment was proving extremely difficult, as further structural changes in the world economy kept taking place. One was the inroads that foreign goods, especially Asian, had by now made in American markets. With the dollar falling in value, Japanese exporters defended their U.S. market shares by raising prices less than the appreciation of the yen even if it meant lower profits—while U.S. firms in Japan preferred to enlarge profit margins rather than cut prices and expand market share.[48] Another was the entrenched practice of making products in the United States with imported parts and materials, with 88 percent of American manufacturers sticking with some foreign ingredients even as they became costlier in dollar terms.[49] The world demand situation was also making adjustment harder, as American exports were held back by ongoing economic stagnation in Western Europe and the debt crisis in Latin America. To shrink the American trade deficits, an even greater depreciation of the dollar seemed necessary, perhaps followed up by the time-honored policy solution, an engineered recession, to reduce imports of consumer goods.

The result of unilateral U.S. economic policies was not only trade deficits but, inevitably, larger inflows of foreign funds to finance them. As trade deficits piled up, totalling $400 billion from 1980 through 1985 alone, Americans had to borrow or sell assets to pay for the deficits, as is always the case when consumption outruns income. Capital inflows from abroad were needed to cover both the trade deficit and the federal budget deficit; the United States had to borrow in excess of its domestic savings, or sell off factories, bonds, stocks, and other property to foreigners, to finance its high level of private consumption (its import surplus) and public consumption (its federal deficit, with spending exceeding tax revenues). Had the capital inflows been used to finance real investment, as during the nineteenth century, America's economy might have emerged in a stronger position, with improved productivity and higher income levels that could easily defray the service charges on the debt. But during the Reagan years, the United States borrowed to pay for private consumption and military spending.

The net foreign borrowing quickly ended seventy years for the United States as a creditor nation. In 1981-82, U.S. residents owned $140 billion more in foreign assets than foreigners held in the United States. This margin dwindled to $4 billion in 1984; in 1985 it turned into a debtor balance of $112 billion. By 1987 the United States was the world's largest debtor nation, with a negative balance of $368 billion (Table 8.2). This was a debt greater than that of the three previous leaders combined (Brazil, Mexico, Argentina), although America's holdings abroad provided investment income, and leverage, beyond the means of any poorer nation. But the American standard of living would likely be affected as the bill came due for the fiscal irresponsibility of the Reagan era. Billions of dollars would have to be transferred to foreigners simply to pay interest on the debt, only the start of a process in which the taxes not paid and the goods not exported during the 1980s would have to be made good. Working people would almost certainly bear the brunt of higher taxes, higher interest rates, higher prices for imports, or some combination thereof.

In the 1960s U.S. foreign policymakers overextended their power in Vietnam, resulting in the collapse of the dollar as key currency and the end of their ability to intervene anywhere in the world at times of their choosing. In the 1980s U.S. policymakers overreached their capacity to redistribute income to the rich and to reestablish strategic military superiority over the Soviet Union. This time the result was the mortgaging of the nation's future.

The United States in the World Economy: New Role, Old Habits

The relative decline of U.S. economic power has created a more polycentric order among high-income capitalist nations, if a somewhat asymmetric one with the United States still the strongest nation. The interdependencies among individuals and social organisms rarely if ever exist on a basis of equality, but in an era of increasing economic interdependence they become less lopsided. Since 1960-64, the U.S. foreign trade ratio, or the share of the GNP involved in exports and imports, has doubled (Table 8.5). Twenty percent of U.S. industrial output is exported; sales to foreign consumers have constituted 20 to 30 percent of total farm receipts in recent years; exports provide one of every eight jobs in manufacturing.[50]

Direct investment abroad by U.S. corporations grew from $90 billion in 1972 to $309 billion in 1987, with three-quarters of it in developed countries with high-income markets and stable political systems (Table 8.3). In the mid 1980s the 150 largest American MNCs, ranked by foreign-based sales, on average derived 34 percent of their total profits from operations abroad.[51] Meanwhile, direct investment in the United States by foreign firms was growing much more rapidly, accelerating to 25 percent per year from 1978 through 1980 and reaching $262 billion in 1987 (Table 8.2). The three biggest investors as of 1987 were Great Britain with 28.6 percent of the total, the Netherlands with 18 percent, and Japan with 12.7; Canada and West Germany held about 8 percent each. By several estimates, 10 percent of all corporate takeovers in the United States have been executed by foreign companies since the late 1970s, and as much as 18 percent of all banking assets are foreign-owned. In the late 1980s nearly 20 percent of the national debt held outside commercial banks was owned by foreigners (and some of the bank holders too were foreign).[52] Americans, it appears, have ceased to dominate international investment flows and capital markets.

The American campaign to promote capitalist development in all corners of the globe has likewise come full circle, through fiercer international competition. The system the United States erected in the early postwar years to rebuild Western Europe and Japan as investment and trading partners and anticommunist bastions has spread to parts of Asia. The flow of U.S. funds to Western Europe was followed in the 1970s by the direct incorporation of third world labor into clothing, footwear, toys, and semiconductor production, supported by a reverse movement of Western capital into developing countries. The goal was a more opportunistic division of labor—specialized foreign affiliates with wages ten or twenty times lower, workdays much longer, strikes and trade unionism virtually nonexistent. The post–1970 corporate sector drive to reduce employee wages and benefits has been accompanied by warnings that labor is still too costly to permit U.S. industries to regain their competitive footing in international markets. Comparative advantage apparently is to be reestablished by "equalizing factor returns"—lowering the compensation standards of American workers. It must be stressed, however, that this "restructuring" drive has to do with profits, and not with any frantic search for low-wage havens as such. In some cases, where the assembly of goods or the fabrication of component parts is manual, with a high ratio of labor costs to total costs, it pays to locate in countries like Mexico, Hong Kong, the Philippines, or Brazil. In most others, the target of foreign investment continues to be nations with growing consumer goods markets and social stability. At the same time capitalist development in Japan and other Pacific rim nations has put down independent roots. A milestone was passed in 1982 when, for the first time, the United States conducted more trade across the Pacific than the Atlantic. By 1985 U.S. exports and imports across the Pacific totalled $193 billion, against $142 billion with all of Europe.[53]

A "scissors effect" has been taking place. The United States has simultaneously become more dependent on the world economy and less able to dictate the course of international affairs. Global economic reach is more critical to U.S. corporations and less susceptible to their influence. It means that the formulation and execution of international economic policy must be conducted with greater skill and subtlety than ever before. It also means that a large-scale expansion of public sector programs and social services at home, along with a planned recapitalization of progressive industries, will be necessary to protect the interests of working people in an age of international economic competition.

To state the conditions is to perceive the dangers. The U.S. leadership and its corporate constituency seem to be as wedded to the idea of control of their economic environment and unfettered freedom of action as they were in the 1890–1914 years. The policy implications seem straightforward: the United States may be more economically and financially "open," but it is no less unilateral. Trade is a case in point. In the past decade the major economic powers have been fighting over the benefits of reduced economic growth. In this zero-sum world, nearly all American industries feel competitive pressure from abroad. This can lead to an outburst of protectionism, or an opportunistically managed one, or both.

In fact U.S. administrations have been waging trade war against Japan and the EC ever since the 1971 fall from grace; this was the first line of defense of their imperial prerogatives.[54] The list of American "initiatives" in trade is a long one. It runs from President Nixon's 1971 import surtax to the "orderly marketing agreements" reached with South Korea, Hong Kong, and Taiwan "voluntarily" to limit their exports of cotton and synthetic textiles (1973), with Japan to slow its automobile exports (1981), and with the EC to curb steel shipments (1982). In 1982 the Reagan administration ruptured the Atlantic alliance with an embargo on exports of turbines and other equipment by U.S.-affiliated firms in Britain, France, West Germany, and Italy to the Soviet Union for its Siberian gas pipeline to Europe, an exercise in extraterritoriality that drew an angry rejection even from Prime Minister Margaret Thatcher. In 1983 Washington put on new sugar quotas, subsidized a large sale of wheat flour, butter, and cheese to Egypt, a French customer, to punish the EC for its tariff protection of its own farmers; increased the U.S. tariff on motorcycles tenfold; doubled duties on specialty steel and stainless steel plate; and placed restrictions on 40 categories of garments from several Asian countries including China. In 1986 the Reagan administration set new ceilings on imports of European whisky, wine, pork, hams, chocolates, and olives to retaliate for food sales the United States allegedly lost to Spain and Portugal when they joined the EC; it also imposed a five-year tariff on Canadian cedar shingles and shakes, drawing immediate retaliation from Ottawa against American books, periodicals, and computer parts and a reminder that Canada remains the largest U.S. trading partner. In 1987 the Reagan administration slapped 100 percent tariffs on certain Japanese computers, television sets, and power tools. In the late 1980s it was taking aim at a high-tech rival, Airbus Industrie, a European consortium whose passenger jets were challenging Boeing and McDonnell Douglas in the hotly competitive international aircraft market.

Protectionism has never been a one-way street. America's trade competitors practice it, and the EC's Common Agricultural Policy that subsidizes exports and prevents imports from coming in at low prices, has long been targeted by Washington as discriminating against U.S. farm exports. In 1986 new EC measures adversely affected American sales of corn, sorghum, wheat, and soybeans (and the Reagan administration retaliated against a range of EC products). Two years later the United States renewed its all-out campaign against the EC's agricultural policies, refusing to discuss gradual steps toward freer farm trade and stalemating the General Agreement on Tariffs and Trade (GATT) negotiations well into 1989. By several measures, though, more goods consumed in the United States are protected in the 1980s than at any time in the postwar period, and "protectionism has probably risen more in the United States than in any other market."[55] The U.S. initiatives, coming as they did during a time of growing interdependence among capitalist nations, embodied a typical American "shoot-out" approach to problem resolution, with a blend of unilateralism, impatience, and conviction that the adversary will yield rather than test American resolve.

The American illusion of omnipotence has been costly and threatens to become costlier than ever. U.S. international power has actually followed an inverted U-shaped course, rising after the 1880s, peaking in the 1950s and 1960s, declining since. True American hegemony lasted only twenty years, 1945 to 1965, if one views the 1920–1940 period as one of "power without responsibility," when the United States had taken over Britain's industrial, financial, and commercial mantle but failed to support the reality of its new role with an appropriate foreign policy.[56] While Japan and West Germany do not possess the power to supplant the United States as the strongest capitalist nation and (erstwhile) guarantor of the rules of the game, neither do they feel the need to acquiesce in every demand from Washington.

America's belligerence in the international economy springs from domestic forces—a practically unshakable corporate command over the income-generation process and a business-oriented view of the world unique to American capitalism. In the policymaking sphere, it has led to a mechanistic extension of the "no nonsense" corporate ethic to international affairs, a policy that has been virtually unchallenged at home. The strongest challenges, when they do occur, seem to come from the political right with its emotional calls for "victory" over communism and for "getting tough" with our trade partners (although the right is frequently joined by mainstream liberals covering themselves against accusations of softness on communism or seeking a wider labor constituency).

The quick payoff approach to foreign relations invariably reduces complex matters of international economics and diplomacy to the formula apparently successful in managing corporate enterprise. What we see is a set of criteria to test results against the imperatives of big-business efficiency. The world must be reduced to a few predictable, regimented processes that produce profits, or "outcomes favorable to our side" in the political sphere, without undue risk or delay. The strategy is anything but riskless for what Veblen called "the underlying populations," for the externalization of military and political costs by the business community is very great. But this has never posed any serious threat to U.S. policymakers, except when they miscalculate badly enough to dump unacceptable costs on the public at large—as in Vietnam after 1967.

The decline of American power is symbolized by the weakening or destruction of multilateral trade and dollar-based liquidity, the levers of U.S. domination of the international economy until the 1970s. From 1945 through the mid 1960s, the United States had the power to stabilize the world system through its hegemonic functions. It established rules and standards of conduct through its "international leadership" (as it was almost universally referred to). It provided such "public goods" as a secure status quo, market outlets for nations that must export or stagnate, guaranteed availability of capital for would-be borrowers, a stable foreign exchange rate system, and a forum for coordinating macroeconomic policies.[57] Now the United States no longer can regulate international economic relations through unilateral action—it can only destabilize them. And it can prevent any other rules of the game from materializing if it so chooses.

The U.S. struggle to shape the international economy in its own image has come full circle, for stabilization of the international economy depends upon genuine stabilization of the major capitalist economies, especially the United States. The new interdependence requires macroeconomic policy to be conceived in a global rather than a purely national context, as the 1979–84 imbroglio over U.S. interest rate policy shows. The case becomes even more convincing the moment one considers the predicaments of international debtor nations like Mexico, Brazil, and Argentina. But the managers of the world's largest single economy are not likely to renounce the pursuit of what they conceive to be their vital interests for the sake of genuine international cooperation, otherwise they might have done it years ago.

The United States is walking a tightrope, stretched between harsher rivalry with its allies for world markets and growing economic interdependencies. Yet it remains to be seen whether American capitalism can trade off the remnants of hegemony for genuine cooperation with Japan, Canada, Europe, and increasingly the Soviet Union. "Capitalism in one country" is a long-term impossibility whether it comes about because of socialist revolutions or capitalist trade wars.

With less support from the other industrial powers for its unilateral policies, military or economic, the United States may have to address the domestic structural problems it has preferred to ignore or regard as marginal cases of "inadaptability of resources."

But whether a future administration is forced to do this will depend, as it always has, on domestic politics. Since the Second World War, the constituency favoring "national security" through a "strong defense" has been the same one that has had a stranglehold over the nation's resources, funneling them away from social spending and toward the military-industrial complex. A basic change toward a new international order will depend on a basic change in the corporate-dominated structure of U.S. politics.

Economic Growth in the Corporate Era: Trends, Triumphs, Paradoxes

A nation's macroeconomic history is largely the product of two forces, sometimes complementary, other times antagonistic. The first is private economic initiative, the second, public policy. There is, of course, the additional influence of international economic relations. In the case of the United States its impact was less significant than for the other industrial capitalist countries, although the relative American immunity to foreign trade and investment effects appears to have ended in the 1970s.

As the twentieth century—the first full century of corporate-led growth—approaches its end, how have the giant business organization and the concentration of economic power affected the structure and functioning of the U.S. economy? What adjustments have occurred in the public sector, and what are the implications for American economic growth and welfare?

A Century of Monopolization: Change and Continuity

It is tempting to focus on the four merger movements from 1890 through 1990 as the pivotal episodes in the development of big business. But mergers must not be thought of as something qualitatively different from any of the other operations of modern capitalism, which has always been a cyclically-driven system with waves of expansion and contraction. Though mergers may not have any distinctive effects on the functioning of the U.S. economy, they do play the very important role of speeding up the growth of large-scale capital and altering the structure of industries where merger activity and financial reshuffling of assets have been heavy. The effects become cumulative over time, as each new merger series is superimposed upon a base of concentration built up in previous years. For the

Table 9.1

Concentration in Industry and Manufacturing, Percentage Shares of Total Assets, 1909–1987

	Share of all industrial assets, 100 largest industrial firms		Share of all manufacturing assets	
			100 largest manufacturing firms	200 largest manufacturing firms
1909	17.7%			
1919	16.6			
		1925	34.5%	
1929	25.5	1929	38.2	45.8%
1939	27.7	1939	41.9	48.7
1948	26.7	1950	39.7	47.7
1958	29.8	1960	46.4	56.3
1967	31.8	1970	48.5	60.4
1977	29.5	1980	46.7	59.7
		1987	50.0	61.8

Sources: Niemi (1980), 336; Herman (1981), 192; U.S. Bureau of the Census (1985), 524, updated from unpublished data furnished by the Federal Trade Commission.

Note: Industrial assets include manufacturing, mining, wholesale and retail trade, services, and construction. For manufacturing assets, data prior to 1980 are not strictly comparable with later years.

acquiring firm, "the potential internal expansion of each of the merged companies has been merged into the actual internal expansion of the [new] combination. . . . [Hence] the merger may be indirectly responsible for the overwhelming size of many present-day corporations which ostensibly have grown primarily by internal expansion."[1] In capitalist growth, the two processes go on side by side and reinforce each other—mergers and growth of individual firms through internal accumulation.[2]

Concentration of industrial production and capital assets rose rapidly between the 1880s and the first decade of the twentieth century and has not retreated in any substantial way from the levels reached around 1905. The long-term drift may be upward, although the data must be approached with caution. Table 9.1 shows rising concentration of assets in industry as a whole and its manufacturing base.It is consistent with studies showing an irregularly increasing oligopoly share of output over much of the present century.[3]

In any event, through the 1980s effective concentration remained as great as ever. Well-established oligopoly practices, the inevitable shakeouts and rising barriers to entry in high-tech industries, and a homogeneity of political outlook among the corporate leadership all make for resilient market power in the face of any dips in measured concentration ratios. So does the tendency for concentration to spread beyond the manufacturing base:

• In 1984 there were 272,037 active corporations in the manufacturing sector; 710 of them (one-fourth of 1 percent) held 80.2 percent of total manufacturing assets. In the service sector, the redoubt of small business, 95 firms of the total of 899,369 owned 28 percent of the sector's assets.[4]

• In 1985 there were 14,600 commercial banks. The 50 largest held 45.7 percent of all assets in the system and the 100 largest held 57.7 percent.[5]

• In 1986 in agriculture, 29,000 large farms (1.3 percent of all farms in the country) with annual sales of more than $500,000 accounted for one-third of total farm sales and 46 percent of all profits. The raising of chickens, hogs, and cattle is becoming even more concentrated than these figures indicate.[6]

• The industrial sector keeps changing, as older industries give way to new. Nonetheless, concentration among the giants remains high. The share of the total sales of the *Fortune* 500 largest industrial firms accounted for by the top 50 was 54.2 percent in 1954, 46.2 percent in 1970, and 54.4 percent in 1987.[7]

Concentration, however, must not be thought of as a one-way process leading toward ever fewer firms controlling greater proportions of industries and the entire economy. Countervailing forces repose in the political economy of the accumulation process itself.

One such force that limits monopolistic power, and may not be reflected in concentration ratios like those of Table 9.1, is international competition. Starting in the 1970s, dozens of industries were hit hard by imports, with steel, automobiles, tires, textiles and footware, cameras, and consumer electronics particularly affected. Such incursions do make the economy more competitive, but it may not follow that the large oligopolists suffer more than peripheral firms. In restructured markets, U.S. corporations could hold their own through competitive adjustments or alliances with foreign capital, as the GM-Toyota and Ford-Mazda projects of the 1980s suggest.[8] In the 1980s U.S. automakers were also helped by import quotas on Japanese cars; their market share losses would have been more severe without the quotas.

A second force is antitrust policy stemming from opposition to big business, sometimes in parts of the business community itself. It was actively pursued during 1904–1913, again in the 1930s and late 1960s. Although its overall impact was limited, it maintained competition in aluminum, tobacco, telephone equipment and services, trucking, shoe machinery, and food marketing, inhibited large horizontal mergers, and stopped old-time predatory practices in a number of markets.[9]

Third and most importantly, technologies and markets constantly change, offering new profit opportunities. These changes trigger a rush to enter the new field, an ensuing round of shakeouts, and, finally, oligopolistic adaptation, or competition among the few. Such competition normally takes nonprice forms, through "the sales effort."[10]

In this respect Table 9.2 should be compared with Table 3.2 to comprehend the changes in markets during the era of stable oligopoly. In 1939, five of the leading industries were newcomers to the top ten after 1900—motor vehicles, electrical machinery, bread and bakeries, petroleum, chemicals—and all except possibly baked goods were oligopolized. Over the next four-odd decades, another upheaval in technologies and markets occurred, dropping all 1939 leading industries out of the top ten, except for automobiles and petroleum. The rise of modern electronics and communications, the third, fourth, and fifth-place industries in 1982, mirrored the decline of the old manufacturing base (primary metals and heavy machinery). Except for plastics, the other leading 1982 products were made in 1939 but expanded rapidly as a result of the Second World War and subsequent life-style changes, with soft drinks driving beverages into the top ten. The greater complexity of the twentieth-century economy, and the correspondingly greater number of opportunities up for grabs, may be judged by the smaller share of total net output held by the top ten industries. They had approximately 27 percent of all value added in 1939 and 1982 against 44 to 46 percent in 1860 and 1900 (Table 3.2).

New products, enlargement of markets, and changes in organization through mergers and other restructurings keep present-day capitalism intensely competitive. It is this aspect of the accumulation process that a host of economists and business historians cite to explain, or justify, the giant corporation. For Chandler, the "managerial revolution" took place because only large-scale organizations could turn out enormous volumes of goods and accomplish the "administrative coordination" required to handle the related production and marketing functions. Galbraith, a critic of corporate power and behavior, agrees that the big corporation is an outgrowth of the "imperatives of technology and organization" and the need for "planning."[11]

The benefits conferred on society by large-scale enterprise were most imaginatively put forth by Schumpeter. In conventional microeconomic theory, the static inefficiencies created by monopoly power are excessively high prices and too little output, compared with the efficiencies of marginal cost pricing under pure competition. For Schumpeter, however, these costs are far smaller than the dynamic benefits of "the perennial gale of creative destruction," as giant firms ceaselessly compete and try to destroy each other's market position by introducing new products and processes.[12] The "Chicago School" goes further, acknowledging no costs of corporate power: unless thwarted by misguided government intervention, the free market will guarantee that large company size will be the reward for efficiently, and continually, satisfying consumer demand. The only

Table 9.2

Output and Employment in Leading Manufacturing Industries, 1939 and 1982

1939	Value added (million dollars)	Employment (thousands)	1982	Value added (million dollars)	Employment (thousands)
Motor vehicles	1,319	398	Motor vehicles & equipment	34,294	616
Steel works & mills	1,148	369	Aircraft & parts	29,402	539
Electrical machinery	798	211	Communication equipment	28,299	601
Publishing & printing	671	97	Office & computing machines	23,386	404
Bread & bakery products	644	202	Electronic components, accessories	21,214	516
Petroleum refining	528	73	Petroleum refining	19,247	108
Chemicals	471	60	Misc. plastics products	17,935	479
Cotton textiles	438	312	Drugs	16,981	166
Meat packing	422	120	Beverages	16,684	194
Sawmills & wood	413	265	Construction & related machinery	16,453	326
Manufacturing, total	24,683	7,887	Manufacturing, total	824,118	19,094

Sources: U.S. Bureau of the Census (1942), 46–48 and (1987), 702–706.

barriers to entry of new firms are those created by government, and collusive private behavior is not viable in a truly competitive market.

Nobody can deny that the accumulation process has generated untold amounts of wealth and that it has driven human productivity far higher than the levels Marx and Engels extolled in their *Communist Manifesto* of 1848—"The bourgeoisie, during its rule of scarce one hundred years, has created more massive and more colossal productive forces than have all preceding generations together." The question concerns the price paid for these benefits, and whether the optimistic interpretations of Chandler, Schumpeter, and the Chicago School allow us even to think about the opportunity costs of organizing virtually an entire economy to accommodate the goals of corporate enterprise.

The answer begins with the premise that the goal of the modern corporation is *profitable growth*. That goal is compatible with a search for efficiency, but it is much more extensive and does not depend upon efficiency improvements. Corporations will usually make efficiency adjustments that increase total profits, but profits are influenced by many factors unrelated to efficiency.

1. Most significantly, the annals of business history are laden with examples of combinations that *decreased* efficiency. This occurred when the drive for market control gave rise to unwieldy behemoths requiring improved administration not so much to reap potential economies of scale as to avoid internal chaos and to allow the new collectivity to approximate the efficiency of the previously separate companies. Examples are the Western Union Telegraph monopoly after 1866, the Standard Oil Trust after 1885, and the Penn Central railroad merger of 1968. In the early 1900s the stifling effect of bigness on efficiency was frequently commented upon.[13]

Efficiency is also impaired when achieved market power so reduces competitive pressures that needed administrative reforms can be dispensed with. One notorious case was Morgan's 1901 blockbuster, U.S. Steel. Nevertheless, the company was hardly a commercial failure, effective market control endured for decades, and above-normal returns were made on the watered stock. Once these objectives were attained, the stage was set for a long era of technological stodginess. Another such case was Ford. The company survived the 1930s only because of cash reserves socked away in its glory days. "Ford provides an excellent illustration of the fact that a really large business organization can withstand a surprising amount of mismanagement."[14]

2. Considerable evidence indicates that economies of scale, important as they are in mass-production, do not account for the high concentration levels in U.S. industry. What was true at the turn of the century remains true today: in most cases scale economies are exhausted at sufficiently small plant sizes—and market shares—so that something other than tight oligopoly would be feasible.[15] IBM, the "most valuable company" in America, may be the prime example of a firm whose domination of its industry resulted not from declining costs of production but from monopolistic power and the price discrimination tactics employed to

preserve it, as documents from the 1969–1982 antitrust prosecution reveal.[16]

3. Studies of invention show that giant companies are not the fountainhead of technological progress. The largest firms do not support R&D more intensively relative to their size.[17] Small, independent inventors, unaffiliated with any industrial research facilities, supply a disproportionate number of inventions like air conditioning, the jet engine, insulin. "Radical new ideas," *Business Week* concluded in a 1976 survey, "tend to bog down in big-company bureaucracy. This is why major innovations—from the diesel locomotive to Xerography and the Polaroid camera—often come from outside an established industry."[18]

4. The bigger the corporation in size of assets or the larger its market share, the higher its rate of profit: these findings confirm the advantages of market power in view of the facts of corporate life described above.[19] Furthermore, "large firms in concentrated industries earn systematically higher profits than do all other firms, about 30 percent more . . . on average," and there is less variation in their profit rates too.[20]

The foregoing analysis suggests that the "strategy-structure" or the "creative destruction" model might be turned on its head. The revised sequence would be that, for big business, profitable growth strategies are linked to the attainment of market power, which often engenders bureaucratic management and conservative policies. Excess profits can accrue long enough to lull corporate giants into a false sense of security. Among the predictable results would be technological lag, periodic attempts to shore up profits and power through mergers, and administrative hypertrophy. This is probably why the United States "is the most over-supervised country in the world. American companies—the big ones—average 12 management levels between the president and those who deal directly with workers and customers. The largest Japanese companies . . . have only 7 levels at most."[21]

Galbraith has observed that "in its mature form the corporation can be thought of as an instrument principally for perpetuating inequality."[22] During the 1980s this was true in the most elemental way: widespread unemployment and import penetration of U.S. markets were the occasion for spectacular salary and bonus increases the top managerial layer awarded itself. On average its members earned five times as much as their Japanese counterparts, three times as much as the top Swiss executives, the highest paid in Europe.[23]

Long-Term Growth:
A Comparative Perspective

Though many Americans might agree that concentrations of economic power create serious problems for a democratic political system, if not for economic equity and efficiency, many would also point to the "bottom line"—the record of economic growth in the United States.

Sheer numbers make the secular growth of the American economy look like the ultimate success story. Over the century following the Civil War, real GNP expanded some 35 times. Judged against the records of other countries, this rate of increase in the volume of production was "extraordinarily rapid."[24] Population growth too was extraordinary compared to other industrializing nations. Between the 1870s and the 1970s America's population grew nearly five times, while Japan's slightly more than tripled; the populations of the United Kingdom and France did not even double. But the wide margin of America's GNP growth over its population growth brought very large rises in the material standard of living. From 1840 through the 1960s output per head doubled every forty or fifty years. Over the hundred years from 1869–78 through 1969–78 it grew between six and seven times.[25]

For most economists, the latter measure—growth of real income per person—is the most important gauge of economic progress. It usually comes as a surprise to learn that the American record, dazzling as it looks with increases of six to sevenfold over the past hundred years or so, is "about average when compared with rates of growth in other developed countries during the last century."[26] "The puzzling finding," Simon Kuznets wrote in 1964, "is a rate of growth of per capita product that was not significantly higher than in France and Germany, only slightly higher than in England, and significantly lower than in Sweden."[27] In later research Kuznets added the Netherlands and Australia to the list of countries with slower per capita product growth than the United States, and Japan and Russia to the list of faster-growing nations, with Switzerland, Denmark, Norway, Italy, and Canada sharing the middle of the range.[28]

Thus, superior productivity and income levels in the United States have been accompanied by a mediocre performance in the rise of these levels over time. The implication is no longer puzzling: if U.S. per capita incomes did not grow particularly fast but Americans on average enjoy living standards equal to or above those of citizens of other developed nations, then the American starting point must already have been higher 100 to 150 years ago. We now know that before the Civil War per capita incomes in the United States were high by contemporary standards, surpassed through the 1870s only by the British (see pp. 26–27). To a great extent this initial advantage was a gift of nature. North America offered its European settlers an almost inconceivable abundance of fertile land and other natural resources for agriculture and industry. These were the factors that placed the United States ahead of other nations economically, after which the corporate-led growth of the past century produced only "about average" growth rates.

There are several explanations why the commonly held visions of the United States as the most successful economic experiment in history are illusory. "The national economic myth . . . that America was a precocious leader" founders on some serious problems that the nation had to face throughout the nineteenth century, and beyond in some instances.[29] One was the exceptional rate of population growth, which diverted resources into less directly productive social overhead capital, especially during periods of rapid economic expansion and low reserves of unemployed labor: investments in residential housing, farm and household equipment, and municipal services probably yielded lower returns than in industry and may have retarded growth in the absolute mass of profits available to the most dynamic sectors of the new industrial capitalism. Another problem was the sheer size of America or "the disadvantages of space." The westward movement of population entailed heavy overhead costs. Clearing and settling new territory was an expensive process. From the 1850s coal, iron, zinc, copper, and lead supplies shifted further west, often ending in the inaccessible Rocky Mountains. "The superficial picture was one of such natural abundance that it would have been hard then (and is still difficult now) to realize that the nation was growing in per capita income no more rapidly than France and less so than Germany."[30]

Another unique American feature, the distrust and vilification of national government that started in the 1840s and 1850s, also hampered economic performance. "Disadvantages of space" were aggravated in the nineteenth century by sectional rivalries, competing state governments, and notoriously inefficient public administration. Local banking systems, for example, were designed to restrict competition from other areas as well as from metropolitan centers of their own states, impeding the fluid movement of funds anywhere investors might want them. Lack of a central banking system until the Federal Reserve Act of 1913 made financial panics worse and business cycle swings more severe in the United States. "Corrupt state and city government enabled some businesses to buy special favors in the way of franchises or permits but produced expensive governments that were a burden to business as a whole."[31]

The legacy of hostility to a legitimate role for government in the economy extended into the twentieth century. Franklin Roosevelt's New Deal and Lyndon Johnson's Great Society substantially increased the role of the federal government and its effectiveness in dampening the most socially injurious tendencies of unrestrained capitalism. But each advance was fiercely attacked, halted, and partially rolled back. The result is a comparatively small national government, except for its military functions. In an age when the integration of the world economy makes economic problems international in scope, permanent and professionally staffed public bodies will be required to deal with them. Admittedly, it is questionable whether even national solutions are possible, if the aim is to control MNCs or the new international financial system with its ocean of funds flowing in and out of world financial centers seeking maximum short-term returns and dodging government regulations and taxes.

Defenders of American capitalism might acknowledge that U.S. economic growth has not been extraordinary in a comparative context, but they would insist that the free enterprise system has delivered impressive standards of living to countless numbers of men and women. They would add that the United States was, and still is, the world's greatest social magnet, attracting droves of people seeking a better life.

A body of literature supports these beliefs. It began early in the nineteenth century, with European visitors who marveled at the sense of bustle and newness in American society, as well as the undeniable absence of social class barriers by old world standards. Many of these writers were aristocrats who knew little about what was happening in the economies of their own countries, which they nonetheless compared unfavorably with the United States. Several others, English in particular, were engineers who were struck by American ingenuity in overcoming shortages of labor and durable machinery, by substituting abundant natural resources for both.

There were elements of truth in all these observations, mixed with "the paradox of qualitative judgment."[32] The fact is that social class divisions were hardening throughout the nineteenth century, and a sharp rise in wealth and income differentials occurred between 1820 and 1860 (see pp. 24–25). The American prowess in mechanization techniques was actually an adjunct of the favorable natural resource base that had given the United States a head start in economic growth. Resource abundance manifested itself in relatively cheap land, wood, and metal ores, which Americans used in staggering quantities by European standards. The free market pointed the way: plentiful resources mean low prices, as if such supplies will last indefinitely, or else, as they dwindle, producers will smoothly adjust to new cost-price ratios. As matters turned out, wasteful practices became ingrained in American resource allocation. The ultimate example may have been the suburbanization and "full size" automobile boom of the 1950s and 1960s. It is by no means clear that the abundance syndrome has been overcome, even after the lessons learned during the oil crises of the 1970s and the balance of trade difficulties of the 1980s.

Similar paradoxes came with the "huddled masses yearning to breathe free." Heavy immigration into the United States began in the 1840s. From the start the underlying force was economic conditions in Europe as the "push" rather than the inherent attractiveness of the United States as the "pull."[33] The explosion in population growth in Europe associated with the first stages of industrialization began to limit the economic opportunities available by virtue of death or retirement of relatives. Much larger numbers of young men were forced to seek new livelihoods including work abroad. People in countries experiencing demographic pressure, coupled with occasional catastrophic events, responded most sensitively to a strong upswing in the demand for labor in the United States. The Irish immigration following the potato famine of 1845–49 was the first, and classic, case. The timing of the migration flows was influenced by the U.S. business cycle, with peak emigration to the United States occurring during prosperous conditions here. But it was also stimulated by U.S. employers, who were confronted with the high cost of native white labor, some of it being siphoned off by western agricultural opportunities; they aggressively recruited cheaper foreign hands by publicizing jobs in the United States.

The lesser-known part of this history is the return flow of immigrants to their native lands. Many newcomers intended to remain in America only temporarily, and others found the working and living conditions no better than back home, especially in the cities. Between 1870 and 1900, it appears that more than one-fourth of all immigrants eventually returned home. The proportion rose to nearly 40 percent in the 1890s and remained at that level until the legislative restrictions of 1921–24. From 1900 to 1980, the 30 million legal immigrants admitted to the United States must be balanced against 10 million emigrants who left to settle elsewhere.[34]

The Distribution of Income and Wealth

The structural changes in capitalism over the past ten or twelve decades have flowed from its needs for bigger markets, greater quantities of productive resources, and more efficient command over the economic process and its side effects. The answer to these demands, the modern corporation, arose as a means of maintaining private control over production and marketing in an age of industrialization, technological dynamism, and internationalized business. The capitalist mode of production is thus preserved in the face of powerful forces making for constant change. Its durability is reflected by the persistent inequality of income and wealth in the United States, and the other free market economies.

For income distribution, data in Table 7.4, as well as for earlier years, show that the top 20 percent of all households receives much more pretax income than the bottom 60 percent put together, and that it gets eight times as much income as the poorest fifth. The top 5 percent takes in three times as much as the poorest fifth, or more.[35] The post-tax distribution differs little from these pretax figures, with any nominally progressive features of the federal income tax undercut by loopholes and by regressive state and local taxes: "it is clear that the tax system has very little effect on the distribution of income."[36]

Data on distribution of wealth, or property, usually evoke more surprise than income distribution figures, which not only suffer from overexposure by comparison, but may seem just to many Americans who retain faith in the rewards of individualistic striving. For this reason, among others, it is important to note that income from property—profits, dividends, rents, interest—has always been more concentrated among the rich than earned income from wages and salaries. Money makes money, so that left alone, inequalities of income and wealth become cumulative.

Table 9.3 presents findings from a Federal Reserve Board survey of financial assets held by "families" of one-person units or more, corrected for inflation. "Total financial assets" include liquid assets (checking, savings, and money-market accounts; certificates of deposit; savings bonds), plus corporate stocks and bonds, nontaxable bonds (state and local), mutual funds and trusts. They *exclude* equity held in personal residences; it does not generate disposable income

Table 9.3

Distribution of Total Financial Assets by Dollar Amounts Owned, in 1983 Prices

	Percent of families	
	1970	1983
None	16%	12%
$1–999	22	27
$1,000–4,999	22	22
$5,000–9,999	11	10
$10,000–24,999	12	12
$25,000–49,999	7	7
$50,000–99,999	5	5
$100,000 and more	5	5
Total	100%	100%
Mean	$23,295	$24,128
Median	$ 2,307	$ 2,300

Source: Federal Reserve Bulletin, September 1984, 685.

and is not a deployable asset, since it cannot be turned into cash without rendering the seller homeless. Private homes account for 30 percent of gross assets held by America's families, but for the bottom 90 percent of all families, nearly 60 percent of their wealth is tied up in the equity in their homes.[37]

Table 9.3 discloses that three-fifths of all families owned less than $5,000 of financial assets in 1983 and that half possessed $2,300 worth or less. Only one household in twenty has managed to amass the kind of wealth that might furnish a living income in case of unemployment or disability or retirement: $100,000 prudently invested earns, depending on prevailing interest rates, a $5,000 to $8,000 annual return—if that much can be described as adequate at a time when the official poverty threshold was $10,178 for a family of four.

This means that substantial wealth, which by itself can yield independent incomes, is limited to a tiny percentage of the American population. In 1983, the richest 0.5 percent of all households—one in 200—owned more than 45 percent of the nation's privately held net wealth, excluding equity in personal residences. This included 47 percent of all corporate stock, 62 percent of nontaxable bonds, 77 percent of all trusts, 10 percent of all cash balances.[38] For these 420,000 "super rich households," the average amount of net assets held was $8.9 million. The next richest 420,000 households, or the second half of the top 1 percent, owned assets ranging from $1.4 to $2.5 million; they owned 7 percent of the nation's net wealth. Thus, the top 1 percent of the nation's households owned about 53 percent of all income-producing wealth; the top 10 percent owned 83 percent. The bottom nine-tenths of the nation's families owned the rest—less than 17 percent of net private wealth.

It appears that between the late 1940s and the 1980s the distribution of wealth in the United States became more unequal, with the share held by the top one-half of one percent of the population rising, especially after 1969–70.[39] The trend is consistent with findings of an earlier study indicating that since 1922 wealth became distributed somewhat more equally only in the 1930s and early 1940s— "two periods of massive government intervention in the marketplace . . . when the market system was functioning under duress or was in administrative abeyance."[40]

The Public Sector in the United States

The size and role of government have grown significantly since the Great Depression. But that growth left the United States with a small public sector by international standards. As a proportion of the GNP, total expenditures by all three levels of government in the United States run about 34 percent. This is the lowest public spending-GNP ratio of any industrial capitalist nation in the world save Japan. But Japan has small armed forces, and its social spending is much more a private function than in most developed countries. Despite these differences, Japan's public spending was approaching American proportions in the late 1980s. Ratios of public expenditure to GNP for Western Europe average 44 to 46 percent, with France, Germany, and the Netherlands running higher.[41] In terms of social spending the United States ranks even lower, with a larger share of its public expenditures going for outlays on the military. Taxes too are light in the United States, equivalent to a smaller percentage of GNP than in any advanced nation except Japan (catching up here too), Switzerland, and Australia.[42]

These low levels of aggregate public activity are matched by "an extremely small amount of state ownership" in the economy.[43] In the United States, public enterprise has been confined to the Post Office, a reduced rail passenger service, and a minimal position in the utilities (mainly water but some electricity too). In other advanced countries government ownership is common in rail and air transport, telecommunications, gas and electricity, coal, petroleum, steel, shipbuilding, motor vehicles, and aerospace. In the late 1970s public enterprises accounted for an average of 13.5 percent of total capital formation for a variety of noncommunist countries, both developed and third world. Excluding the United States, "whose share is untypically low" at about 4.4 percent, the average capital formation share exceeded 16.5 percent.[44]

The "welfare state" completes the picture of limited government in the United States. Social expenditures have risen since the 1930s. They were not driven up by government bureaucrats seeking to expand their own power, as American conservatives claim, but grew belatedly, after the private sector was unwilling or unable to provide old-age support and other human services. They were responses to demands that originated in popular agitation and social movements and were only later enacted into law. The list embraces social security, unemployment insurance, medicare, educational assistance, aid for families with dependent children, food stamps, and rental housing subsidies. Several of these programs have proven to be politically untouchable because they are directed toward middle-class Americans, with social security the prime example. This is why, for the most part, government benefits are distributed independent of income and depend upon characteristics like being a senior citizen or a veteran, attending a state university, or being a farmer or disabled. Most benefits are not directed primarily toward lower-income people.

But the welfare state is not only nonredistributive in the United States. It is modest indeed compared to the welfare societies of northern Europe with their full range of income maintenance and social service programs, from cash benefits and subsidized day care for children to universal medical insurance. The Great Society programs of 1964–67 were breakthroughs in the American context, but they were underfinanced to begin with and frozen by 1970 to help pay for the Vietnam War. Among industrialized nations, the United States alone does not have family income supplements for child support. It is also the sole nation without some form of health care system for all citizens.

In short, more than a century ago the United States began evolving toward a society of wage and salary workers with little property and even less income from property to cushion their own security. No other capitalist nation has so persistently extended the rule of profit to all corners of social life, and in no other case has the regime of capital so fully permeated labor markets in particular. Related to this is the weakness of working-class organization, lacking even a social democratic-type party that can keep progressive, reformist measures on the public agenda.[45] At the same time the United States lacks public economic institutions that not only moderate the rule of capital but are becoming more crucial for a well-functioning capitalist economy itself in the late twentieth century. "There is little question that in cross-national comparison the United States does not promote business enterprise to the degree that its international competitors do or that the U.S. itself did earlier in its history."[46]

Across the capitalist world, the counterattack of the right in the 1980s, featuring an aggressive promotion of free market ideology, was not confined to Reaganomics. In Great Britain, the Thatcher government succeeded in reducing the size of the welfare state. But Thatcherism still leaves Britain with a wider network of social benefits than the United States, including an intact if impaired national health service, and the possibility that the cutbacks will be restored by a future Labour government. Caps on health and unemployment insurance were attempted in other nations, as was privatization of public enterprises, particularly in France under the Chirac government (March 1986-May 1988). Denationalization of state-owned industries was also undertaken to some degree in Canada, Japan, West Germany, Italy, and the Netherlands. In many of these cases, the impetus was the attractive example of the United States. European conservatives, and social democrats like François Mitterrand and Bettino Craxi, could point to a "miracle" of employment creation under Reagan. But the attraction was fading by the late 1980s, as the differences in macroeconomic policies responsible for rapid growth of GNP in the United States from 1982 to 1985 and economic stagnation in much of Western Europe were narrowing. Privatization in Britain and France was also losing its glitter, especially after the worldwide panic in stock markets of October 1987. Conservatives stopped growth of the public enterprise-welfare state in Europe and chipped away parts of it, but it remains more extensive than its American counterpart.

What Hath Capitalism Wrought:
The American "Social Welfare Function"

The starting point for constructing a "social welfare function" must be real income per head. Americans still enjoy, on average, the highest per capita incomes in the world, rivaled only by citizens of Switzerland (although comparative measurements of national products are extremely sensitive to exchange rate fluctuations, which have been large in recent years).[47] Per-capita income figures must then be compared with other indicators, since every economics textbook cautions students that GNP alone is not meant to be a measure of human economic welfare. A study of the U.S., Japanese, West German, and Swedish economies for 1960 to 1985 employs 17 indicators of quality of life and economic performance to assess how well each country provides its people with "adequate income, good health, a secure livelihood, leisure time, adequate shelter, a long life, and freedom from harm." On the basis of the indicators, the U.S. performance was the worst, while Sweden's was the best.[48]

A more concrete view of the American social welfare function comes from comparing "number one" per capita incomes with specific facts of everyday life: among advanced industrial nations, the United States is "number one," or close to it, in the following categories:[49]

• Lowest level of job security for workers, with greatest chance of being dismissed without notice or reason. Other advanced nations generally prohibit sudden or arbitrary firings or plant closings.

• Greatest chance for a worker to become unemployed without adequate unemployment and medical insurance. The United States has the lowest unemployment income-compensation ratio of all major industrial countries. In 1986, of all Americans employed or unemployed, 18 percent had no health insurance at all.

• Less leisure time for workers, with an average of two-and-one-half weeks annual vacation. Newly hired workers in most European countries receive a minimum of four weeks paid vacation. After twenty years on the job, only 64 percent of U.S. workers are entitled to four weeks.

• Lowest combined level of working-class mobilization, percent of the labor force unionized, and percentage of the electorate voting in national elections. The United States ranks at the bottom of a list of 18 advanced noncommunist nations.

• While sharp income inequalities exist in all industrial capitalist countries, the United States appears to have one of the most lopsided income distribution profiles. In particular, the share of total income going to the poorest percentiles is exceptionally low in the United States.

• Lowest ratio of female to male earnings, with American women typically earning 64 percent of the male wage, only one percentage point higher than in 1939. In Europe the figures are not only much higher, but the wage gap has closed in recent years.

• Combined worst ranking for life expectancy and infant mortality, with this record due in part to extreme inadequacy of health care for minorities. The United States spends more on health care than any other nation—11 percent of GNP in 1988. But in 1986 it ranked sixteenth in infant mortality among the 21 wealthiest nations. If only whites were counted, the United States would be in twelfth place.

• Highest teenage pregnancy rate of any industrial nation, twice that of runner-up Great Britain.

• Highest incidence of poverty in the industrial world, with exceptionally high infant and preschool child poverty. The rate exceeded 17 percent for everyone below eighteen years of age in 1986, not a recession year, and reached 40 percent for black children. Also in 1986, 2 million adults were poor even though they worked year-round at full-time jobs.

• Among worst rankings of all advanced industrial nations for levels of pollutant emissions into the air.

• Greatest likelihood for a citizen to be killed by another person, nearly three times as likely as a resident of Finland, which has the second highest murder rate.

Whither American Capitalism?

American capitalism exhibits considerable social stability—one might say remarkable in view of the way the system distributes its economic chances and rewards. Private enterprise has succeeded better than the state in imposing its coercions because they are disguised as free choices. Mainly these choices come down to personal consumption within one's income level. This by no means denies the political and personal freedoms Americans enjoy. But those freedoms were gained through a long struggle against the power of capital. "Capitalists have no interests *as capitalists* in promoting the cause of freedom. They are indeed more likely to have opposed interests, insofar as freedom may create subversive attitudes toward the regime of capital."[50]

"High mass consumption," driven by technology and heavy doses of household debt, has been a great social stabilizer for advanced capitalism. But it is part of a larger phenomenon, since it embodies, for most Americans, the incentives of the free market system. In general Americans seem to feel that the rewards generated by the system are reasonable and not arbitrary. Even during times of skepticism about the fairness of free market outcomes, most people are still convinced that they would have more to lose if the system were replaced by "government bureaucracy" or "economic planning." This structure of beliefs has strong roots in history and the culture of individualism, but political demobilization, or the near-total exclusion of alternatives from public discourse, also plays a very important role. Ideas like worker control, cooperative institutions, job entitlement, and public enterprise will not be placed on the political agenda by either of the two major parties, at least in the foreseeable future.

The other force making for capitalist stability is, paradoxically, capitalist crisis itself. Every recession leaves American workers, bereft of a strong political voice and a trade union movement that both supports and is supported by it, with little alternative but to hope for a quick economic recovery and a return to the *status quo ante*. "The illusion is that when the crisis disappears, the conditions prompting it must have disappeared."[51] A crisis mentality sees a problem as solved when life goes back to normal, so that within the boundaries of acceptable public debate any other outcome is "unrealistic" or worse.

But the central contradiction of American life—record-high per capita incomes coexisting with appalling social problems—does not result from random shocks to the system or bad luck. The contradiction is far too profound for that, and too enduring. If the analysis in the preceding chapters holds, the dilemmas of American society flow mainly from the nature and exercise of corporate power.

This must not be construed as an argument for attributing all social maladjustment or every case of criminal behavior to the policies of corporate business. The point is that, throughout the present century, the corporate sector has controlled well over half of the economy's resources and output, and it has been the chief arbiter of how we live, where we live, what we consume, whether we can find a job, how we get to work and what we do on the job, how we use our leisure time, what we read, and what we watch on television. A moment's reflection will reveal how one (or more) of these aspects of life is degraded by the constant clash between personal and public welfare and private profit.

There have been times when progress was made in reducing the size of this social breach. During the 1930s it took a massive breakdown of the system to bring about economic reforms. Three decades later, the consensus over the Great Society was shattered by the Vietnam War, itself an outgrowth of global interventionism that had long been the cornerstone of a corporate-shaped foreign policy.

Foreign involvement on the scale of a Vietnam or a Korea no longer seems likely, although it is not to be ruled out completely. Beyond that, however, prospects for basic changes in the corporate order seem small. Such changes will again become possible only when the existing power equation is reversed—only when popular discontent and public power combine as the main element forcing change in the corporate order at large.

Endnotes

All works cited below are found in the References section, except for publications cited in abbreviated form as follows:

BW: Business Week
CT: Chicago Tribune
EE: Employment and Earnings
FRB: Federal Reserve Bulletin
IHT: International Herald Tribune
NYT: New York Times
PI: Philadelphia Inquirer
SCB: Survey of Current Business
WSJ: Wall Street Journal

Chapter 1

1. For appraisals of the new economic history, see Woodman (1972); Fishlow (1974); Fogel (1966), reprinted in Fogel and Engerman (1971).
2. Davis, Easterlin, and Parker (1972), 9.
3. New economic historians "have devoted virtually no attention to the subject of big business at all. . . . The neglect seems to have resulted from the Cliometricians' belief that the merger movement [of 1895–1904] was not important." Lamoreaux (1985), 8–9.
4. See Davis and North (1971).
5. Temin (1973), 8.
6. Fishlow (1974), 461, 463; emphasis in original.
7. On what follows, see Chandler (1977) and Du Boff and Herman (1980).
8. Bowles and Edwards (1985), 86.
9. See Heilbroner (1985), ch. 3.
10. Sweezy (1956), 80.
11. Keynes (1937), 213–14; emphasis in original.
12. For present-day "dirty tricks," see "Business Sharpens its Spying Techniques," *BW*, August 4, 1975. Applying military strategy to marketing is another development, at

least in a formal educational setting, the Marketing War College in New York. Executives are taught "how to wage defensive, offensive, flanking, or guerilla warfare against the enemy in the battle for consumers' minds and pocketbooks." "The reason the war analogy is so useful," one of the college's directors stated, "is that business is now in a much more warlike mode." Ewart Rouse, "In the Trenches with Corporate America," *PI*, November 9, 1986.

13. Marshall (1920), 537.
14. Marx (1984), 586.
15. This is the classic definition of Robbins (1935), 16.
16. Hirsch (1978), 6–7.
17. Marx (1984), 586.
18. Polanyi (1944), 66.
19. As Schumpeter concluded in (1950), 84.
20. Perroux (1964), 106; my translation (RBD).
21. Marx (1984), 555 and (1967), 873.
22. Robinson (1962), 37.
23. Robinson (1962), 37–38.
24. Marx (1967), 245, 256.
25. Keynes (1936), 30–31, 249–50.

Chapter 2

1. Henretta (1973), 79.
2. Chandler (1977), 15, 18.
3. Warner (1968), 5–7, 13, 18.
4. Sherry (1976), 54.
5. On foreign trade during this period, see Douglass North, "The U.S. Balance of Payments, 1790–1860," in National Bureau of Economic Research (1960) and Niemi (1980), 39–42.
6. Chandler (1977), 57–60.
7. Ferguson (1979), 7.
8. Lebergott (1964), 510.
9. Robert Gallman in Davis, Easterlin, and Parker (1972), 27–29.
10. On the above, see Cochran (1974).
11. Cochran (1974), 1461–63; Albert Fishlow in Davis et al. (1972), 472–85; U.S. Bureau of the Census (1975), 805.
12. Chandler (1977), 15.
13. Fishlow in Davis et al. (1972), 485–88.
14. Cochran (1972), 76–80; Evans (1948), 12.
15. Lebergott (1964), 510.
16. Gallman in Davis et al. (1972), 21–29, 33–34.
17. U.S. Bureau of the Census (1931), 9.
18. Henretta (1973), 198, 200.
19. Chandler (1977), 48.
20. Chandler (1977), 109–20; Vatter (1975), 174–77.
21. See Chandler (1977), ch. 3.
22. Fishlow (1965), 115–18.
23. Fishlow (1965), 132–60; Fogel (1964), 111–46, 228–37. As Fogel notes, these percentages are not insignificant, but not large enough to suggest that the railroads alone sparked a "take-off" in the antebellum years, contrary to the thesis of Rostow (1960).
24. Fishlow (1965), 163–204, 230–36. The quotation is from Bruchey (1975), 51–52.
25. Fishlow in Davis et al. (1972), 508–13.

26. On this paragraph and the next two, see Du Boff (1980).

27. Porter (1973), 43.

28. On this and what follows, see Du Boff (1984b).

29. Lindstrom (1978), vii.

30. Niemi (1980), 51–53; also Fishlow (1965), 215, 263–66.

31. Fishlow (1964), 359–60 for this and the following figures.

32. Fishlow (1964), 363–64. In 1860 the South's export earnings percentage was highest of all, at 29, but in an export-dependent, plantation economy context, as should be evident in these pages.

33. Anderson and Gallman (1977).

34. Lindstrom (1978), 3–8, 72–76.

35. Engerman (1966), Table 1, reprinted in Fogel and Engerman (1971).

36. Niemi (1980), 104–05; Bruchey (1975), 53–54.

37. U.S. Bureau of the Census (1975), 209, 899.

38. The reference is to the debate over whether slavery "paid"; see Fogel and Engerman (1974), 67–94.

39. Goldin and Sokoloff (1982), 746.

40. Lance Davis and Robert Gallman, "Capital Formation in the United States during the Nineteenth Century," Table 1, in Mathias and Postan (1978).

41. Williamson and Lindert (1980), 67–75, 94–95.

42. Lebergott (1964), 161–62; Williamson (1974), 232–34.

43. Robert Gallman, "Trends in the Size Distribution of Wealth in the Nineteenth Century," in National Bureau of Economic Research (1969), 6.

44. Goodrich (1950).

45. On this and what follows, see Du Boff (1984a), 59–61.

46. Niemi (1980), 83–85.

47. Gallman in Davis et al. (1972), 33, 40; Gallman, "Gross National Product in the United States, 1834–1909," in National Bureau of Economic Research (1966), 4–7.

Chapter 3

1. The reference again is to Rostow (1960), none of whose "take-off" criteria withstood quantitative testing.

2. On this, see Engerman (1966), reprinted in Fogel and Engerman (1971); also Robert Gallman in Davis, Easterlin, and Parker (1972), 56–57.

3. Abramovitz and David (1973), 429, 437. The term Grand Traverse comes from Paul David, "Invention and Accumulation in America's Economic Growth," in Brunner and Meltzer (1977).

4. On the investment and national product figures in this paragraph, see Robert Gallman, "Gross National Product in the United States, 1834–1909," Table 3, in National Bureau of Economic Research (1966) and Lance Davis and Robert Gallman, "Capital Formation in the United States during the Nineteenth Century," Table 1, in Mathias and Postan (1978).

5. The supply curve of investible savings was moving rightward faster than the investment demand curve. On this and what follows, see Davis and Gallman in Mathias and Postan (1978), 22–54, 59–69 and Lance Davis, "Savings and Investment," in Porter (1980), 187–200. In Davis et al. (1972), 303 Davis states that "the aggregate supply of capital appears to have been affected primarily by savings considerations."

6. Gallman in National Bureau of Economic Research (1966), 14–15, 34.

7. See p. 15. By 1850 there were more than 900 commercial banks in the country.

8. Schumpeter (1934), ch. 3.

9. Williamson (1979), 234–38; David in Brunner and Meltzer (1977), 208–11.

10. David in Brunner and Meltzer (1977), 189, 196, 207; Williamson (1974), 142, 292.

11. Abramovitz and David (1973), 430, 434, 437.

12. Moulton (1935), 47.

13. Schumpeter (1934), 68–74, 95–115.

14. Abramovitz and David (1973), 437.

15. Williamson (1979), 246.

16. David in Brunner and Meltzer (1977), 207.

17. Albert Fishlow in Davis et al. (1972), 526; Vatter (1975), 158–59.

18. Robert Gallman and E. S. Howle, "Trends in the Structure of the American Economy since 1840," in Fogel and Engerman (1971), 32.

19. Creamer, Dobrovolsky, and Borenstein (1960), 22, 25.

20. Computed from Kuznets (1961), 198 and Ulmer (1960), 256.

21. Kuznets (1961), 327–41.

22. U.S. Bureau of the Census (1975), 627.

23. Baran and Sweezy (1966), 219–21. See also Foster (1986), 83–93 and Nell (1988), ch. 7.

24. David in Brunner and Meltzer (1977), 189; Williamson (1974), 140–43.

25. See D. Gordon, Edwards, and Reich (1982), 91–94, 112–21.

26. Williamson (1979), 233–34 and (1974), ch. 11.

27. See Table 2.1.

28. U.S. Bureau of the Census (1931), 9.

29. See Pred (1966), 19–24.

30. Abramovitz and David (1973), 430.

31. This is why income elasticities are the key microeconomic demand-side variable for analyzing growth. "Favorable" price elasticities have little to do with long-run growth; they are functions of community tastes or cultural modes that change with every new wave of consumer goods.

32. U.S. Bureau of the Census (1975), 693–94.

33. This section is based on Du Boff (1979), 57–64, 138–54, 225.

34. Marx (1984), 354.

35. Ross Robertson, "Changing Production of Metalworking Machinery, 1860–1920," in National Bureau of Economic Research (1966), 484–90.

36. See Rosenberg (1972), 97–102.

37. Davis and North (1971), 167–71 and Chandler (1977), 244–83.

38. For one account, see Passer (1953).

39. Du Boff (1979), 96–103.

40. Robert Gallman, "Commodity Output, 1839–1899," in National Bureau of Economic Research (1960), 43; U.S. Bureau of the Census (1975), 654, 667.

41. See Lebergott (1964), 510.

42. Niemi (1980), 85; Lamoreaux (1985), 29; Du Boff (1979), 40, 218.

43. J.W. Markham, "Survey of the Evidence and Findings on Mergers," in National Bureau of Economic Research (1955), 156.

44. U.S. Bureau of the Census (1975), 200–01, 208–09.

45. For the dating of business cycles since 1854, see U.S. Bureau of the Census (1985), 531 or (1987), 511, or Sherman and Evans (1984), 26.

46. Foster and Szlajfer (1984), 65.

Chapter 4

1. For summaries, see Vatter (1975), 169–74; Cochran and Miller (1961), 135–53, 188–202; Scherer (1980), 118–22; Lamoreaux (1985), 1–5.

2. Computed from Chandler (1965), 16.

3. Burgess and Kennedy (1949), 298, 313, 375, 801–02.

4. U.S. Bureau of the Census (1895), 28–29, 130–37 and (1975), 804–05, 1102.

5. Chandler (1977), 204.

6. Chandler (1977), 79.

7. Kolko (1965), 4.

8. Cochran (1977b), 477–79.

9. Chandler (1977), 148–59.

10. Quoted by Kolko (1965), 39.

11. Danielian (1939), 3–4, 15.

12. See Chandler (1977), 287–99.

13. U.S. Bureau of the Census (1975), 164–65; Lebergott (1964), 178–79.

14. Crocker (1887), 362–63. A year earlier U.S. Labor Commissioner Carroll Wright made the same point about "machinery and overproduction," in U.S. Department of the Interior (1886), 80–90. See also Eichner (1969), 10–15.

15. See Chandler (1977), 350–53, 418–26.

16. Thorelli (1955), 294–303.

17. Quoted in Passer (1953), 326.

18. See Mattes (1969) and Noble (1977), 92–93. In 1961 the two electrical giants, along with Allis-Chalmers, Ingersoll-Rand, and 25 other producers, were prosecuted in the biggest price-fixing conspiracy in U.S. history, with seven company executives given prison sentences.

19. Chandler (1977), 299.

20. This section draws heavily on Du Boff and Herman (1980).

21. Chandler (1977), 79, 89, 489.

22. See James (1983).

23. Edwards (1979), 217–18 and James (1983), 450. See also Eichner (1969), 102–19.

24. Chandler (1977), 364–65; emphasis added.

25. Chandler (1977), 224–33.

26. Bridge (1903), 135.

27. Chandler (1977), 322.

28. Chandler (1977), 419–24.

29. Cochran (1977a), 68.

30. U.S. Congress (1940), Monograph no. 21, 68. The author, Clair Wilcox, describes American Tobacco Company's similar tactics as amounting to "relentless war on its competitors" (66).

31. Taussig (1964), 136.

32. See David (1970).

33. Bils (1984), 1045.

34. David (1970), 599–600.

35. See Noble (1977).

36. Noble (1977), 98.

37. Chandler (1977), 375.

38. Noble (1977), ch. 6. Chandler's own account, in (1977), 374–75 does not seem inconsistent with this statement.

39. Noble (1977), 19.

40. Nelson (1959), 37.

41. Thorelli (1955), 294–303.

42. Nelson (1959), 53.

43. Nelson (1959), 100–03.

44. Cochran (1977a), 67. See also Lamoreaux (1985), 144–52.

45. See Navin and Sears (1955), 116–21.

46. See Lamoreaux (1985), 50–86, 187–89.
47. Chandler (1977), 333.
48. Navin and Sears (1955), 129–30.
49. U.S. Industrial Commission (1900), 1033.
50. Nelson (1959), 94, 99.
51. Navin and Sears (1955), 135–36.
52. Porter (1973), 32–33.
53. Herman (1981), 65–68, 114–21, 324–25.
54. Keller (1963), 158–63.
55. See U.S. Congress (1913).
56. The legislation referred to takes in the Federal Reserve Act of 1913, Clayton Act of 1914, Glass-Steagall (Banking) Act of 1933, Securities and Exchange Act of 1934, and Banking Act of 1935. In all, they placed formal control of the money supply in a central bank, banned interlocking directorates, separated investment banking (underwriting and promoting) from commercial banking so that no single bank could do both, and regulated securities markets.
57. Chandler (1977), 187.
58. Veblen (1904), 54.
59. Porter and Livesay (1970), 378–79.
60. Quoted in Klemm (1959), 354.

Chapter 5

1. U.S. Bureau of the Census (1987), 411 and U.S. Department of Commerce (1986), 57–59. Proprietorships, partnerships, nonprofit institutions, and government account for most of the rest.
2. Pitelis (1987), ch. 5. Private sector income consists of household consumption and saving plus corporate profits (retained earnings and dividends). Corporate profits have also grown substantially relative to total private sector income.
3. Hall (1986), 285–87. See also Nell (1988), ch. 5 and 190–97 on "demand-determined production."
4. The share of investment accounted for by the top 100 or 200 firms must be about the same as shares of total assets in Table 9.1.
5. See Kalecki (1965), ch. 1 and Sawyer (1985), ch. 2. The most comprehensive treatment is Eichner (1976), ch. 3, on the "corporate levy."
6. On the "financial instability" hypothesis, see Minsky (1982); also Wolfson (1986), chs. 1–3.
7. See Rosenberg (1969), 12–17.
8. See Cain and Peterson (1986) and Thurow (1968).
9. Paul Uselding, "An Early Chapter in the Evolution of American Industrial Management," in Cain and Uselding (1973), 73–80.
10. Foster (1986), 245.
11. See Robert Pollin, "Structural Change and Increasing Fragility in the U.S. Financial System," in Cherry et al. (1987), 151–56.
12. Keynes (1936), 161–63.
13. Kalecki (1965), chs. 3–5. On this topic, see also Foster and Szlajfer (1984).
14. On the Harrod-Domar model, see Sherman and Evans (1984), 238–40 or other macroeconomic textbooks.
15. Keynes (1936), ch. 12.
16. U.S. Bureau of the Census (1975), 135.
17. Kuznets (1961), 576–77.
18. Ulmer (1960), 256.

19. U.S. Industrial Commission (1900), 340. In window glass, production exceeded domestic demand for ten years, with capacity growth so rapid that workers were employed six or eight months a year: (1901), 896, 925–27. Other testimony on high ratios of underutilized capacity included sugar, whiskey, and tin plate: (1900), 109–10, 125–26, 169–70, 925–26.

20. Kendrick (1961), 293–94.

21. U.S. Bureau of the Census (1975), 224; Kendrick (1961), 294.

22. Du Boff (1977), 13, 23.

23. On this period, see Baran and Sweezy (1966), 226–34.

24. Mills (1932), 121–22, 133. These conclusions seem confirmed by Vatter (1975), 300, 303 and U.S. Bureau of the Census (1975), 164–66.

25. Kendrick (1961), 294.

26. Kendrick (1961), 294; Kuznets (1961), 577–78, 596–97.

27. U.S. Bureau of the Census (1975), 224, 884, 887. See also Soule (1947), 7–8.

28. See Baran and Sweezy (1966), 88–92.

29. U.S. Bureau of the Census (1975), 8; investment figures from Table 3.1.

30. Chandler (1977), 337–44; Edwards (1979), 218–19. Chandler's data show that of the 152 mergers large enough to affect the market structures of the industries in which they operated, 41 percent failed. Of the others, Chandler states that they were "rarely" profitable unless they "used the resources under [their] control more efficiently than had the constituent companies before they joined the merger." The statement conflicts with Edwards's chi-square test indicating that market power increased the chances of success by half, as well as with evidence cited in this chapter and in pp. 51–52.

31. Porter (1973), 79.

32. Joe Bain, "Industrial Concentration and Anti-Trust Policy," in Williamson (1951), 627–28.

33. Edwards (1975), 450.

34. Chandler (1977), 401.

35. Edwards (1975), 429. See also Herman (1981), 68–70 and Scherer (1980), 54–56.

36. Edwards (1975), 442–45.

37. Porter (1973), 23.

38. Cochran (1972), 230–37.

39. Nelson (1959), 121.

40. Address in Cleveland, June 26, 1934, quoted in Edwards (1940), 167. On the nonenforcement of the Sherman and Clayton Acts by both the Justice Department and the Federal Trade Commission in the 1920s, see Eis (1969), 288–90.

41. Thorp (1931), 86.

42. Eddy (1937), 79, 84.

43. U.S. Congress (1945), 84.

44. Jesse Markham, "Survey of the Evidence and Findings on Mergers," in National Bureau of Economic Research (1955), 168.

45. Chandler (1977), 233–35 and Markham in National Bureau of Economic Research (1955), 168–69.

46. Quoted in *Fortune*, July 1962, 251.

47. See Eis (1969) and Chandler (1977), 464–76.

48. Niemi (1980), 336 and Blair (1972), 266.

49. R. A. Gordon (1974), 23–27.

50. Kendrick (1961), 294, 299.

51. U.S. Bureau of the Census (1975), 224; Kendrick (1961), 294; Board of Governors of the Federal Reserve System (1986), 171.

52. R. A. Gordon (1974), 24–25.

53. Computed from Ulmer (1960), 33, 256–57, 320–21, 374–75, 405–06.

54. Its total was $1.22 billion of gross investment of $16.62 billion (Table 3.1), less public nonmilitary outlays of $2.66 billion.

55. Du Boff (1979), 48.

56. U.S. Bureau of the Census (1975), 238, 240, and Kuznets (1961), 198.

57. Quoted in Du Boff (1979), 95.

58. Du Boff (1979), 57–71.

59. Du Boff (1979), 61–63.

60. President's Conference on Unemployment (1929), 322, 324.

61. President's Conference (1929), 58, 324–26; U.S. Bureau of the Census (1975), 401.

62. Calculated from Kendrick (1961), 475.

63. Calculated from U.S. Bureau of the Census (1933), vol. I, 21–35 and vol. II, 1122–33.

64. See Leontief (1951), rear fold-outs.

65. These and motor vehicle statistics subsequently cited are from U.S. Bureau of the Census (1975), 716.

66. U.S. Bureau of the Census (1933), vol. I, 21–35 and vol. II, 1220–23, 1228.

67. Rae (1971), 45–58.

68. Motor vehicle production alone employed 495,000 in 1929, to which a multiplier of 7.5 is applied. This is similar to the procedure used by Rae (1971), 48 adjusted downward to reflect a 52 percent lower motor vehicle per person ratio in 1929.

69. Metzer (1985), 122 puts the figure at 51.9 percent.

70. U.S. Bureau of the Census (1975), 1120, 1128.

71. See Noble (1977), ch. 10.

72. All productivity figures are from Kendrick (1961), 60–71, 147–53, 396, 424. For an earlier similar finding, see Mills (1932), 289–314.

73. Creamer et al. (1960), 25, 38–43.

74. President's Conference (1929), 139.

75. President's Conference (1929), 321–22, 531.

76. U.S. Bureau of the Census (1975), 623, 640; R.A. Gordon (1974), 43–44.

77. Foster and Szlajfer (1984), 205.

78. Nourse et al. (1934), 296–309, 340–58, 415–25.

79. U.S. Bureau of the Census (1975), 137; figures are based on annual averages for 1919–20 and 1928–29.

80. President's Conference (1929), xvi-xvii.

81. U.S. Bureau of the Census (1975), 164, and Lebergott (1964), 163, 523, 528. Soule (1947), 221 cites similar figures from different sources.

82. U.S. Bureau of the Census (1975), 236, 238 and Kravis (1959), 919, 933.

83. Calculated from Holt (1977), 283.

84. See Lindert and Williamson (1976), 89–90; also U.S. Bureau of the Census (1975), 302.

85. Leven et al. (1934), 93–94.

86. These and the following statistics are calculated from U.S. Bureau of the Census (1975), 224, 1117, 1120–21.

87. U.S. Bureau of the Census (1975), 1111, 1118–19. The fiscal policy of the 1920s constituted "one of the most prolonged and successful assaults on the taxation of wealth and privilege in the history of the United States." Its architect, Secretary of the Treasury Andrew Mellon, "clearly stated what has come to be called supply-side economics in the 1980s." See Campagna (1987), 54–60, 587–88.

88. Leven et al. (1934), 55–56.

89. Nystrom (1929), 278–85.

90. Soule (1947), 140.

91. Blair (1972), 419–37; Sherman (1987), 168–70.
92. Dowd (1977), 101.
93. President's Conference (1929), 61, 390–98.
94. U.S. Bureau of the Census (1975), 224, 989, 1009 on these and the data that follow.
95. Devine (1983), 16–20.
96. U.S. Bureau of the Census (1975), 224 and Kendrick (1961), 294.
97. Devine (1983), 14–16; U.S. Congress (1940), Monograph no. 12, 9–11, 22–28; Mills (1932), 482–88. R. A. Gordon (1974), 44 observes that the downturn of 1929 "was clearly not due to an encroachment of costs on profits."
98. R.A. Gordon (1974), 71.
99. This and what follows are based on R. A. Gordon (1974), 40–45, Board of Governors of the Federal Reserve (1986), and other sources.
100. Galbraith (1955), 191.
101. See Hunter (1982).
102. See Temin (1976), 63–83, 170–73 and Mishkin (1978).
103. Calculated from U.S. Department of Commerce (1986), 6; U.S. President (1988), 250, 279; Board of Governors of the Federal Reserve (1986), 171; R.A. Gordon (1974), 47.
104. U.S. Department of Commerce (1986), 1, 135.

Chapter 6

1. The following draws heavily on R.A. Gordon (1974), 90–101.
2. See Schultze (1986), 59–79. As Schultze notes, the greater stability of the economy since World War II has been termed a statistical aberration, a view he rejects. See the debate in *Journal of Economic History* 46 (June 1986), 341–71, 494–96, 507–09.
3. U.S. President (1988), 279. For earlier product per capita statistics, which run close to disposable income, see U.S. Bureau of the Census (1975), 224; the largest earlier quarter-century increases appear to have been 60 to 65 percent.
4. Alan Blinder, "The Level and Distribution of Economic Well-Being," in Feldstein (1980), 433.
5. R. A. Gordon (1974), 97.
6. U.S. Bureau of the Census (1975), 132.
7. Vatter (1963), 46.
8. R. A. Gordon (1974), 102.
9. Arthur Okun, "Postwar Macroeconomic Performance," in Feldstein (1980), 162–69.
10. See J. B. DeLong and L. H. Summers, "The Changing Cyclical Variability of Economic Activity in the United States," in R. J. Gordon (1986), and the comment by Robert Eisner, 719–27; also Hunter (1982), 884, 898–900.
11. See Steindl (1979), 5–10; also Foster and Szlajfer (1984), 167–69 and 189–92, by Steindl.
12. See Eilbott (1966); Lewis (1962), 15–16, 29–31; R.J. Gordon, "Postwar Macroeconomics," in Feldstein (1980), 158.
13. Vatter (1963), 6–7.
14. Quoted in Robert Borosage, "The Making of the National Security State," in Rodberg and Shearer (1970), 31.
15. See Baran and Sweezy (1966), 212–13 and Mosley (1985), ch. 1.
16. Mosley (1985), 9.
17. On NSC–68, see Block (1980).
18. See Stone (1952) and Kolko (1972), ch. 21.

19. See R. A. Gordon (1974), ch. 5 on the cycles of the 1950s. All data cited are from U.S. Department of Commerce (1986).

20. Vatter (1963), 73, 98.

21. U.S. President (1988), 250.

22. Hickman (1965), 8–11, 132–38, 182–89.

23. Mosley (1985), 14.

24. Galbraith (1967), 228–30.

25. Samuelson (1967), 769.

26. Shiskin (1970), 107.

27. See R. A. Gordon (1974), 157–61 and Wolfson (1986), ch. 4.

28. U.S. Department of Commerce (1986), 7, 10.

29. Bernstein (1983), 24.

30. I have expropriated this phrase from Professor David Felix, Washington University.

31. Vatter (1963), 23; *SCB*, February 1985, 26.

32. Rae (1971), 48.

33. Polenberg (1980), 128–29.

34. See St. Clair (1986), ch. 6, and Rae (1971), 187–94; also Du Boff and Herman (1980), 106–09 and references therein.

35. St. Clair (1986), 16–17, 56–80.

36. Lee Mertz, quoted in Dane Smith, "How the Interstates Reshaped Life in the U.S.," *PI*, December 16, 1985. The quotation and data that follow are from this source.

37. Vatter (1963), 12, 163–71; C.E. Nathanson, "The Militarization of the American Economy," in Horowitz (1969).

38. See Judith Reppy, "The United States," in Ball and Leitenberg (1983), 34; also Mosley (1985), 77 who adds that one-third of all full-time research scientists were employed in military and space R&D.

39. Vatter (1963), 166–71; Nathanson, "Militarization of the American Economy," in Horowitz (1969); *SCB*, February 1985, 26.

40. For the Grand Traverse, see p. 29. By 1926 the investment share of GNP exceeded 16 percent, compared to 11 or 12 percent a decade earlier; Kendrick (1961), 294–95. These figures are in 1929 dollars; they are not directly comparable with the proportions cited for the post–1947 period in 1982 dollars.

41. U.S. President (1988), 250. The current dollar figures run slightly lower, with a nearly identical range, 14.0 to 16.8 percent.

42. U.S. President (1988), 250.

43. U.S. President (1988), 336.

44. U.S. President (1988), 279, 336; "Why Consumers are Hitting the Brakes," *BW*, April 28, 1986.

45. U.S. President (1988), 334, 336.

46. Benjamin Friedman, "Increasing Indebtedness and Financial Stability in the United States," in Federal Reserve Bank of Kansas City (1986), 35, 38.

47. See Bowles and Gintis (1976) and Spring (1972).

48. The best summary of these issues is Schwarz (1983). For the poverty rate, see U.S. President (1988), 282.

49. All figures in this paragraph computed from U.S. Federal Trade Commission (1980), 112, 119, 121.

50. Nelson (1959), 4.

51. U.S. Federal Trade Commission (1969), 174, 191–93.

52. See Blair (1972), ch. 12 and Scherer (1980), 128–41.

53. See Du Boff and Herman (1989).

54. Magdoff and Sweezy (1969), 13.

55. Ravenscraft and Scherer (1987), 23–24.

56. Ravenscraft and Scherer (1987), 38–45, 207–10, 217.

57. Mueller (1985).

58. J. J. Abele, "Merger Inquiry Expanded by U.S.," *NYT*, March 7, 1969; Eileen Shanahan, "Antitrust Chief to Combat Reciprocal Business Deals," *NYT*, March 19, 1969.

59. J.J. Abele, "Celler Says Business Urged Merger Investigations," *NYT*, June 13, 1969.

60. Quoted in Magdoff and Sweezy (1969), 19.

61. M. Gordon (1985), 9–11.

62. Henley (1987), 324–28.

63. Henle (1972), 23–25.

64. M. Gordon (1982) and (1985), 7.

65. Veblen (1904), 29, 168, 173.

66. U.S. President (1988), 250, 279.

67. See Du Boff (1977), 11.

68. See Bowles and Edwards (1985), 109, 329, 347; Bowles, Gordon, and Weisskopf (1986), 134–36; Thomas Michl, "An Anatomy of the Reagan Recovery," in Cherry et al. (1987), 260–61.

69. U.S. President (1988), 248–49, 364. The foreign trade ratio here is measured by an average of exports and imports of all goods and services divided by GNP.

Chapter 7

1. See Cypher (1987) and Magaziner and Reich (1982), ch. 18. An integrated circuits program for weapons systems was sold to Congress in the 1970s on the grounds that it would generate commercial spillovers; see W. R. Neikirk, "Military Focus Diverts U.S. Technology," *CT*, December 29, 1987.

2. Computed from *SCB*, September 1987, 21.

3. Data from *SCB*, September 1987, 58–59.

4. See Benjamin Friedman, "Increasing Indebtedness and Financial Stability in the United States," in Federal Reserve Bank of Kansas City (1986), 35; also Magdoff and Sweezy (1987), 16.

5. Friedman in Federal Reserve Bank of Kansas City (1986), 28–33, 49–51; Magdoff and Sweezy (1987), 12–17.

6. *FRB*, January 1988, 1.

7. U.S. President (1988), 325; Robert Pollin, "Structural Change and Increasing Fragility in the U.S. Financial System," in Cherry et al. (1987), 146–47.

8. Calculated from U.S. President (1988), 248–49.

9. Tim Weiner, "Energy Department Leads Nuclear Arms Buildup," *PI*, June 28, 1987 and Michael Gordon, "Most Energy Funds for Military Uses," *NYT*, January 13, 1987.

10. Cypher (1981), 18–19.

11. See Melman (1983).

12. Mosley (1985), 80–84, 137–42; also Markusen (1986).

13. John Finney, "Military Budget Spurs Economy," *NYT*, February 27, 1974.

14. "The Impact of Cuts in Defense Spending," *BW*, January 19, 1976. Military spending, stated Nobel Laureate Lawrence Klein, "has been a large part of the whole expansion of the American economy since World War II."

15. Frank Greve, "Military Cuts Hard to Find in '84 Budget," *PI*, January 10, 1983.

16. "Why Star Wars is a Shot in the Arm for Corporate R&D," *BW*, April 8, 1985 and Huntly Collins, "SDI Work a Bonanza for Colleges," *PI*, April 8, 1987.

17. "Industry Outlook—Aerospace/Defense," *Prudential-Bache Research*, December 8, 1982.

18. "Senator Blames Congress for High Cost of Military," *NYT*, January 11, 1985.

19. On this and what follows, see Du Boff (1972b).

20. U.S. Department of Commerce (1984), xiv, 218–23.

21. See Jeff Gerth, "U.S. Weapons Makers Ring Up Healthy Profits," *NYT*, April 9, 1985; also Mark Thompson, "Report: Big Profit in Defense," *PI*, December 24, 1986, citing a General Accounting Office survey.

22. Wayne Biddle, "45 of 100 Biggest Contractors Being Investigated," *NYT*, April 25, 1985.

23. Mark Thompson, "Major Changes in Arms-Buying Recommended," *PI*, March 1, 1986; also "A Blue Ribbon Assault on the Pentagon," *BW*, March 10, 1986.

24. See "The Defense Scandal," *BW*, July 4, 1988. Senator Grassley was quoted in *IHT*, June 18–19, 1988.

25. Judith Reppy, "The United States," in Ball and Leitenberg (1983), 27.

26. From data compiled by Nuclear Free America, Baltimore and in *Fortune*, April 25, 1988, D11–30.

27. R.D. Hershey Jr., "U.S. Study Finds Nearly 3 of 10 Get Benefits," *NYT*, September 27, 1984.

28. U.S. President (1988), 342.

29. U.S. President (1988), 305; also *FRB*, July 1983, 515–18.

30. For example, Choate and Walter (1981) and "The Decay that Threatens Economic Growth," *BW*, October 26, 1981. See also Martin Tolchin, "Large Infusion of Funds Urged for Public Works," *NYT*, February 25, 1988, on a study by the National Council on Public Works Improvement.

31. Aschauer (1987).

32. U.S. President (1988), 250.

33. See Hartman (1983), 30–53, 99–150.

34. Robert Pear, "Millions Bypassed as Economy Soars," *NYT*, March 16, 1986 and Michel McQueen, "Even with Good Pay, Many Americans are Unable to Buy a Home," *WSJ*, February 5, 1988.

35. U.S. President (1988), 296–97.

36. Calculated from *EE*, January 1988, 13, 167, 196 and earlier January issues of *EE*.

37. Levitan and Conway (1988), 11.

38. See Krashevski (1986); also Summers (1986).

39. U.S. President (1988), 293; also U.S. Bureau of the Census (1987), 383.

40. See Du Boff (1977) on the issues and calculations involved here. Post-1976 figures are from *EE*, January 1988, 13, 199 and earlier January issues of *EE*.

41. U.S. Bureau of the Census (1987), 381.

42. "Market power in many industries opens up . . . vulnerability of total output to many other types of shocks, including shifts in the terms of trade, spontaneous shifts in consumption and investment, and changes in government policy." Hall (1986), 322.

43. See the sources cited Chapter 6, note 68; also U.S. President (1988), 353.

44. Jorgenson (1988) and Bruno and Sachs (1985), 162–69, 176–77.

45. See Wolff (1986) and Henley (1987), 321–23, 327–28; also U.S. President (1988), 274–75, 349.

46. See Baily and Chakrabarti (1988) and Boretsky (1980).

47. Quinn, Baruch, and Paquette (1987); Reubens (1981).

48. Baily and Chakrabarti (1988), ch. 5. See also Keith Schneider, "Services Hurt by Technology," *NYT*, June 29, 1987.

49. See Bowles and Edwards (1985), 94–97, 331–63; also D. Gordon, Edwards, and Reich (1982), 22–26, 165–70.

50. Thurow (1980), 177.

51. See McQuaid (1982), ch. 9 and Herman (1981), 172–86.

52. Quoted in *WSJ*, April 25, 1975. See also Gerald Epstein, "Domestic Stagflation and Monetary Policy," in Ferguson and Rogers (1981).

53. Herbert Stein, former chairman of the Nixon Council of Economic Advisers, took this position, in *WSJ*, September 14, 1977.

54. On the business counteroffensive, see Saloma (1984), chs. 2–4, 6; Ackerman (1984), ch. 9; Edsall (1984), 72–78, 107–40; Ferguson and Rogers (1986), ch. 3; "A Winning Streak for Business," *BW*, February 27, 1978.

55. See Foglesong (1983).

56. See Sanders (1983) and Ackerman (1984), ch. 5; also Holzman (1984).

57. Edwin Dale Jr., "Unemployment: Legacy of the Recession," *NYT*, April 11, 1976.

58. "A Recession as 'Good News,'" *NYT*, May 23, 1979. Years earlier *BW* editorialized (May 17, 1952) that "there's no assurance against inflation like a pool of genuine unemployment. That is a blunt, hard-headed statement, but a fact."

59. See Sherman and Evans (1984), ch. 11; also Sherman (1987), ch. 6.

60. "Political Aspects of Full Employment," reprinted in Kalecki (1972). See also Sawyer (1985), ch. 7.

61. Minsky (1986), 13–33; also Minsky (1982), 44–57.

62. U.S. Bureau of the Census (1987), 402 and earlier editions; also Davis (1986), 127–53.

63. Louis Uchitelle, "Jobless Insurance System Aids Reduced Number of Workers," *NYT*, July 26, 1988.

64. U.S. President (1988), 299.

65. Sheldon Danziger and P. Gottschalk, "Target Support at Children and Families," *NYT*, March 22, 1987 and U.S. Congress (1987), 37–39.

66. See Chris Tilly, "Regenerating Inequality," in Cherry et al. (1988).

67. President Ronald Reagan, message to Congress, February 5, 1985.

68. U.S. President (1988), 314–15, 321.

69. Nariman Behravesh, quoted in "Pentagon Spending is the Economy's Biggest Gun," *BW*, October 21, 1985.

70. Ferguson and Rogers (1986), 130–37 and Ackerman (1984), ch. 4.

71. "Is Deregulation Working?" *BW*, December 22, 1986. On deregulation, see also Campagna (1987), 468–70, 525–28.

72. Matt Spetalnick, "Big Airlines Squeeze Out the Small," *PI*, January 5, 1985; Scott Kilman, "An Unexpected Result of Airline Decontrol is Return to Monopolies," *WSJ*, July 20, 1987; Agis Salpukas, "Air Fare Increases Worry Regulators," *NYT*, September 9, 1987; "The Frenzied Skies," *BW*, December 19, 1988.

73. See, for example, U.S. Bureau of the Census (1987), 504.

74. M. Gordon (1985), 11.

75. Quoted in *NYT*, December 24, 1985.

76. Steve Lohr, "Britons' Buying Spree in U.S.," *NYT*, August 10, 1987.

77. "Getting Top Dollar for Beatrice's Leftovers," *BW*, July 6, 1987; Bryan Burrough and R. Johnson, "Beatrice, Once Hailed Deal of the Century, Proves Disappointing," *WSJ*, November 21, 1988.

78. See Greer (1981) and "When You Say Busch, You've Said It All," *BW*, February 17, 1986. For a similar story in coffee, see Stan Luxenberg, "Folger's Scores in the Coffee Wars," *NYT*, January 28, 1979.

79. Isadore Barmash, "The Merger Spree in Retailing," *NYT*, May 20, 1984.

80. R. A. Bennett, "Chemical is Buying a Big Texas Bank," *NYT*, December 16, 1986; also Federal Reserve Board data.

81. Peter Kilborn, "Corporate Giants Invade the Residential Market," *NYT*, February 4, 1979.

82. Figures from *Financial World*, July 14, 1987, cited in "Big Pay Raises Reported for Wall Street's Top 10," *PI*, June 10, 1987. See also Alison Cowan, "Investment Bankers' Lofty Fees," *NYT*, December 26, 1988. Leveraged buyouts added another layer of profiteering, culminating in the bidding in 1988 to take RJR Nabisco private. See Chris Welles, "The RJR Greedfest Won't Stop LBO Mania for Long," *BW*, December 5, 1988 and James Sterngold, "Managers' Huge Stake in a Private Nabisco," *NYT*, November 14, 1988; also Sarah Bartlett, "RJR: $25 Billion Question," *NYT*, December 2, 1988.

83. On these issues, see Du Boff and Herman (1989).

84. "Deal Mania," *BW*, November 24, 1986. On the objective conditions, see also Magdoff and Sweezy (1987), 93–105, 141–50.

85. See the evidence cited in Du Boff and Herman (1989).

86. Porter (1987). See also "Do Mergers Really Work?" *BW*, June 3, 1985.

87. Magdoff and Sweezy (1988), 4.

88. Walker and Vatter (1986), 525–26.

89. Ferleger and Mandle (1988), 105. The United States is still more "Keynesian" than Western Europe in that aggregate demand fluctuations are the major force behind fluctuations in GNP, investment, and profits, according to Bruno and Sachs (1985), 274.

90. U.S. President (1988), 250. In the 1980s real fixed business investment grew about 2.3 percent per year, compared to the post–1972 trend of 2.8 percent (Table 7.2).

91. This thesis is persuasively stated by Wolff (1987).

92. Walker and Vatter (1986), 520.

Chapter 8

1. Williams (1953), 24.

2. On this and what follows, see Niemi (1980), 53–55 and 70–73 and Douglass North, "The United States Balance of Payments, 1790–1860," in National Bureau of Economic Research (1960).

3. Kravis (1972), 392, 399–400.

4. On this, see Magdoff (1969) and Du Boff and Herman (1972).

5. Robert Lipsey in Davis, Easterlin, and Parker (1972), 557–58.

6. Lipsey in Davis et al. (1972), 568, 572–77.

7. LaFeber (1963), 195.

8. U.S. Bureau of the Census (1975) 869; Lewis (1938), 450.

9. Wilkins (1970), ch. 3.

10. See LaFeber (1963), 81–83, 370–79. See also p. 71.

11. Wilkins (1970), 110; Lewis (1938), 445, 605.

12. Jenks (1927), 334.

13. Feis (1930), 26–29, 57–59, 78–80.

14. Lewis (1938), 605–06.

15. U.S. Bureau of the Census (1975), 903–04.

16. Computed from U.S. Bureau of the Census (1975), 255–57 and Lewis (1938), 450.

17. Wilkins (1970), 207.

18. See Kuznets (1966), 311–14 on this and other data cited in this paragraph.

19. Most of these ideas originated with Stephen Hymer. The best collection of his works is Hymer (1979).

20. On this, see Moran (1973).

21. Kolko (1984), 2, 11.

22. Cochran (1977a), 174.

23. Cochran (1972), 226.

24. See the list of foreign interventions inserted by Senator Barry Goldwater in *Congressional Record* 117 (April 26, 1971), 11913–24.

25. See Kolko (1972), chs. 12–18 and LaFeber (1984), chs. 2–4.

26. Calculated from U.S. Bureau of the Census (1975), 891, 893. See also Bowles, Gordon, and Weisskopf (1986), 142–44 and Riddell (1988).

27. MacEwan (1981), 120–22.

28. See Wolff (1971).

29. William Branson, "Trends in U.S. International Trade and Investment since World War II," in Feldstein (1980), 185–96.

30. See Levitt (1970).

31. Data from *SCB*, June 1986, 28.

32. Calculated from *SCB*, June 1975, 26–27.

33. Source cited in note 29; also Lipsey and Kravis (1987), 151.

34. Cavanagh and Clairmonte (1982), 155 and (1988), 4–5.

35. The European apostle of this view was Servan-Schreiber (1967).

36. The classic statement on this is Hayes and Abernathy (1980).

37. New York Stock Exchange (1984), 18–22; C.H. Deutsch, "U.S. Industry's Unfinished Struggle," *NYT*, February 21, 1988; and other sources.

38. Lipsey and Kravis (1987), 154.

39. See Cowling and Sugden (1987), ch. 5.

40. Cited by Louis Uchitelle, "2 Hard-to-Quit Habits Sustain Trade Deficit," *NYT*, January 14, 1988.

41. New York Stock Exchange (1984), 12–14; Branson in Feldstein (1980), 197–99.

42. Calculated from U.S. President (1988), 366.

43. U.S. President (1988), 330.

44. See, for example, the data in U.S. President (1988), 371.

45. Thomas Michl, "An Anatomy of the Reagan Recovery," in Cherry et al. (1987), 264.

46. See Krugman and Baldwin (1987).

47. U.S. President (1988), 366.

48. Damon Darlin, "Most U.S. Firms Seek Extra Profits in Japan, at the Expense of Sales," *WSJ*, May 15, 1987.

49. Uchitelle, cited in note 40; also Steven Greenhouse, "Few Benefits Yet of Dollar's Drop," *NYT*, April 5, 1986.

50. U.S. President (1988), 358, 362; U.S. Bureau of the Census (1987), 714.

51. "U.S. Companies Ranked by Sales," *BW*, April 18, 1986, 290–96.

52. U.S. President (1988), 348; *SCB*, August 1988, 69.

53. *SCB*, April 1986, S16–S17; R.A. Bennett, "Asia Trade Seen Affecting U.S.," *NYT*, September 5, 1983. See also D. Gordon (1988), 50–63 on determinants of investment flows in the 1980s.

54. See Du Boff (1972a).

55. Lawrence and Litan (1987), 61–62.

56. This is Kindleberger's theme (1973).

57. See Kindleberger (1973) and (1981).

Chapter 9

1. George Stocking, "Comment," in National Bureau of Economic Research (1955), 201–02.

2. Marx was first to analyze these trends, calling them "centralization" and "concentration" respectively, in (1984), 584–89.

3. Porter and Livesay (1969); also Scherer (1980), 69.

4. U.S. Bureau of the Census (1987), 507.

5. *FRB*, February 1987, 90.

6. U.S. Bureau of the Census (1987), 614; William Robbins, "Farm Experts See a Future of Fewer and Larger Tracts," *NYT*, February 17, 1985.

7. Computed from issues of the annual *Fortune* 500.

8. On foreign competition making the U.S. economy more competitive between 1958 and 1980, see Shepherd (1985), 73–75, 200–02; on the limits to the process, see Bowring (1986), 71–78.

9. See Shepherd (1985), 202–04, 330–41.

10. Herman (1981), 235–39 and Baran and Sweezy (1966), 67–72.

11. Galbraith (1967), chs. i-ix and (1973), chs. v, ix-xii.

12. Schumpeter (1950), chs. v-viii.

13. See Bullock (1901), 198–203; also Cochran and Miller (1961), 198–202.

14. Rae (1965), 115.

15. See Scherer (1980), 91–98 and Shepherd (1985), 179–95.

16. DeLamarter (1986). IBM is the most valuable company in terms of the market value of its common stock.

17. See Scherer (1980), 413–24, 433–37 and references therein.

18. "The Breakdown of U.S. Innovation," *BW*, February 16, 1976. Former GE vice-president T.K. Quinn stated in 1953 that he knew of "no original product invention . . . made by any of the giant laboratories or corporations . . . . The record of the giants is one of moving in, buying out and absorbing the smaller creators"; quoted in Baran and Sweezy (1966), 49.

19. See Scherer (1980), 92; Sherman (1987), 174–77; Shepherd (1985), 41–43, 66–67, 129–30.

20. Bowring (1986), ch. 6.

21. Guest (1986), 7.

22. Galbraith (1973), 271.

23. See Patton (1985); also "Executive Pay," *BW*, May 4, 1987 and "Top Executive Pay by Country," *PI*, December 29, 1986.

24. Robert Gallman in Davis, Easterlin, and Parker (1972), 33–35.

25. Gallman in Davis et al. (1972), 40–41 and U.S. Bureau of the Census (1975), 8, 224.

26. Gallman in Davis et al. (1972), 59.

27. Kuznets (1965), 313.

28. Kuznets (1966), 64–65.

29. This paragraph is based largely on Cochran (1975).

30. Cochran (1977a), 52–53.

31. Cochran (1975), 935.

32. Cochran (1975), 929.

33. See Richard Easterlin in Davis et al. (1972), 155–58.

34. Niemi (1980), 256–57; Kolko (1984), 69–71; Warren and Kraly (1985), 1–5.

35. See the sources cited in Table 7.4, as well as U.S. Bureau of the Census (1985), 452 and (1975), 292–93. Beginning in 1975, percentile income distribution data are not strictly comparable with those of earlier years, due to revised procedures.

36. Pechman (1985), 4–5.

37. U.S. Congress (1986), 20–24.

38. All data are from U.S. Congress (1986).

39. U.S. Congress (1986), 31–44.

40. Smith and Franklin (1974), 162–63.

41. See Maddison (1984), 57, 68–71 and Schott (1984), 32–34.

42. See U.S. Bureau of the Census (1987), 810; Magaziner and Reich (1982), 14–16; Schwarz (1983), 90–93.

43. McCraw (1984), 36.

44. Floyd, Gray, and Short (1984), 115–17 and McCraw (1984), 34–35.

45. On this, see Davis (1986).

46. McCraw (1984), 38.

47. See U.S. Bureau of the Census (1987), 805.

48. Gorham (1987). The 17 indicators are: infant mortality, perinatal mortality, female and male life expectancy, overall and youth unemployment, homicide rate, misery index, unemployed eligible for unemployment benefits, equality of income distribution, equality of male/female earnings, physicians per capita, per capita expenditure on medical care, hospital beds per capita, home ownership, living space per capita, average working hours.

49. What follows is drawn from Magaziner and Reich (1982), 13–22, 145–46; Schott (1984), 24–27; Niemi (1980), 399–401; Osberg (1984), 24–29; Maddison (1984); F.M. Hechinger, "Alarm over Alienation of the Young," *NYT*, March 25, 1986; G.M. Gaul, "Health Coverage is Eluding Many," *PI*, December 27, 1987; and other sources.

50. Heilbroner (1985), 128.

51. Richard Sennett, "Profiting from Crisis," *NYT*, January 19, 1978.

References

Abramovitz, Moses, and P. A. David. 1973. "Reinterpreting Economic Growth. Parables and Realities." *American Economic Review* 63 (May): 428–39.

Ackerman, Frank. 1984. *Hazardous to Our Wealth. Economic Policies in the 1980s.* Boston: South End Press.

Anderson, Ralph, and R. E. Gallman. 1977. "Slaves as Fixed Capital: Slave Labor and Southern Economic Development." *Journal of American History* 64 (June): 24–46.

Aschauer, David A. 1987. "Is the Public Capital Stock Too Low?" *Chicago Fed Letter* No. 2 (October): 1–3.

Baily, Martin Neil, and A. K. Chakrabarti. 1988. *Innovation and the Productivity Crisis.* Washington: The Brookings Institution.

Ball, Nicole, and M. Leitenberg, eds. 1983. *The Structure of the Defense Industry.* New York: St. Martin's Press.

Baran, Paul A., and P. M. Sweezy. 1966. *Monopoly Capital.* New York: Monthly Review Press.

Bernstein, Peter L. 1983. "Capital Stock and Management Decisions." *Journal of Post Keynesian Economics* 6 (Fall): 20–38.

Bils, Mark. 1984. "Tariff Protection and Production in the Early U.S. Cotton Textile Industry." *Journal of Economic History* 44 (December): 1033–45.

Blair, John M. 1972. *Economic Concentration.* New York: Harcourt Brace Jovanovich.

Block, Fred. 1980. "Economic Instability and Military Strength: Paradoxes of the 1950 Rearmament Decision." *Politics & Society* 10 (1): 35–58.

Board of Governors of the Federal Reserve System. 1986. *Industrial Production 1986 Edition.* Washington: Federal Reserve System.

Boretsky, Michael. 1980. "The Role of Innovation." *Challenge* 23 (November-December): 9–15.

Bowles, Samuel, and R. Edwards. 1985. *Understanding Capitalism.* New York: Harper & Row.

Bowles, Samuel, and H. Gintis. 1976. *Schooling in Capitalist America.* New York: Basic Books.

Bowles, Samuel, D. M. Gordon, and T. E. Weisskopf. 1986. "Power and Profits." *Review of Radical Political Economics* 18 (Spring-Summer): 132–67.

Bowring, Joseph. 1986. *Competition in a Dual Economy.* Princeton: Princeton University Press.

Braverman, Harry. 1974. *Labor and Monopoly Capital*. New York: Monthly Review Press.

Bridge, James Howard. 1903. *The Inside Story of the Carnegie Steel Company*. New York: Aldine Book Co.

Bruchey, Stuart. 1975. *Growth of the Modern American Economy*. New York: Dodd, Mead.

Brunner, Karl, and A. H. Meltzer, eds. 1977. *International Organization, National Policies and Economic Development*. Amsterdam: North-Holland.

Bruno, Michael, and J. D. Sachs. 1985. *Economics of Worldwide Stagflation*. Cambridge, Mass.: Harvard University Press.

Bullock, C. J. 1901. "Trust Literature: Survey and Criticism." *Quarterly Journal of Economics* 15 (February): 167–217.

Burgess, George H., and M. C. Kennedy. 1949. *Centennial History of the Pennsylvania Railroad Company 1846–1946*. Philadelphia: Pennsylvania Railroad.

Cain, Louis P., and D. G. Paterson. 1986. "Biased Technical Change, Scale, and Factor Substitution in American Industry, 1850–1919." *Journal of Economic History* 46 (March): 153–64.

Cain, Louis P., and P. Uselding, eds. 1973. *Business Enterprise and Economic Change*. Kent, Ohio: Kent State University Press.

Campagna, Anthony S. 1987. *U.S. National Economic Policy 1917–1985*. New York: Praeger.

Cavanagh, John, and F. Clairmonte. 1982. "The Transnational Economy." *Trade and Development* No. 4 (Winter): 149–82.

Cavanagh, John, and F. Clairmonte. 1988. "La puissance américaine au milieu de la bourrasque mondiale." *Le monde diplomatique* No. 406 (Janvier): 4–5.

Chandler, Alfred D., Jr., ed. 1965. *The Railroads. The Nation's First Big Business*. New York: Harcourt Brace World.

Chandler, Alfred D., Jr. 1977. *The Visible Hand. The Managerial Revolution in American Business*. Cambridge, Mass.: Harvard-Belknap.

Cherry, Robert D., et al. 1987. *The Imperiled Economy. Book I: Macroeconomics from a Left Perspective*. New York: Union for Radical Political Economics.

Cherry, Robert D., et al. 1988. *The Imperiled Economy. Book II: Through the Safety Net*. New York: Union for Radical Political Economics.

Choate, Pat, and S. Walter. 1981. *America in Ruins*. Washington: Council of State Planning Agencies.

Cochran, Thomas C. 1972. *Business in American Life*. New York: McGraw-Hill.

Cochran, Thomas C. 1974. "The Business Revolution." *American Historical Review* 79 (December): 1449–66.

Cochran, Thomas C. 1975. "The Paradox of American Economic Growth." *Journal of American History* 61 (March): 925–42.

Cochran, Thomas C. 1977a. *200 Years of American Business*. New York: Basic Books.

Cochran, Thomas C. 1977b. "The Sloan Report: American Culture and Business Management." *American Quarterly* 29 (Winter): 476–86.

Cochran, Thomas C., and W. Miller. 1961. *The Age of Enterprise*, rev. ed. New York: Harper & Row.

Cowling, Keith, and R. Sugden. 1987. *Transnational Monopoly Capitalism*. New York: St. Martin's Press.

Creamer, Daniel, S. P. Dobrovolsky, and I. Borenstein. 1960. *Capital in Manufacturing and Mining*. Princeton: Princeton University Press.

Crocker, Uriel H. 1887. "General Overproduction." *Quarterly Journal of Economics* 1 (April): 362–65.

Cypher, James M. 1981. "The Basic Economics of Rearming America." *Monthly Review* 33 (November): 11–27.

Cypher, James M. 1987. "Military Spending, Technical Change, and Economic Growth." *Journal of Economic Issues* 21 (March): 33–59.

Danielian, N. R. 1939. *AT&T. The Story of Industrial Conquest*. New York: Vanguard Press.

David, Paul A. 1970. "Learning by Doing and Tariff Protection." *Journal of Economic History* 30 (September): 521–601.

Davis, Lance, and D. C. North. 1971. *Institutional Change and American Economic Growth*. New York: Cambridge University Press.

Davis, Lance, Richard Easterlin, and W. N. Parker. 1972. *American Economic Growth*. New York: Harper & Row.

Davis, Mike. 1986. *Prisoners of the American Dream*. New York: Schocken.

DeLamarter, Richard T. 1986. *Big Blue: IBM's Use and Abuse of Power*. New York: Dodd, Mead.

Devine, James N. 1983. "Underconsumption, Over-Investment, and the Origins of the Great Depression." *Review of Radical Political Economics* 15 (Summer): 1–28.

Dowd, Douglas F. 1977. *The Twisted Dream. Capitalist Development in the U.S. since 1776*, second ed. Cambridge, Mass.: Winthrop.

Du Boff, R. B. 1972a. "Dollar Devaluation and Foreign Trade." *Monthly Review* 23 (March): 9–24.

Du Boff, R. B. 1972b. "Converting Military Spending to Social Welfare." *Quarterly Review of Economics and Business* 12 (Spring): 7–22.

Du Boff, R. B. 1977. "Unemployment in the United States: A Historical Summary." *Monthly Review* 29 (November): 10–24.

Du Boff, R. B. 1979. *Electric Power in American Manufacturing, 1889–1954*. New York: Arno Press.

Du Boff, R. B. 1980. "Business Demand and the Development of the Telegraph in the United States, 1844–1860." *Business History Review* 54 (Winter): 459–79.

Du Boff, R. B. 1984a. "The Rise of Communications Regulation: the Telegraph Industry, 1844–1880." *Journal of Communication* 34 (Summer): 52–66.

Du Boff, R. B. 1984b. "The Telegraph in Nineteenth-Century America: Technology and Monopoly." *Comparative Studies in Society and History* 26 (October): 571–86.

Du Boff, R. B., and E. S. Herman. 1972. "Corporate Dollars and Foreign Policy." *Commonweal* 96 (April 21): 159–63.

Du Boff, R. B., and E. S. Herman. 1980. "Alfred Chandler's New Business History: A Review." *Politics & Society* 10 (1): 87–110.

Du Boff, R. B., and E. S. Herman. 1989. "The Promotional-Financial Dynamic of Merger Movements: A Historical Perspective." *Journal of Economic Issues* (March, forthcoming).

Eddy, George. 1937. "Security Issues and Real Investment in 1929." *Review of Economic Statistics* 19 (May): 79–91.

Edsall, Thomas Byrne. 1984. *The New Politics of Inequality*. New York: Norton.

Edwards, Corwin D. 1940. "Preserving Competition versus Regulating Monopoly." *American Economic Review* 30 (March): 164–79.

Edwards, Richard C. 1975. "Stages in Corporate Stability and the Risks of Corporate Failure." *Journal of Economic History* 35 (June): 428–57.

Edwards, Richard C. 1979. *Contested Terrain. The Transformation of the Workplace in the Twentieth Century*. New York: Basic Books.

Eichner, Alfred S. 1969. *The Emergence of Oligopoly. Sugar Refining as a Case Study*. Baltimore: Johns Hopkins University Press.

Eichner, Alfred S. 1976. *The Megacorp and Oligopoly*. New York: Cambridge University Press.

Eilbott, Peter. 1966. "The Effectiveness of Automatic Stabilizers." *American Economic Review* 56 (June): 450–65.

Eis, Carl. 1969. "The 1919–1930 Merger Movement in American Industry." *Journal of Law and Economics* 12 (October): 267–96.

Engerman, Stanley. 1966. "The Economic Impact of the Civil War." *Explorations in Entrepreneurial History* 3 (Spring-Summer): 176–99.

Evans, G. H. 1948. *Business Incorporations in the United States 1800–1943*. New York: National Bureau of Economic Research.

Federal Reserve Bank of Kansas City. 1986. *Debt, Financial Stability, and Public Policy*. Kansas City: Federal Reserve Bank of Kansas City.

Feis, Herbert. 1930. *Europe the World's Banker, 1870–1914*. New Haven: Yale University Press.

Feldstein, Martin, ed. 1980. *The American Economy in Transition*. Chicago: University of Chicago Press.

Ferguson, Eugene S. 1979. "The American-ness of Technology." *Technology and Culture* 20 (January): 3–24.

Ferguson, Thomas, and J. Rogers. 1981. *The Hidden Election. Politics and Economics in the 1980 Presidential Campaign*. New York: Pantheon.

Ferguson, Thomas, and J. Rogers. 1986. *Right Turn. The Decline of the Democrats and the Future of American Politics*. New York: Hill and Wang.

Ferleger, Louis, and J. R. Mandle. 1988. "Managing the Next Economy." *Socialist Review* 18 (January-March): 105–10.

Fishlow, Albert. 1964. "Antebellum Interregional Trade Reconsidered." *American Economic Review* 54 (May): 352–64.

Fishlow, Albert. 1965. *American Railroads and the Transformation of the Ante-Bellum Economy*. Cambridge, Mass.: Harvard University Press.

Fishlow, Albert. 1974. "The New Economic History Revisited." *Journal of European Economic History* 3 (Fall): 453–67.

Floyd, Robert H., C. S. Gray, and R. P. Short. 1984. *Public Enterprise in Mixed Economies*. Washington: International Monetary Fund.

Fogel, Robert W. 1964. *Railroads and American Economic Growth*. Baltimore: Johns Hopkins University Press.

Fogel, Robert W. 1966. "The New Economic History." *Economic History Review* 19 (December): 642–63.

Fogel, Robert W., and S. L. Engerman, eds. 1971. *The Reinterpretation of American Economic History*. New York: Harper & Row.

Fogel, Robert W., and S. L. Engerman. 1974. *Time on the Cross. The Economics of American Negro Slavery*. Boston: Little, Brown.

Foglesong, Richard E. 1983. "Business Against the Welfare State." *Challenge* 26 (November-December): 38–45.

Foster, John Bellamy. 1986. *The Theory of Monopoly Capitalism*. New York: Monthly Review Press.

Foster, John Bellamy, and H. Szlajfer, eds. 1984. *The Faltering Economy*. New York: Monthly Review Press.

Galbraith, J. K. 1955. *The Great Crash 1929*. Boston: Houghton Mifflin.

Galbraith, J. K. 1967. *The New Industrial State*. Boston: Houghton Mifflin.

Galbraith, J. K. 1973. *Economics and the Public Purpose*. Boston: Houghton Mifflin.

Goldin, Claudia, and K. Sokoloff. 1982. "Women, Children, and Industrialization in the Early Republic." *Journal of Economic History* 42 (December): 741–74.

Goodrich, Carter. 1950. "The Revulsion against Internal Improvements." *Journal of*

Economic History 10 (November): 145–69.

Gordon, David M. 1988. "The Global Economy." *New Left Review* No. 168 (March/April): 24–64.

Gordon, David M., R. Edwards, and M. Reich. 1982. *Segmented Work, Divided Workers. The Historical Transformation of Labor in the U.S.* New York: Cambridge University Press.

Gordon, Myron J. 1982. "Corporate Bureaucracy, Productivity Gain, and Distribution of Revenue in U.S. Manufacturing, 1947–77." *Journal of Post Keynesian Economics* 4 (Summer): 483–96.

Gordon, Myron J. 1985. "The Postwar Growth in Monopoly Power." *Journal of Post Keynesian Economics* 8 (Fall): 3–13.

Gordon, Robert Aaron. 1974. *Economic Instability and Growth: The American Record.* New York: Harper & Row.

Gordon, Robert J., ed. 1986. *The American Business Cycle.* Chicago: University of Chicago Press.

Gorham, Lucy. 1987. *No Longer Leading. A Scorecard on U.S. Economic Performance and the Role of the Public Sector.* Washington: Economic Policy Institute.

Greer, Douglas F. 1981. "The Causes of Concentration in the U.S. Brewing Industry." *Quarterly Review of Economics and Business* 21 (Winter): 87–106.

Guest, Robert H. 1986. "Management Imperatives for the Year 2000." *California Management Review* 28 (Summer): 62–70.

Hall, Robert E. 1986. "Market Structure and Macroeconomic Fluctuations." *Brookings Papers on Economic Activity* No. 2: 285–322.

Hartman, Chester, ed. 1983. *America's Housing Crisis.* Boston: Routledge & Kegan Paul.

Hayes, Robert H., and W. J. Abernathy. 1980. "Managing our Way to Economic Decline." *Harvard Business Review* 58 (July-August): 67–77.

Heilbroner, Robert L. 1985. *The Nature and Logic of Capitalism.* New York: Norton.

Henle, Peter. 1972. "Exploring the Distribution of Earned Income." *Monthly Labor Review* 95 (December): 16–27.

Henley, Andrew. 1987. "Labor's Shares and Profitability Crisis in the U.S." *Cambridge Journal of Economics* 11 (December): 315–30.

Henretta, James A. 1973. *The Evolution of American Society, 1700–1815.* Lexington, Mass.: D. C. Heath.

Herman, Edward S. 1981. *Corporate Control, Corporate Power.* New York: Cambridge University Press.

Hickman, Bert G. 1965. *Investment Demand and U.S. Economic Growth.* Washington: The Brookings Institution.

Hirsch, Fred. 1978. *Social Limits to Growth.* Cambridge, Mass.: Harvard University Press.

Holt, Charles F. 1977. "Who Benefited from the Prosperity of the Twenties?" *Explorations in Economic History* 14 (July): 277–89.

Holzman, Franklyn D. 1984. "Myths that Drive the Arms Race." *Challenge* 27 (September-October): 32–36.

Horowitz, David, ed. 1969. *Corporations and the Cold War.* New York: Monthly Review Press.

Hunter, Helen Manning. 1982. "The Role of Business Liquidity During the Great Depression and Afterwards." *Journal of Economic History* 42 (December): 883–902.

Hymer, Stephen. 1979. *The Multinational Corporation: A Radical Approach.* New York: Cambridge University Press.

James, John A. 1983. "Structural Change in American Manufacturing, 1850–1890." *Journal of Economic History* 43 (June): 433–59.

Jenks, Leland. 1927. *The Migration of British Capital to 1875.* New York: Knopf.

Jorgenson, Dale W. 1988. "Productivity and Economic Growth in Japan and the United States." *American Economic Review* 78 (May): 217–22.

Kalecki, Michal. 1965. *Theory of Economic Dynamics*, rev. second ed. London: Unwin University Books.

Kalecki, Michal. 1972. *The Last Phase in the Transformation of Capitalism*. New York: Monthly Review Press.

Keller, Morton. 1963. *The Life Insurance Enterprise, 1885–1910*. Cambridge, Mass.: Harvard University Press.

Kendrick, John W. 1961. *Productivity Trends in the United States*. Princeton: Princeton University Press.

Keynes, J. M. 1936. *The General Theory of Employment Interest and Money*. New York: Harcourt, Brace.

Keynes, J. M. 1937. "The General Theory of Employment." *Quarterly Journal of Economics* 51 (February): 209–23.

Kindleberger, Charles P. 1973. *The World in Depression 1929–1939*. Berkeley: University of California Press.

Kindleberger, Charles P. 1981. "Dominance and Leadership in the International Economy." *International Studies Quarterly* 25 (June): 242–54.

Klemm, Friedrich. 1959. *A History of Western Technology*. New York: Scribner's.

Kolko, Gabriel. 1965. *Railroads and Regulation, 1877–1916*. Princeton: Princeton University Press.

Kolko, Joyce and Gabriel. 1972. *The Limits of Power. The World and U.S. Foreign Policy, 1945–1954*. New York: Harper & Row.

Kolko, Gabriel. 1984. *Main Currents in Modern American History*. New York: Pantheon.

Krashevski, Richard S. 1986. "What is Full Employment?" *Challenge* 29 (November-December): 33–40.

Kravis, Irving B. 1959. "Relative Income Shares in Fact and Theory." *American Economic Review* 49 (December): 917–49.

Kravis, Irving B. 1972. "The Role of Exports in Nineteenth-Century United States Growth." *Economic Development and Cultural Change* 20 (April): 387–405.

Krugman, Paul R., and R. E. Baldwin. 1987. "The Persistence of the U.S. Trade Deficit." *Brookings Papers on Economic Activity* No. 1: 1–43.

Kuznets, Simon. 1961. *Capital in the American Economy*. Princeton: Princeton University Press.

Kuznets, Simon. 1965. *Economic Growth and Structure*. New York: Norton.

Kuznets, Simon, 1966. *Modern Economic Growth*. New Haven: Yale University Press.

LaFeber, Walter. 1963. *The New Empire. An Interpretation of American Expansion 1860–1898*. Ithaca: Cornell University Press.

LaFeber, Walter. 1984. *America, Russia, and the Cold War 1945–1980*, fifth ed. New York: Knopf.

Lamoreaux, Naomi R. 1985. *The Great Merger Movement in American Business, 1895–1904*. New York: Cambridge University Press.

Lawrence, Robert Z., and R. E. Litan. 1987. "Why Protectionism Doesn't Pay." *Harvard Business Review* 65 (May-June): 60–67.

League of Nations. 1945. *Industrialization and Foreign Trade*. Geneva: League of Nations.

Lebergott, Stanley, 1964. *Manpower in Economic Growth: The American Record since 1800*. New York: McGraw-Hill.

Leontief, Wasily W. 1951. *The Structure of the American Economy, 1919–1939*. New York: Oxford University Press.

Leven, Maurice, H. G. Moulton, and C. Warburton. 1934. *America's Capacity to Consume*. Washington: The Brookings Institution.

Levitan, Sar, and E. Conway. 1988. "Part-Timers: Living on Half-Rations." *Challenge* 31 (May-June): 9–16.

Levitt, Kari. 1970. *Silent Surrender. The Multinational Corporation in Canada*. Toronto: Macmillan.

Lewis, Cleona. 1938. *America's Stake in International Investments*. Washington: The Brookings Institution.

Lewis, Wilfred Jr. 1962. *Federal Fiscal Policy in the Postwar Recessions*. Washington: The Brookings Institution.

Lindert, P. H., and J. G. Williamson. 1976. "Three Centuries of American Inequality." *Research in Economic History* 1 (1976): 69–117.

Lindstrom, Diane. 1978. *Economic Development in the Philadelphia Region, 1810–1850*. New York: Columbia University Press.

Lipsey, Robert E., and I. B. Kravis. 1987. "The Competitiveness and Comparative Advantage of U.S. Multinationals 1957–1984." *Banca Nazionale del Lavoro Quarterly Review* No. 161 (June): 147–65.

MacEwan, Arthur. 1981. "International Economic Crisis and the Limits of Macropolicy." *Socialist Review* 11 (September-October): 113–38.

McCraw, Thomas K. 1984. "Business & Government: The Origins of the Adversary Relationship." *California Management Review* 26 (Winter): 33–52.

McQuaid, Kim. 1982. *Big Business and Presidential Power*. New York: William Morrow.

Maddison, Angus. 1984. "Origins and Impact of the Welfare State, 1883–1983." *Banca Nazionale del Lavoro Quarterly Review* No. 148 (March): 55–87.

Magaziner, Ira C., and R. B. Reich. 1982. *Minding America's Business*. New York: Harcourt Brace Jovanovich.

Magdoff, Harry. 1969. *The Age of Imperialism*. New York: Monthly Review Press.

Magdoff, Harry, and P. M. Sweezy. 1969. "The Merger Movement: A Study in Power." *Monthly Review* 21 (June): 1–19.

Magdoff, Harry, and P. M. Sweezy. 1987. *Stagnation and the Financial Explosion*. New York: Monthly Review Press.

Magdoff, Harry, and P. M. Sweezy. 1988. "The Stock Market Crash and its Aftermath." *Monthly Review* 39 (March): 1–13.

Markusen, Ann. 1986. "The Militarized Economy." *World Policy Journal* 3 (Summer): 495–516.

Marshall, Alfred. 1920. *Industry and Trade*, 3rd ed. London: Macmillan.

Marx, Karl. 1967. *Capital: A Critique of Political Economy. Vol. III*. New York: International Publishers.

Marx, Karl. 1984. *Capital: A Critique of Political Economy. Vol. I*. New York: International Publishers.

Mathias, Peter, and M. M. Postan, eds. 1978. *The Cambridge Economic History of Europe. Vol. VII, Part 2*. New York: Cambridge University Press.

Mattes, W. F. 1969. "GE's Great Bulb Caper." *The Nation* 208 (June 30): 823–25.

Matthaei, Julie A. 1982. *An Economic History of Women in America*. New York: Schocken.

Melman, Seymour. 1983. *Profits without Production*. New York: Knopf.

Metzer, Jacob. 1985. "How New was the New Era? The Public Sector in the 1920s." *Journal of Economic History* 45 (March): 119–26.

Mills, Frederick C. 1932. *Economic Tendencies in the United States*. New York: National Bureau of Economic Research.

Minsky, Hyman. 1982. *Can "It" Happen Again? Essays on Instability and Finance*. Armonk, N.Y.: M.E. Sharpe.

Minsky, Hyman. 1986. *Stabilizing an Unstable Economy*. New Haven: Yale University Press.

Mishkin, Frederic S. 1978. "The Household Balance Sheet and the Great Depression." *Journal of Economic History* 38 (December): 918–37.

Moran, Theodore H. 1973. "Foreign Expansion as an 'Institutional Necessity' for U.S. Corporate Capitalism." *World Politics* 25 (April): 369–86.

Mosley, Hugh G. 1985. *The Arms Race: Economic and Social Consequences*. Lexington, Mass.: D.C. Heath.

Moulton, Harold G. 1935. *The Formation of Capital*. Washington: The Brookings Institution.

Mueller, Dennis C. 1985. "Mergers and Market Share." *Review of Economics and Statistics* 67 (May): 259–67.

National Bureau of Economic Research. 1955. *Business Concentration and Price Policy*. Princeton: Princeton University Press.

National Bureau of Economic Research. 1960. *Trends in the American Economy in the Nineteenth Century*. Princeton: Princeton University Press.

National Bureau of Economic Research. 1966. *Output, Employment, and Productivity in the United States after 1800*. New York: Columbia University Press.

National Bureau of Economic Research. 1969. *Six Papers on the Size Distribution of Wealth and Income*. New York: Columbia University Press.

Navin, Thomas R., and M. V. Sears. 1955. "The Rise of a Market for Industrial Securities, 1887–1902." *Business History Review* 29 (June): 105–38.

Nell, Edward. 1988. *Prosperity and Public Spending*. Boston: Unwin Hyman.

Nelson, Ralph L. 1959. *Merger Movements in American Industry 1895–1956*. Princeton: Princeton University Press.

New York Stock Exchange. 1984. *U.S. International Competitiveness: Perception and Reality*. New York: New York Stock Exchange.

Niemi, Albert W. Jr. 1980. *U.S. Economic History,* second ed. Chicago: Rand McNally.

Noble, David F. 1977. *America by Design. Science, Technology, and the Rise of Corporate Capitalism*. New York: Knopf.

Nourse, Edwin G., et al. 1934. *America's Capacity to Produce*. Washington: The Brookings Institution.

Nystrom, Paul H. 1929. *Economic Principles of Consumption*. New York: Ronald Press.

Osberg, Lars. 1984. *Economic Inequality in the United States*. Armonk, N.Y.: M. E. Sharpe.

Passer, Harold C. 1953. *The Electrical Manufacturers 1875–1900*. Cambridge, Mass.: Harvard University Press.

Patton, Arch. 1985. "Those Million-Dollar-a-Year Executives." *Harvard Business Review* 63 (January-February): 56–62.

Pechman, Joseph A. 1985. *Who Paid the Taxes, 1966–1985?* Washington: The Brookings Institution.

Perroux, François. 1964. *L'économie du XXe siècle*. 2e éd. Paris: Presses Universitaires de France.

Pitelis, Christos. 1987. *Corporate Capital*. New York: Cambridge University Press.

Polanyi, Karl. 1944. *The Great Transformation*. New York: Holt, Rinehart.

Polenberg, Richard. 1980. *One Nation Divisible: Class, Race, and Ethnicity in the U.S. since 1938*. New York: Viking Press.

Porter, Glenn. 1973. *The Rise of Big Business, 1860–1910*. New York: Crowell.

Porter, Glenn, ed. 1980. *Encyclopedia of American Economic History*. New York: Scribner's.

Porter, Michael E. 1987. "From Competitive Advantage to Corporate Strategy." *Harvard Business Review* 65 (May-June): 43–59.

Porter, P. G., and H. C. Livesay. 1969. "Oligopolists in American Manufacturing and Their Products, 1909–1963." *Business History Review* 43 (Autumn): 282–98.

Porter, P. G., and H. C. Livesay. 1970. "Oligopoly in Small Manufacturing Industries." *Explorations in Economic History* 7 (Spring): 371–79.

Pred, Allan R. 1966. *The Spatial Dynamics of U.S. Urban-Industrial Growth, 1880–1914.* Cambridge, Mass.: MIT Press.

President's Conference on Unemployment, National Bureau of Economic Research. 1929. *Recent Economic Changes in the United States.* New York: McGraw-Hill.

Quinn, J. B., J. J. Baruch, and P. C. Paquette. 1987. "Technology in Services." *Scientific American* 257 (December): 50–58.

Rae, John B. 1965. *The American Automobile.* Chicago: University of Chicago Press.

Rae, John B. 1971. *The Road and the Car in American Life.* Cambridge, Mass.: MIT Press.

Ravenscraft, David J., and F. M. Scherer. 1987. *Mergers, Sell-Offs, and Economic Efficiency.* Washington: The Brookings Institution.

Reubens, Edwin P. 1981. "The Services and Productivity." *Challenge* 24 (May-June): 59–63.

Riddell, Tom. 1988. "U.S. Military Power, the Terms of Trade, and the Profit Rate." *American Economic Review* 78 (May): 60–65.

Robbins, Lionel. 1935. *An Essay on the Nature and Significance of Economic Science.* 2nd ed. London: Macmillan.

Robinson, Joan. 1962. *Essays in the Theory of Economic Growth.* London: Macmillan.

Rodberg, Leonard S., and D. Shearer, eds. 1970. *The Pentagon Watchers.* Garden City, N.Y.: Doubleday.

Rosenberg, Nathan. 1969. "The Direction of Technological Change." *Economic Development and Cultural Change* 18 (October): 1–24.

Rosenberg, Nathan. 1972. *Technology and American Economic Growth.* New York: Harper & Row.

Rostow, W. W. 1960. *The Stages of Economic Growth.* New York: Cambridge University Press.

St. Clair, David J. 1986. *The Motorization of American Cities.* New York: Praeger.

Saloma, John S. III. 1984. *Ominous Politics. The New Conservative Labyrinth.* New York: Hill and Wang.

Samuelson, Paul. 1967. *Economics.* 7th ed. New York: McGraw-Hill.

Sanders, Jerry W. 1983. *Peddlers of Crisis. The Committee on the Present Danger and the Politics of Containment.* Boston: South End Press.

Sawyer, Malcolm C. 1985. *The Economics of Michal Kalecki.* Armonk, N.Y.: M. E. Sharpe.

Scherer, F. M. 1980. *Industrial Market Structure and Economic Performance.* 2nd ed. Chicago: Rand McNally.

Schott, Kerry. 1984. *Policy, Power, and Order. The Persistence of Economic Problems in Capitalist States.* New Haven: Yale University Press.

Schultze, Charles L. 1986. *Other Times, Other Places. Macroeconomic Lessons from U.S. and European History.* Washington: The Brookings Institution.

Schumpeter, J. A. 1934. *The Theory of Economic Development.* Cambridge, Mass.: Harvard University Press.

Schumpeter, J. A. 1950. *Capitalism, Socialism, and Democracy.* 3rd ed. New York: Harper & Row.

Schwarz, John E. 1983. *America's Hidden Success. A Reassessment of Twenty Years of Public Policy.* New York: Norton.

Servan-Schreiber, Jean-Jacques. 1967. *Le défi américain.* Paris: Denoël, 1967 (translation, *The American Challenge*, 1968).

Shepherd, William G. 1985. *The Economics of Industrial Organization.* 2nd ed. Englewood Cliffs, N.J.: Prentice-Hall.

Sherman, Howard J. 1987. *Foundations of Radical Political Economy*. Armonk, N.Y.: M.E. Sharpe.

Sherman, Howard J., and G. R. Evans. 1984. *Macroeconomics. Keynesian, Monetarist, and Marxist Views*. New York: Harper & Row.

Sherry, Robert, 1976. "Independent Commodity Production versus Petty Bourgeois Production." *Monthly Review* 28 (May): 52–60.

Shiskin, Julius. 1970. "The 1961–69 Economic Expansion in the United States." *Business Conditions Digest* 10 (January): 101–12.

Smith, James D., and S. D. Franklin. 1974. "The Concentration of Personal Wealth, 1922–1969." *American Economic Review* 64 (May): 162–67.

Soule, George. 1947. *Prosperity Decade. From War to Depression*. New York: Rinehart.

Spring, Joel H. 1972. *Education and the Rise of the Corporate State*. Boston: Beacon Press.

Steindl, Josef. 1979. "Stagnation Theory and Stagnation Policy." *Cambridge Journal of Economics* 3 (March): 1–14.

Stone, I. F. 1952. *The Hidden History of the Korean War*. New York: Monthly Review Press.

Summers, Lawrence H. 1986. "Why is the Unemployment Rate So Very High Near Full Employment?" *Brookings Papers on Economic Activity* No. 2: 339–83.

Sweezy, Paul M. 1956. *The Theory of Capitalist Development*. New York: Monthly Review Press.

Taussig, F. W. 1964. *The Tariff History of the United States*. 8th rev. ed. New York: Capricorn Books.

Taylor, George R. 1967. "American Urban Growth Preceding the Railway Age." *Journal of Economic History* 27 (September): 309–39.

Temin, Peter, ed. 1973. *New Economic History*. Harmondsworth, England: Penguin Books.

Temin, Peter. 1976. *Did Monetary Forces Cause the Great Depression?* New York: Norton.

Thorelli, Hans B. 1955. *The Federal Antitrust Policy*. Baltimore: Johns Hopkins University Press.

Thorp, Willard L. 1931. "The Persistence of the Merger Movement." *American Economic Review* 21 (March): 77–89.

Thurow, Lester C. 1968. "Disequilibrium and Marginal Productivity of Capital and Labor." *Review of Economics and Statistics* 50 (February): 23–31.

Thurow, Lester C. 1980. *The Zero-Sum Society*. New York: Basic Books.

Ulmer, Melville J. 1960. *Capital in Transportation, Communications, and Public Utilities*. Princeton: Princeton University Press.

U.S. Bureau of the Census. 1865. *Eighth Census of the United States. Manufactures of the United States in 1860*. Washington: U.S. GPO.

U.S. Bureau of the Census. 1895. *Eleventh Census 1890. Transportation by Land. Part I*. Washington: U.S. GPO.

U.S. Bureau of the Census. 1902. *Twelfth Census of the United States. Manufactures. Part I*. Washington: U.S. GPO.

U.S. Bureau of the Census. 1913a. *Thirteenth Census of the United States 1910. Abstract of the Census*. Washington: U.S. GPO.

U.S. Bureau of the Census. 1913b. *Thirteenth Census of the United States 1910. Vol. VIII: Manufactures 1909*. Washington: U.S. GPO.

U.S. Bureau of the Census. 1931. *Fifteenth Census of the United States. Population. Vol. I*. Washington: U.S. GPO.

U.S. Bureau of the Census. 1933. *Fifteenth Census of the United States. Manufactures: 1929*. Washington: U.S. GPO.

U.S. Bureau of the Census. 1942. *Sixteenth Census of the United States: Manufactures 1939. Vol. I.* Washington: U.S. GPO.

U.S. Bureau of the Census. 1975. *Historical Statistics of the United States. Colonial Times to 1970.* Washington: U.S. GPO.

U.S. Bureau of the Census. 1985. *Statistical Abstract of the United States: 1986.* Washington: U.S. GPO.

U.S. Bureau of the Census. 1987. *Statistical Abstract of the United States: 1988.* Washington: U.S. GPO.

U.S. Congress, 62nd. 1913. House Report 1593. *Report of the Committee Appointed Pursuant to House Resolutions 429 and 504 to Investigate the Concentration of Control of Money and Credit.* Washington: U.S. GPO.

U.S. Congress, 76th. 1940. Temporary National Economic Committee. *Investigation of Concentration of Economic Power.* Washington: U.S. GPO.

U.S. Congress, 79th. 1945. House Document 158. *Tenth Annual Report of the Securities and Exchange Commission.* Washington: U.S. GPO.

U.S. Congress, 99th. 1986. Joint Economic Committee. *The Concentration of Wealth in the United States.* Washington: Joint Economic Committee.

U.S. Congress, 100th. 1987. Congressional Budget Office. *The Changing Distribution of Federal Taxes: 1975-1990.* Washington: Congressional Budget Office.

U.S. Department of Commerce. 1984. *The Detailed Input-Output Structure of the U.S. Economy, 1977. Vol. I.* Washington: U.S. GPO.

U.S. Department of Commerce. 1986. *The National Income and Product Accounts of the United States, 1929-82.* Washington: U.S. GPO.

U.S. Department of the Interior. 1886. *The First Annual Report of the Commissioner of Labor, March 1886.* Washington: U.S. GPO.

U.S. Federal Trade Commission. 1969. *Economic Report on Corporate Mergers.* Washington: U.S. GPO.

U.S. Federal Trade Commission. 1980. *Statistical Report on Mergers and Acquisitions 1978.* Washington: Federal Trade Commission.

U.S. Industrial Commission. 1900. *Preliminary Report on Trusts and Industrial Combinations, Vol. I.* Washington: U.S. GPO.

U.S. Industrial Commission. 1901. *Report on the Relations and Conditions of Capital and Labor Employed in Manufactures and General Business. Vol. VII.* Washington: U.S. GPO.

U.S. President. 1988. *Economic Report of the President. Transmitted to the Congress February 1988.* Washington: U.S. GPO.

Vatter, Harold G. 1963. *The U.S. Economy in the 1950s.* New York: Norton.

Vatter, Harold G. 1975. *The Drive to Industrial Maturity. The U.S. Economy, 1860-1914.* Westport, Conn.: Greenwood Press.

Veblen, Thorstein. 1904. *The Theory of Business Enterprise.* New York: Scribner's.

Walker, John F., and H. G. Vatter. 1986. "Stagnation—Performance and Policy." *Journal of Post Keynesian Economics* 8 (Summer): 515-30.

Warner, Sam Bass, Jr. 1968. *The Private City. Philadelphia in Three Periods of Growth.* Philadelphia: University of Pennsylvania Press.

Warren, Robert, and E. P. Kraly. 1985. *The Elusive Exodus: Emigration from the United States.* Washington: Population Reference Bureau.

Wilkins, Mira. 1970. *The Emergence of Multinational Enterprise.* Cambridge, Mass.: Harvard University Press.

Williams, John H. 1953. *Economic Stability in a Changing World.* New York: Oxford University Press.

Williamson, Harold F., ed. 1951. *The Growth of the American Economy.* 2nd ed. New York: Prentice-Hall.

Williamson, Jeffrey G. 1974. *Late Nineteenth-Century American Development*. New York: Cambridge University Press.

Williamson, Jeffrey G. 1979. "Inequality, Accumulation, and Technological Imbalance." *Economic Development and Cultural Change* 27 (January): 231–53.

Williamson, Jeffrey G., and P. H. Lindert. 1980. *American Inequality. A Macroeconomic History*. New York: Academic Press.

Wolff, Edward N. 1986. "The Productivity Slowdown and the Fall in the U.S. Rate of Profit, 1947–76." *Review of Radical Political Economics* 18 (Spring-Summer): 87–109.

Wolff, Edward N. 1987. *Growth, Accumulation and Unproductive Activity*. New York: Cambridge University Press.

Wolff, Rick. 1971. "The Foreign Expansion of U.S. Banks." *Monthly Review* 23 (May): 15–30.

Wolfson, Martin H. 1986. *Financial Crises. Understanding the Postwar U.S. Experience*. Armonk, N.Y.: M. E. Sharpe.

Woodman, Harold D. 1972. "Economic History and Economic Theory." *Journal of Interdisciplinary History* 3 (Autumn): 323–50.

Index

About the Author

Richard B. Du Boff, Professor of Economics at Bryn Mawr College, received his A.B. from Dartmouth College, and a Ph.D. from the University of Pennsylvania. He has written extensively on American economic history, foreign policy, and the political economy of military spending, including previous books and numerous articles in scholarly journals and popular periodicals.